▼ A2 MEDIA STUDIES
THE ESSENTIAL INTRODUCTION

Building on the groundwork laid by AS Media Studies: The Essential Introduction, A2 Media Studies: The Essential Introduction develops key topics in greater depth and introduces students to the notion of independent study. The book is designed to support students through the transition from a focus on textual analysis to the consideration of the wider contexts and theoretical perspectives that inform any study of the media.

Individual chapters cover the following key areas:

- wider contexts
- independent study and research
- genre
- representation
- audience
- news
- comparative textual analysis
- theoretical perspectives
- passing exams.

Specially designed to be user-friendly, A2 Media Studies: The Essential Introduction includes:

- activities
- practical assignments and exam questions
- further reading
- a glossary of key terms and resources
- case studies.

Peter Bennett is former Head of Communications at Rowley Regis College, Chief Examiner for Communication Studies at A Level, co-editor of Communication Studies: The Essential Resource (2003), and co-author of AS Communication Studies: The Essential Introduction (2002) and Framework Media: Channels (2003). **Jerry Slater** is a freelance consultant in media and communication education, Chair of Examiners for VCE and GNVQ Media, Principal Examiner for Communication Studies at A Level and a reviser and examiner for A Level Media Studies. **Peter Wall** is Chair of Examiners for Media and Communication Studies at A Level, Chief Examiner for GCSE Media Studies and GNVQ Media, co-editor of Media Studies: The Essential Resource (2004), co-author of AS Media Studies: The Essential Introduction (2004) and AS Communication Studies: The Essential Introduction (2002), author of Media Studies for GCSE (2002) and co-author of Framework Media: Channels (2003).

'A much needed addition to the A Level Media Studies canon. The trio have produced a book that will rapidly become the bible of choice for teachers and students alike. Anyone considering work at A2 should invest in a copy.'

Les Grafton, A Level teacher, North Leamington School

'Methodical, well presented and thoroughly accessible . . . the perfect bridge between AS and A2, widening and deepening the conceptual framework, steering students beyond media texts into the broader contextual issues and media theoretical approaches, and encouraging and empowering them to develop the critical skills required in the second year of the A Level course . . . Teachers and students have been waiting for this book for a long time, and they won't be disappointed.'

Julia Burton, Principal Examiner and Principal Moderator for two GCE Media Units

Other books for Media and Communication Studies

Series Editor: Peter Wall

Media Studies: The Essential Resource
Philip Rayner, Peter Wall and Stephen Kruger

AS Communication Studies: The Essential Introduction
Andrew Beck, Peter Bennett and Peter Wall

Communication Studies: The Essential Resource
Andrew Beck, Peter Bennett and Peter Wall

A2 MEDIA STUDIES

THE ESSENTIAL INTRODUCTION

Peter Bennett, Jerry Slater
and Peter Wall

Routledge
Taylor & Francis Group

LONDON AND NEW YORK

First published 2006
by Routledge
2 Park Square, Milton Park, Abingdon, Oxon OX14 4RN

Simultaneously published in the USA and Canada
by Routledge
270 Madison Ave, New York, NY 10016

Routledge is an imprint of the Taylor & Francis Group

© 2006 Peter Bennett, Jerry Slater and Peter Wall

Typeset in Novarese and Bell Gothic by Keystroke, Jacaranda Lodge, Wolverhampton
Printed and bound in Italy by Printer Trento

British Library Cataloguing in Publication Data
A catalogue record for this book is available from the British Library

Library of Congress Cataloging in Publication Data
A catalog record for this book has been requested

ISBN 0–415–34767–X (hbk)
ISBN 0–415–34768–8 (pbk)

▼ CONTENTS

List of figures   ix
Acknowledgements   xi
Figure acknowledgements   xiii

Introduction   1

Chapter 1 Wider contexts   4
Reality TV   7
Sport in the media   10
Getting at these wider contexts   14
Further reading   18

Chapter 2 Independent study/research   19
Making a start   22
Title   24
Structure   31
Bibliography and references   34
Presentation   35
Some more on AQA Unit 5   36
Further reading   36

Chapter 3 Genre   37
Genre: codes and conventions   37
Pinning down the identities and meanings of genre   40
Genre studies   43
Hybrids   50
Case study: celebrity lifestyle magazines   56
Case study: British television crime fiction   64
Ideas for exploring genre   72

Chapter 4   Representation   74

What is representation?   74
Mediation as a process   76
Stereotypes and minorities   78
Alternative representations   83
Types of realism   84
Ideology and representation   87
Introduction to case studies   92
Case study: 'In a Big Country': the meanings of Scotland   93
Case study: 'Slugs and snails and puppy dogs' tails': the meanings of men   101
Reality TV   109

Chapter 5   Audience   113

Introduction   113
Who is interested in the audience and why?   117
Public service broadcasting and the audience   129
The segmented audience versus the mass audience   129
Audience theories   131
Active audiences   134
Audiences and hegemony   142
Reception theory   148
Television schedules and the audience   150
Beyond the active audience   151
Further reading   154

Chapter 6   News   155

News room roles   162
Construction of a news story   168
Television news presentation   171
Case study   179
Further reading   185

Chapter 7   Comparative textual analysis   186

Places to take off from: comparative critical strategies   186
Postmodernist readings   201
The conditions of production   206
The contexts of consumption   207
Putting it all together   208

Chapter 8   Theoretical perspectives   215

The popular culture debate   217
The toolkit of theory   219
Semiotics   219
Structuralism   221

Poststructuralism   223
Postmodernism   224
Feminism   226
Queer theory   230
Marxism   231
Liberal pluralism   236
Cultural imperialism and postcolonialism   237
Further reading   239

Chapter 9   Passing exams   240

Why do we have exams?   240
Common sense prevails . . .   243
Concepts and contexts: the Media Studies focus   245
Unseen text exams   247

Chapter 10   Crime fiction   251

Historical background   251
Some gender issues   254
Enter the expert   257
Economics of scale and locations of choice   258
Intertextuality: the knowing audience   259
The Bill and *The Cops*   259
Further reading   261

Resources   262
Glossary   263
Bibliography   271
Index   274

▼ FIGURES

2.1	MCS site	25
3.1	The audience–producer–text triangle of dependency	41
3.2	Poster for *Paycheck* (2003)	43
3.3	Moore's paraphernalia in *Watchmen*	44
3.4	Top ten sitcoms	45
3.5	The top ten British sitcoms as voted by the great British public	51
3.6	Chris Tarrant and his family taking a well-deserved holiday	57
3.7	Jordan and Peter Andre	59
3.8	Ben Affleck and Jennifer Lopez	62
3.9	Flavio Briatore in the sun	63
4.1	Gay deaf sign	90
4.2	Graham Norton	91
4.3	Scottish shortbread	96
4.4	Scene from the film *Trainspotting* (1996)	97
4.5	Mel Gibson in *Braveheart* (1995)	99
4.6	Scottish football fan (painted in the flag of St Andrew)	99
4.7	Liam Neeson in *Rob Roy* (1995)	99
4.8	Gallery of Modern Art, Glasgow	100
4.9	Loch Ness website	100
4.10	Cover of the *Observer* Music Monthly	102
4.11	Scene from *The Godfather* (1972)	104
4.12	U2 in *Q Magazine*	105
4.13	'Tops-Off Totty' Gary Lucy	106
4.14	NHS careers advertisement	108
4.15	Advertisement for *Queer Eye for the Straight Guy*	108
5.1	Cover of *Prima*, December 2004	123
5.2	Cover of *Country Living*, December 2004	124
5.3	Advertisement in the *Evening Gazette*, 15 October 2004	126
5.4	DVD cover of *The Missing* (2003)	128
5.5	Still from *I'm a Celebrity Get Me Out of Here*	131
5.6	Still from *Triumph of the Will* (1935)	132
5.7	*We Love Telly* magazine, week ending 5 November 2004	136
5.8	John Kerry and George Bush	138
5.9	Publicity poster for *Fahrenheit 9/11* (2004)	144

5.10	Black and white minstrels	145
5.11	'Heroin Screws You Up'	146
5.12	BAFTA ceremony	148
6.1	Teletext news index	157
6.2	*The Guardian Unlimited*	158
6.3	National newspaper circulation	160
6.4	News desk	175
6.5	'Posh wants UK tot'	177
7.1	Coolio, *Gangsta's Paradise*	188
7.2	1960s LP cover: Cliff Richard, *21 Today*	192
7.3	Front page of the *Sun*	194
7.4	'The *Sun* Says'	196
7.5	Front page of the *Stourbridge News*	199
7.6	Still from the original *Thunderbirds*	202
7.7	Still from *Thunderbirds* (2004)	203
7.8	Front cover of *The Movies: An Illustrated History of the Silver Screen* (2000)	210
7.9	DVD cover for *La Dolce Vita*. © Nouveaux Pictures	211
7.10	Front cover of *etc.*, issue 8	212
7.11	Front cover of *The People's Friend*	213
9.1	Planning grid for textual comparisons	248
10.1	*Prime Suspect*	255
10.2	*Blue Murder*	256
10.3	Publicity still, *55 Degrees North*	256
10.4	*Cracker*	257
10.5	*Inspector Morse*	259

▼ ACKNOWLEDGEMENTS

The authors would like to express their thanks to Katrina Chandler, Development Editor at Routledge, her predecessor, Kate Ahl, Anna Hines, Production Editor at Routledge, Heather Vickers at Picture Research and Rosamund Howe, our copy editor, for their considerable help in the preparation of this book. Thanks are also due to Shirley Hart, Sarah Casey and the Media students at Colchester Sixth Form College. Their constructive criticism and support made a vital contribution.

▼ FIGURE ACKNOWLEDGEMENTS

Every attempt has been made to obtain permission to reproduce copyright material. If any proper acknowledgement has not been made, we would invite copyright holders to inform us of the oversight.

2.1	MCS site. Hosted by the University of Wales, Aberystwyth. Source: www.aber.ac.uk/media	25
3.2	Poster for *Paycheck*. Courtesy of Dreamworks Pictures	43
3.3	*Watchmen* No. 5. © 1987 DC Comics. All rights reserved. Used with permission	44
3.4	Top ten sitcoms. © BBC	45
3.5	The top ten British sitcoms as voted for by the great British public. © BBC	51
3.6	Chris Tarrant and his family taking a well-deserved holiday. Source: *Hello* magazine, courtesy of Hello magazine	57
3.7	Jordan and Peter Andre. Source: *OK* magazine, 2 March 2004. Courtesy of EMAP	59
3.8	Ben Affleck and Jennifer Lopez. Source: *Heat* magazine, week ending 31 October 2003. Courtesy of Heat magazine	62
3.9	Flavio Briatore in the sun. Source: *Hello* magazine, courtesy of Hello magazine	63
4.1	Gay deaf sign. Courtesy of the LET'S SIGN Dictionary / www.deafsign.com	90
4.2	Graham Norton. © Andrew Williams	91
4.3	Scottish shortbread. Courtesy of Duncan's of Deeside	96
4.4	Scene from the film *Trainspotting* (1996). Source: The Kobal Collection	97
4.5	Mel Gibson in *Braveheart*. Source: The Kobal Collection	99
4.6	Scottish football fan. © Jeff Gilbert	99
4.7	Liam Neeson in *Rob Roy* (1995). © The Kobal Collection	99
4.8	Gallery of Modern Art, Glasgow. Courtesy of Greater Glasgow & Clyde Valley Tourist Board	100
4.9	Loch Ness website. Source: www.lochness-centre.com	100
4.10	The *Observer* Music Monthly, February 2004, no. 6. Courtesy of the *Observer*	102
4.11	Scene from *The Godfather* (1972). Source: The Kobal Collection	104
4.12	U2 in *Q Magazine*. November 2004. Courtesy of *Q Magazine*	105

4.13	'Tops-Off Totty' Gary Lucy. Courtesy of *J17*	106
4.14	NHS careers advertisement. Courtesy of the NHS	108
4.15	Advertisement *for Queer Eye for the Straight Guy*. Courtesy of Scout Productions	108
5.1	Cover of *Prima*, December 2004. Courtesy of National Magazines	123
5.2	Cover of *Country Living*, December 2004. Courtesy of National Magazines	124
5.3	Advertisement in the *Evening Gazette*, 15 October 2004. Courtesy of Newsquest Newspapers	126
5.4	DVD cover of *The Missing* (2003). Courtesy of Columbia Pictures	128
5.5	Still from *I'm a Celebrity Get Me Out of Here*. Courtesy of ITV	131
5.6	Still from *Triumph of the Will* (1935). Source: British Pathe News	132
5.7	*We Love Telly* magazine, week ending 5 November 2004. Courtesy of the *Daily Mirror*	136
5.8	John Kerry and George Bush. © Reuters/Jim Bourg	138
5.9	Publicity poster for *Fahrenheit 9/11* (2004). Courtesy of www.michaelmoore.com	144
5.10	Black and white minstrels. © Corbis	145
5.11	Anti-drug advertising campaign: 'Heroin Screws You Up'. Source: The Advertising Archive	146
5.12	BAFTA ceremony. © Ken McKay/Rex Features	148
6.1	Teletext news index.	157
6.2	The Guardian Unlimited. © The Guardian	158
6.3	National newspaper circulation. Source: *Guardian*	160
6.4	News desk. © Sam Barcroft/Rex Features	175
6.5	'Posh wants UK tot'. Source: *News of the World*, 22 August 2004	177
7.1	Album cover of Coolio, *Gangsta's Paradise*. Courtesy of Tommy Boy Records	188
7.2	LP cover of Cliff Richard, *21 Today*. Courtesy of Columbia Records	192
7.3	Front page of the *Sun*, 15 October 2004. Courtesy of the *Sun*	194
7.4	'The *Sun* Says', 15 October 2004. Courtesy of the *Sun*	196
7.5	Front page of the *Stourbridge News*, 5 August 2004. Courtesy of the *Stourbridge News*	199
7.6	Still from the original *Thunderbirds*. © BBC	202
7.7	Still from *Thunderbirds* (2004). © Universal Studios	203
7.8	Front cover of *The Movies: an Illustrated History of the Silver Screen* (2000). Courtesy of Hermes House	210
7.9	DVD cover for *La Dolce Vita*. © Nouveaux Pictures	211
7.10	Front cover of *etc.*, issue 8. Courtesy of *etc.* magazine	212
7.11	Front cover of *The People's Friend*, Christmas special, 9 October 2004. Courtesy of DC Thompson	213
10.1	*Prime Suspect*. © Granada Television	255
10.2	*Blue Murder*. © ITV plc	256
10.3	Publicity still from *55 Degrees North*. © BBC	256
10.4	*Cracker*. © Granada Television	257
10.5	*Inspector Morse*. © Carlton Television	259

AQA examination questions are reproduced by permission of the Assessment and Qualifications Alliance.

▼ INTRODUCTION

This book is intended to be a follow-on volume from AS *Media Studies: The Essential Introduction* and is designed to help you with the transition from a focus on textual analysis to a consideration of the wider contexts that inform any study of the media. This is an important transition that you will need to make as your study of the media progresses, be it from AS Level to A2 or from the introduction to a Media Studies degree to a more sophisticated level of understanding. However, it is important for you to bear in mind that the work you did as part of your study using AS *Media Studies* should form an important foundation for the work you are being asked to undertake in this book.

Those central concepts which we explored in AS *Media Studies* – reading the media, audiences and institutions – will remain integral to your study at this level as well. However, you may well find that textual analysis, although still important, becomes subordinate to the opportunity to explore some of the wider contexts in which texts are created and consumed. Study of audiences and institutions is likely therefore to become much more prominent.

Another important step forward that this book should help you take is in the application of media theory. Although with Media Studies as an academic discipline there is no specific body of theory that needs to be learned, there are a number of important theories which offer you perspectives for serious consideration of the media and broader cultural issues. Some of these theories are considered in detail throughout this book. However, it is important to offer a word of caution at this point. Not all the theories that you become acquainted with are likely to be equally useful or relevant. There is often a temptation for students to apply a theory they have learned simply to show off the fact that they know it. A more confident student, however, would not feel the need to do this. In fact the best students are those who are prepared to question or even challenge the orthodoxy that these theories offer. Indeed there is a compelling argument that suggests that in a world that is changing so rapidly, many of the theories that had credibility a short time ago are now outdated or even outpaced by the many advances made by media technology. Certainly a lot of the audience study produced by researchers and academics in the 1980s has dubious relevance today in light of the plethora of choice offered to the consumer in today's media-saturated world.

Of course it is important that you are able to demonstrate that you have grasped and understood such theories before you dive headlong into questioning their validity. One of the things that this book aims to do is to offer you a theoretical framework in which to explore the media. Without some understanding of relevant theories, the perspectives you yourself can offer have no greater value than those of a person who has never studied Media or Cultural Studies. Just as you might reasonably expect a doctor to have some grasp of the theoretical side of anatomy before practising, so it is incumbent on the Media student to have some grasp of theory.

Needless to say, that begs the question 'What do I do with this theory once I have learned it?' Well, certainly, knowing theories for their own sake is of little use. What you need to be able to do is to apply them. This is where one of the biggest steps that this book invites you to take comes in. What we are asking you to do is to be prepared to take the risk of letting go of your teacher's hand and having the confidence to look independently at media texts by seeking out those that interest or intrigue you and then applying the theoretical framework that you have learned. For example, as part of this book we will explore some of the theories that underpin the concept of genre. It is quite likely that you will also explore this concept, say, by looking at a particular example of a film or television genre in class. Many students will go into an examination knowing only how to apply genre theory to the texts that they have studied. This often leads to half-understood ideas being regurgitated in the exam with little attempt to answer the question being asked. An independent student, on the other hand, will have taken the trouble to absorb and understand the theory and then gone on to see how it can be applied to texts beyond those considered in the classroom. In the process s/he may even have reached the point of beginning to question the value of theory or at the very least have identified its limitations.

So, for example, you may learn that genre can be seen as an organising principle for the production and consumption of texts by which those with similar features can be classed together. The western is a particularly good and often used example of a film genre. This is due largely to the fact that a good deal of the genre research carried out in the early 1970s was focused on the western, not least because many of the ideas behind genre theory neatly fitted this particular category of text. However, the western is no longer the popular film genre that it once was. In fact Clint Eastwood's *Unforgiven*, released in 1992, did a great deal in a self-referential way to offer its own critique of the western, perhaps to the point where it had the last word on the genre itself. You may find that often media texts provide a more meaningful critique than a library of academic writing. Genre theory is much less easily applied to more contemporary media texts, not least because so many have developed into hybrids to which simple formulas are difficult to apply.

Finally, you may have noted the emphasis on contemporary texts implicit in the previous paragraph. A specification like the AQA GCE Media Studies places a lot of importance on engagement with contemporary texts. This is not a denial of the importance of media history but another attempt to develop student independence and autonomy in engaging with texts that are in some way current and specifically relevant to today. In consequence you will find that unlike the western, contemporary texts tend not to have extensive theories already attached to them. Few contemporary texts come, like the western, with a long bibliography of academic study.

This is not, of course, to say that such academic study is of no value. Clearly, much of what has been written about such an important genre as the western is bound to be of value and importance. However, it is important that you see such material as background to your own exploration of the media. What this book encourages you to do is to immerse yourself in specific aspects of media study, ideally over a period of time so that you can explore first hand some of the key issues and debates. The theoretical framework we seek to provide you with should act as a guide, not an obstacle to this exploration. This way you have the opportunity to come up with fresh ideas about the ever changing world of the media rather than allowing yourself to reproduce second-hand and often out-of-date ideas you have learned from various sources. For instance, you may be interested in the representation of young people in soap operas. In order to undertake such a study you probably need to find out about representation as a broad concept, representation of people in general and perhaps something about soap opera itself. Once you have done this background work, you should then take a close look at the texts, the soap operas themselves, not just for a single episode but over a period of, say, two to three weeks. It might also be a good idea to keep a check on secondary sources, the tabloid press and television listings magazines. You might also conduct some audience research to find out how people react to soaps and the representation of young people specifically. By so immersing yourself in the topic you are likely to gain an insight that no textbook or learned journal can ever offer you.

▼ 1 WIDER CONTEXTS

In this chapter we consider the importance of theoretical concepts and wider contexts as tools for providing insight into media texts, issues and debates.

At the beginning of your study of the media you will probably have placed a lot of emphasis on textual analysis. Looking closely at texts and how they are constructed and interpreted is a valuable way of finding out about how the media work. However, textual analysis is rarely a useful end in itself. Despite their complexity, media texts are probably more valuable for what they can tell us about the society in which they are created and consumed than they are for their own intrinsic aesthetic worth. This is one way in which a study of the media and other popular cultural forms differs from subjects like Literary Studies, where a great deal of emphasis is placed on the value of individual texts. A study of genre when applied to media texts generally takes us beyond the scrutiny of individual texts into a wider scrutiny of the collective qualities and impact of a group of similar texts.

You will read many textbooks, especially from the early days of Media Studies, that show great virtuosity in the analysis of individual texts. However, you will also notice that many of these analyses try to draw some conclusion about the significance of these texts within a social and cultural context. They seek in fact to place the texts within their wider contexts; this not only takes cognisance of how they are produced and consumed but also considers how they relate to the prevailing social, political, economic and cultural conditions surrounding their production and consumption.

Consider the question 'What is the best meal you ever had?' How would you attempt to answer? One possible way is to make your response 'text-based' – a seven-course blow-out in a Michelin starred restaurant – the truffles were superb. The more likely possibility is a context-based response: 'The night I first met Kim and we shared a bag of chips in the bus shelter on the way home.' Now consider how you might apply these two approaches to the question: 'What's the best film you ever saw?'

This engagement with the issue of wider contexts should be a key feature of your study of the media at this level. The problem is that it is not always easy to get access to or come to an understanding of these wider contexts, especially when you are asked to

analyse previously unseen texts under exam conditions. However, where you do have the opportunity to conduct research into these wider contexts, it is important that you attempt to do so.

Wider contexts of course involve more than just the conditions in which media texts are consumed. They must also engage with the conditions in which media texts are produced as well as the broader social and cultural forces that are at play. As we have said, one of the important reasons for studying media texts is the fact that they allow us to engage with and think about the broader social themes reflected in them. Of course this brings us to consider yet again that key debate around how far media texts reflect social conditions and how far they contribute to them. Whatever position you choose to adopt on that thorny issue, it is difficult to deny the significant role played by the media in the transmission of culture and values within Western society. Let us therefore assume that media texts do to some significant degree reflect the conditions in which they are produced and consumed; then we need to find some way of both identifying and understanding these wider contexts.

Often this will mean to a lesser or greater extent engaging with social and political history. Later in this chapter we look at some of the ways in which you can attempt to do this but let us start by looking at a couple of examples and considering how the wider context might not only be relevant to our consideration of a text, but also enrich our experience of it.

Of course there is no real substitute for a genuine act of engagement that stems naturally from finding something in a text that really interests you. This engagement is in itself a key context which is also a channel to other texts. You may, for example, be led to consider music or films of the 1960s by way of a contemporary text: by the references to the spring and summer of 1968 in Bernardo Bertolucci's *The Dreamers*, or the key 1960s soundtrack of TV's *Heartbeat* or even by watching the tribute show for the latest member of the Beatles or The Who to die. At first sight the texts might seem a little old-fashioned, dependent on rather obsolete technology, and may generally offer you the sense of being something of a historical document. Then again you may be an avid lover of 1960s music, British films of the 1960s or maybe you are just a fan of retro, in which case you might actually feel quite excited about the texts you are looking at. If you do a little digging into what life was like in the 1960s, perhaps by simply asking someone who was around at the time, you might discover some of the reasons why the texts you are looking at are like they are. The 1960s was a time of great social change in Britain. It was marked by a period of great postwar prosperity in which people had surplus cash to spend on luxury goods such as televisions, cars and fashion. On the back of this came the emergence of 'youth culture' in which teenagers became important, not least because they had money to spend on things like records, clothes, concerts and films. In addition, there was a new emphasis on provincial working class as opposed to the bourgeois London-based classes that had dominated British cultural life for most of the twentieth century. The idea of 'youth culture' and the attention paid to young people through the media are clearly well accepted these days, but in 1960s Britain bands like the Rolling Stones were seen as a serious threat to society because of their seemingly anarchic attitudes. This came to a head with the arrest in 1967 of Mick Jagger, now Sir Mick Jagger, on drugs charges.

If you look at media texts such as British films of the 1960s or popular music of the period, you will see how they reflect this social shift. Films of the period celebrate northern working class life and deal with earthy social issues such as teenage pregnancies and conflict with parents and authority. The films are gritty and realistic, often shot in monochrome to give them impact. Similarly, popular music of the period dealt with the corresponding need for self-expression. If 1960s film provided a model of young men wrestling, sometimes literally, with issues of identity and masculinity, popular music gave them a microphone and a stage.

For a brief period in the late 1960s this stage became a platform for a, for the first time youth-led, discussion of 'the way we live now', a project previously reserved for high cultural forms. This was for some an overdue evaluation of the values of postwar Britain, for others a democratisation of the channels of communication, while some saw it as a visionary project which produced various blueprints for a new order (and the cynical saw it as essentially a confidence trick designed to sell consumer goods and revive an ailing ruling class). To research these issues is relatively straightforward: a good look at the development of song lyrics across the period will certainly open this up.

Not only did the pop song 'grow up' in the 1960s, but also in doing so it changed its function (and mode of address). The Beatles, for example, progressed from the modest formulaic of 'I want to hold your hand' to the frank directness of 'Why don't we do it in the road', but more significantly published their collected lyrics (illustrated!). Here was something that looked like a poetry book proclaiming 'in the end' that 'the love you take is equal to the love you make' and being read (and listened to). The lyrics of 1960s rock and pop performed a chaotic but cohesive narrative that spoke only superficially of sex and drugs and rock and roll but more significantly through them of a new dispensation. Here is part of that 'symphony':

> She just can't be chained
> To a life where nothing's gained
> And nothing's lost
> At such a cost.
>> ('Ruby Tuesday': The Rolling Stones)

> There is no other day
> Let's try it another way.
>> ('See Emily Play': Pink Floyd)

> I hear a very gentle sound,
> With your ear down to the ground.
> We want the world and we want it,
> We want the world and we want it,
> Now, Now? NOW!
>> ('When the Music's Over': The Doors)

> Things they do look awful cold.
> Hope I die before I get old!
>> ('My Generation': The Who)

What might the lyrics on p. 6 suggest about the key concerns of the 1960s? Where else might you go to pursue these 'leads'?

In film the late 1960s was notable for its fascination with 'swinging London' and the return of colour following the stark but beautiful monochrome of the Free Cinema projects. Mini-skirted 'chicks' and cats in cravats replaced desperate northern men and their pregnant girlfriends and everyone was having sex and on the pill and enjoying themselves. For film-maker Alan Parker this was the nadir of British film which had all too quickly replaced the zenith of A Taste of Honey and Billy Liar. All films at this time, Parker suggested, had a red London bus in shot in them and this was a sign you were in for a bad time. Where Billy Liar had offered fantasy as a means of exploring Billy's delusional desperation, films like What's New Pussycat? presented fantasy as an end in itself and the essence of entertainment. Reality was no longer the prize when 'ratings' called the shots. Billy Liar, for all his schemes, has to go back home at the end of the film, back to an inescapable reality, and so do we. The modern idiom is less clean.

REALITY TV

A more recent example of the way in which wider contexts can be explored is in the genre of reality TV programmes. These are a relatively new media phenomenon that proliferated at the beginning of this century. Clearly programmes like Big Brother and I'm a Celebrity Get Me Out of Here satisfy a huge appetite for reality TV among audiences. It is interesting to explore some of the economic, social and cultural forces that gave rise to the popularity of this genre, which has been dismissed by such noteworthy commentators as John Humphrys as 'mediocre, pointless, puerile even'.

Perhaps the first and most significant of these is the 'digital revolution' in media technology. This revolution has a created a proliferation of television channels through the satellite, cable and freeview networks. A viewer with full digital satellite access now has access to over 100 channels. In contrast, in the early 1980s, prior to the advent of BSkyB, there were just four channels, two of which were publicly funded. All channels, but most especially the commercial channels, need to be competitive in this media-saturated environment. A mainstream commercial channel such as ITV must do all it can to remain competitive and maintain its share of the mass market if it is to continue to attract advertisers prepared to pay top rates for prime-time slots.

One inevitable outcome of increased competition is that the cost of making pro-grammes will be driven down. Two ways of achieving this are to reduce the fees paid to expensive performers and to ensure a maximum return on capital investment. One way of reducing the cost of expensive performers is to get rid of them and rely on members of the public as a source of entertainment. Similarly, investment in studio facilities or locations requires expensive capital outlay. One way to make this more cost effective is to ensure that the set is used to fill the maximum number of

broadcasting hours possible, ideally several hours a day for several weeks. Consider, for example, how many reality TV shows occupy both a prime-time slot on one of the major terrestrial channels and by an ancillary 'behind the scenes' programme on the digital networks.

Two formats that have successfully exploited the participation of audiences and sought to maximise their initial investment are the quiz show and the game show. Formats such as *Who Wants to Be a Millionaire?* are exported to television networks worldwide. A show such as *Countdown*, C4's long-running afternoon show, is produced on what amounts to a conveyor belt in Yorkshire Television Studios. With a purpose-built set, a studio audience and a steady supply of contestants, several shows a day can be produced using the same presenters and crew, hence keeping costs to a minimum. This principle is readily extended to reality television for a show like *Big Brother* where the house and the prize money represent the basic capital investment. The involvement of established celebrities is strictly limited, with the stars of the programme being 'ordinary' members of the viewing public.

This principle is further extendable from wannabe members of the public to minor celebrities hoping to advance or to relaunch their careers, prepared to accept high levels of humiliation to achieve this in a programme like *I'm a Celebrity Get Me Out of Here*. The Australian rainforest set of the programme incidentally is used for both British and US versions of the programme.

The Internet is another aspect of communications technology that has had an important influence on the way in which we consume television. In essence there are three primary ways in which the Internet has affected the production and consumption of reality television programmes:

- voyeurism
- celebrity
- interactivity.

The Internet is essentially a voyeuristic medium. The audience is generally anonymous but able to access a whole range of images and information about other people's lives. It is hardly surprising that the solitary, voyeuristic nature of the Internet means that a high proportion of its traffic is to pornographic sites. It is noteworthy that much of the interest in reality television programmes surrounds the audience's voyeuristic interest in people having sex in front of cameras. The reverse side of voyeurism is, of course, exhibitionism. The Web encourages people to behave in an exhibitionist way that they might not consider in public. The webcam, a small camera connected to a PC, allows Web users to give worldwide access to the intimate details of their daily lives. A significant amount of webcam usage is for pornographic purposes but there are also sites where people celebrate the ordinariness of their daily lives by allowing all of it to be transmitted across the Internet.

This technology enables people to achieve fame and notoriety for no reason other than their willingness to allow other people access to their lives. In a similar way, the participants in reality television shows achieve celebrity status and attempt to build successful media careers on the strength of their involvement with the show.

Celebrity has become central to our everyday lives. Celebrity status was once reserved for those who had achieved highly in their field, Hollywood actors and sports stars for example. In a media-saturated society there is an insatiable demand for celebrity to fill television airtime and the columns of the newspapers and magazines. The manufacture of celebrities, some with painfully short-lived careers, is essential to fuel this demand and reality television is one way of doing this.

Another important dimension that the Internet has brought to television viewing is that of interactivity. When using the Web, audiences have an important degree of control over what appears on screen. They are also able to change what is on screen by the click of a mouse. The ability to do this is inevitably going to make viewers dissatisfied with any passive role of simply receiving whatever television broadcasters choose to send them. Email, telephone lines and text messaging are methods by which an audience can influence what is on screen, primarily by voting for characters and personalities they do or do not like. By voting for an unpopular or abrasive personality to remain on the show they can add to the narrative conflict and increase the level of excitement in a programme. The use of expensive premium-rate phone lines is also another important source of income for television companies. Potentially the most telling technological innovation is the capacity of digital satellite receivers to respond directly to televisual output by direct interaction through the remote control. This technology allows such direct engagement that, as the technology becomes more widely available in homes, it is likely to mean the development of more and more interactive opportunities in broadcasting, not least through advertising and sponsorship. This phenomenon, known as convergence technology, will ultimately bring all of our communication devices together, allowing us full interactivity through the television screen.

The voyeurism and exhibition that we now see as central to much of our culture has its origins in and is a reflection of our society's fixation with surveillance. Postmodern culture has taken surveillance and turned it into fun although potentially it is a serious threat to all our civil liberties. Programmes such as *Police Camera Action*, which employed footage shot by traffic police during car pursuits for example, have done much to popularise a genre of programme which relies on real-life surveillance. Rather than a threat to our liberty, the existence of surveillance cameras has become an opportunity for people to become stars in their own films, often for ridiculous or even anti-social behaviour. Reality TV becomes an inevitable extension of the idea of playing with surveillance, welcoming cameras to witness our most intimate and often embarrassing exploits.

SPORT IN THE MEDIA

So once we investigate a text such as reality TV it becomes obvious that there are forces well beyond popularity with audiences that shape the nature of these programmes. Moreover, it is often the case that these forces operate best unseen and unconsciously, with 'reality' as a well-tried disguise. George Orwell once said that propaganda 'hits below the intellect': much of what the mass media 'peddle' works in this way. Orwell also foresaw the popularity of the national lottery in his seminal work *Nineteen Eighty-Four*, but couldn't have predicted the continuing power of professional sport as an ideological engine, a new 'opiate of the people'. The political agenda of a newspaper is often first revealed or betrayed by its sports headlines and much can be gleaned about our society from an encounter with Sven's latest dilemma.

Sports news is of course, these days, very often simply 'news': hold the front page: read all about it. David Beckham is as likely to be staring from the front page as the back. Even his admission of a deliberate booking in a World Cup qualifier against Wales in October 2004 had a crossover function as the integrity of the whole nation seemed for a short period to depend on 'the living endorsement'. Would Bobby Moore, the England captain who lifted the World Cup in 1966, have done such a thing, or more pertinently, would he have admitted it?

'Becks' takes his primary meaning and infamous nickname from football but you can also see that his other life as a brand is sending messages back. His 'meaning' has been through a storm in recent years with stories of his infidelities ironically shaking the 'Charles and Di' fantasy of 'Posh and Becks', while at the same time also undermining the ordinary Essex boy and girl 'take'. The meanings of 'Becks' are in this way woven into a series of narratives in which he is variously celebrated and pilloried but also maintained and perpetuated as a sign (and, cynically, as a brand). As a media figure Beckham also finds himself continually contextualised by tabloid headlines: from 'GOLDEN-BALLS' to 'TEN BRAVE HEROES AND ONE STUPID BOY'.

The coverage of sport, and particularly football, has always been a reasonable barometer of society's priorities. The fact that Beckham, shortly before the 2002 World Cup, introduced a good many people to the metatarsal bone gives credence to Bill Shankly's line (quoted in full on p. 14) about football and 'life and death'. Certainly the amount of passion and money spent on football by many football fans stands in bleak contrast to the amount of both spent on their partners or even with them. Moreover, the cosmopolitan nature of much football at the highest level in this country means that in all but exceptional cases the old relationships between players and their constituencies, the fans, are breaking or have broken down. And all this, because of a model of economic dependency, in the glare of the media spotlight. With every action scrutinised from any angle, everything becomes potentially significant and part of an argument or narrative. For example, the kissing of the club badge was once a ritual reserved for local boys made good, lifelong supporters living their dream. Now, it has simply become a handy reminder to highly paid mercenaries of who is paying their wages; and this all brought to you through the convention of the close-up. Think how goal celebrations have increased in sophistication and frequency: it's because they know we're watching and so we, the audience, become implicated in the charade.

In other words, in terms of wider contexts sports coverage is already a promising area of study. One of these is the economic context. Where once you might have expected to find in a book like this one a graphic detailing the ownership of media institutions, it is now as interesting to detail involvement in sporting franchises. From the point where Sky attempted to gain control of one of the world's leading sporting brands, Manchester United, a new era had dawned. The intervening period has seen Russian multibillionaire Roman Abramovitch buy both Chelsea and a couple of teams of highly paid performers, including a manager. Meanwhile Arsenal have agreed to call their as yet unbuilt new stadium after a leading Middle Eastern airline, in what may prove to be a completely new 'futures' market. It seems likely that we are lurching towards an American model of ownership with franchises so insecurely 'rooted' that they could even be moved from East to West Coast or from anywhere to anywhere else. In fact, arguably the job has begun: in principle in terms of the replacement of Wimbledon F.C. with 'M.K. Dons' and in effect with the Chelsea side who turned up overnight and might disappear just as quickly.

These trends have many implications for both the mass media and the society they serve. International sports franchises are likely to have media divisions or at least to be media 'savvy'. In television, for example, there is already talk of the next Premier League licence as the next important watershed since there is a good chance it will mean an end to collective bargaining, wherein each club has an equal stake. With MUTV and Chelsea TV already offered (though not taken up) in more than 50 per cent of homes, the danger is obvious. In a business already skewed by massive discrepancies in achieved revenue, any further redistribution in favour of the bigger clubs would be disastrous, and not only financially.

Yet if we look for the reasons why more tabloid inches are devoted to sport, especially football, than to any other topic, talk of multinational superstars is somewhat misplaced. The reasons why this has been the case since at least the 1960s are much more pertinent to you as Media Studies students. The 1960s, as we have noted, was a decade of change. One of the contexts of these changes was clearly economic. A generation that had grown up with the war and then postwar rationing was suddenly affluent (well off) in a way that it had never been before. What happened therefore in the late 1950s and early 1960s was the creation of a need, a potential, a vacuum. A new audience of teenagers was emerging which was eager to consume whatever it could find. British popular culture of the 1960s in all its sometimes tawdry glory was the answer to this need.

Alongside popular music, television and film, newly accessible fashion and popular fiction sat a redefined and reconstructed idea of sport as a stylish (and healthy) embodiment of all we stood for. And football was the essence of an essence, producing both England's most significant sporting moment in 1966 and the first genuine 'cross-over' celebrity, George Best, who when featured returning from a European fixture was christened 'El Beatle' (the Beatles at this moment were allegedly more popular than Christ). As a result of an air crash that had wiped out half their team in 1958, Manchester United were the only real nationwide 'brand' at this time but the advent of *Match of the Day* in 1964 changed all this. Television gave extra prominence to top clubs and made celebrities out of their players. The image of Bobby Moore lifting the World Cup in 1966 was given extra impact by the fact that everyone knew who he was, because they'd seen him play (on the telly).

Football also tapped into that other 1960s strand: regionalism. In the same way that a generation of northern working-class actors became the faces and voices of the era, so it was that another cultural (and social) contest was being fought out between the North-West (Liverpool and Manchester) and London in a sporting sense. Suddenly football was a key component of contemporary culture and down-market tabloids like the *Sun* were 'born' partly to contextualise the 'new' sport in its relationship to television, celebrity and sexuality. Now, '15 pages of supersun sport' is the norm, roughly 20 per cent of the whole and a place where the ideological stance of the paper is often given freest expression. In a set of sports headlines you will usually find a clear indication of a paper's ideological mode of address or at least what it assumes about its audiences. Matches against Germany in any sport are an explicit example of this: 'Herr we go!', 'This time it's war' and 'England expects' are three of the milder versions. A selection of sports headlines for any given day will prove a number of points. Listen to the *Sun* for a moment:

- FERGIE'S HISTORY
- GLAZER BID IN TATTERS
- BUTTON IT, BECKS
- WE'RE GOING HYPER
- REYES CAN STOP US FALLING APART
- STRACH TO THE FUTURE
- GEREMI'S BLAST; NO WAY JOSE
- HUCK UP FOR RUCK
- IT'S ALL GO FOR BOW
- KEV'S FOWL PLAY

ACTIVITY...

What do you notice about the language used across these headlines? What clues do you get about the stories they 'anchor'?

WARNING! Anchorage is hardly an appropriate term in many cases: KEV'S FOWL PLAY, for example, which appears to suggest wrongdoing, is in fact a story about Manchester City manager KEVin Keegan deciding to PLAY striker Robbie FOWLer in City's next game.

There are a number of readings that might be given to this set of 'titles' but what must be addressed is the animated language which suggests extreme emotions and, beyond this, a specifically created context of consumption. What is often granted by the media to all manner of sporting events is a vocabulary and register which seems

straightforwardly exaggerated, if not simply inappropriate. This is the language of high drama: notions of 'tragedy', the routine assignment to a sporting event of the stature 'classic', 'titanic' or even 'historic'. Emotions then take their cues from this, so 'woe', 'fury' and 'despair' are used to crank things further and sport is asked to assume a sort of cathartic function, a way of working through and working out our passions and repressions. Postmodernists might see this as a textbook hyperreality where repro-duced values and emotions function only in their own contexts. Marxists, on the other hand, would probably sense the ideological manipulation, the disabling set of false needs and values that supply our 'addiction'. George Orwell (2000) was perhaps implicitly aware of both when he pointed out in more straightforward terms the impli-cations of relaxing the discipline which connects meanings with words (his best advice was 'let the meaning choose the word'). He believed that the 'slovenliness of our language makes it easier for us to have foolish thoughts'.

Sport is now clearly a branch of the entertainment industry, channelled by the media to our homes. But it is also a powerful set of metaphors which relate to all aspects of our social life. These are in the first place issues of representation and are classically part of what Antonio Gramsci called hegemony (see p. 234), in which ideological positions are made to appear natural and unproblematic. Ideas about competition being part of human nature and of the inevitable dominance of the able and the strong are good examples of this. Where do we learn as effectively about the 'real' meaning of social class or ethnicity or gender in Britain today other than in the complex set of hierarchies or 'pecking orders' established by sports journalism? This is news without the implicit caveats (warnings): interested opinions masquerading as inconsequential facts. In the crudest test, sports measure their credibility and prestige from the amount of money Sky is prepared to pay for television rights and that in turn depends on the gender, class and cultural contexts.

The Norwegian media theorists Johan Galtung and Mari Holmboe Ruge identified four trends in newsgathering and presentation, all of which are amply evidenced by a look at any national sports broadcast or print or moving image:

- reference to elite personnel
- reference to elite nations
- personalisation
- negativity.

ACTIVITY...

How far are these the dominant themes of sports reporting? What does this tell us about the meanings of sport in the media?

And this story is extended if you simply ask a few obvious but pertinent questions. These are designed to open to examination the implicit matrix of values that 'scaffold' the reporting of sporting events. It was suggested by J.K. Galbraith (1969) that

advertising is 'a relentless propaganda on behalf of goods in general'. It is hard at times not to see the media's treatment of sport in the same light.

ACTIVITY . . .

Answer the following questions for a clearer context.

- What differences are there in the way that supposedly 'middle-class' sports like golf and rowing are presented compared with something like football?
- Why are so few women's sports adequately covered?
- What does the coverage of international events like the World Cup or the Olympic Games say about Britain's position in and attitude to the wider world?
- Why is Rugby Union covered more extensively than Rugby League?
- Comment on the increase in the percentage of female presenters of sports programmes: is this a positive sign for the promotion of sport among females or are there other factors? Compare male and female sports presenters.
- What are the factors that make some sports stars into significant celebrities?
- What are the values that sports coverage asks us to invest in?

Karl Marx famously asserted in *Contribution to the Critique of Hegel's Philosophy of Right* [1848] that 'Religion is the sigh of the oppressed creature, the heart of a heartless world . . . the opium of the people.' That other great champion of the British working class, former Liverpool manager Bill Shankly, wryly observed that 'Some people say football is a matter of life and death – it's not, it's much more important than that.' Ideologically, it may be that these two statements are not dissimilar.

GETTING AT THESE WIDER CONTEXTS

You need to find a strategy for exploring such wider contexts for yourself in a similar way to how we have looked at those in this chapter. Unfortunately there is no magic formula to help you do this. The solution lies in research and most specifically in knowing where to look. Knowledge is not so much about knowing things as about knowing where to find out about things. On the plus side technology, particularly in the form of the PC and the Internet, has never been more user-friendly than it is today. Using it for searchable newspaper databases such as *Guardian Unlimited* cut out a lot of painstaking searching of back issues of print sources, for example.

So how do you go about getting information on wider contexts? Well, in many ways the answer to that question is wider than the scope of this book but the guidance that follows should at least get you started. It is to be hoped that your study of the media has in some ways awakened in you a curiosity that goes beyond media texts into broader social issues. Also, there will be other units in your course that might help sketch in some of the background information. What you have learned elsewhere may well have some bearing on the wider contexts of media texts. Remember that the skills other courses equip you with, for example historical research, will have an application in exploring these contexts. Similarly, you should be prepared to ask for help. Teachers, fellow students, family, friends and work colleagues will represent a variety of ages, backgrounds and world views that can be invaluable in helping you to contextualise your study of the media. So be prepared to go out and ask some questions; what you know is often less important than your ability and skills to go and find new information.

Getting started

The best starting point for finding out about contexts is the text itself. Within the text there are likely to be a number of clues that will enable you to move out into exploring some of the wider contexts that have informed its production and consumption. As part of your textual analysis you will be exploring the 'messages' contained within the texts. What is the text about? What is it saying? Also you need to look within a text for the broader social backdrop it might be reflecting. For example, where and when is it set? The geographical location of a text, for example, might contain some significant clues to its nature.

Next, it might be useful to consider how this text might relate to others of a similar type. You will read in 'Crime Fiction', Chapter 10, how different texts reflect the social background against which they were created. You need to think about how the texts you are looking at relate to other texts, which might be either contemporary or from a different historical period. If the texts are significantly different from each other, you need to decide how far this difference is due to the different contexts in which they were produced and consumed.

At this point you may find there is a need to dig deeper into some of the background or context of the text(s). This is going to involve you in doing some research. Fortunately a lot of background information is readily available on the Internet. Certainly this is a good starting point, although you may also find it necessary to seek out additional sources of information. For many students, however, the Internet can be as much of a hindrance as it is a help. Using it effectively requires both a degree of self-discipline and the ability to discriminate between what is useful and what is not. Try to take advantage of the many shortcuts that the Web offers. As we have already mentioned, searchable newspaper databases are a rapid way of unearthing information, especially if you focus on such areas as their media coverage. Similarly a site like The Internet Movie Database (http://www.imdb.com/) provides fast access to a vast film resource with invaluable hypertext links for tracking down details of actors, producers and directors. Such sites are also valuable in that they offer reasonably objective and reliable information. Where opinion is being expressed, this is readily identifiable. Similarly academic media sites such as Media and Communication Studies (MCS) and the Communication, Cultural and Media Studies (CCMS) website can be useful for sketching in background detail and providing contexts in a reliable way.

You need to be cautious, however, with fan sites and forums as, though generally well intentioned, these rarely contain objective and factual information, so it is important that you verify what you obtain from them. There are several sites that offer interesting background information and have a focus on media history. One of the best of these is TV Ark, which offers a vast range of television programme extracts sorted helpfully by genre. The BBC website also offers archive materials as well as some invaluable background information and links.

Remember that key concepts are potentially really helpful tools for exploring wider contexts in just the same way that they are for exploring the text itself. Here are some ideas to get you started.

- Media language: How is the text constructed? Does it have high production values? Is there evidence of sophisticated use of technology? What genre conventions are evident and how do these relate to those used in texts of the same genre?
- Representation: What does the text represent? How prevalent are these representations in other media of the time?
- Institution: Where does the text come from? Is it produced by a large media organisation? Is it commercially produced or made by the BBC or some alternative producer? Is it produced on behalf of a specific interest group?
- Audiences: What audience is targeted? How is the audience addressed? Is it a mass audience or a niche audience? What context was the text distributed in? How does it relate to audience expectations?
- Values and ideology: What value system is evident in the text? How might the ideology implicit in the text relate to the period when it was current? Does it reflect the mainstream or some counter-culture?

Of course if you are exploring two or more different texts, possibly from different eras, it becomes possible to see how their differences reflect some of the social change that has taken place. If, for example, you look at a situation comedy produced in the 1970s you may well be taken aback by the degree of racism and sexism it contains in comparison with a modern-day sitcom. Whether you draw the conclusion that racism and sexism are less prevalent in modern society is quite another issue. Certainly you might say that overt prejudice is less acceptable in the mass media. As a counter to much of our latter-day obsession with political correctness, many lads' magazines make a point of being overtly sexist and 'incorrect', supposedly in an 'ironic' way.

NOTEBOX

One advantage of living in such a media-saturated society is that it is relatively easy to get access to non-contemporary texts. Most video rental and sales outlets have extensive back catalogues of both feature films and television series. Also it is worth keeping an eye on the listings for the many digital satellite channels. A number of these are theme- or genre-based and transmit programmes from previous eras. Sources such as the BFI Film Library have back catalogues of more esoteric material.

Similarly if you are looking at two or more texts from the same era, you may find it useful to explore how differently they reflect that era. It may be that they represent different ideological viewpoints; for example, the *Daily Mail* and the *Guardian* are quite a long way apart ideologically on many issues and each would report a story about asylum seekers, for example, very differently.

NOTEBOX

One area that some students find difficulty with is understanding the political context in which media texts exist. It is useful if you equip yourself with a basic grasp of political systems, if you don't already have one. Politics is a complex business and political practices change and evolve over time.

Political positions are often represented as right and left wing. At its simplest, left-wing politics are aligned with those of Karl Marx, who gave his name to the political philosophy we call Marxism. Marx believed in an egalitarian society in which wealth was distributed equally and fairly according to the needs of individuals rather than their power to earn money. Marxism implies a powerful state, with state ownership of industry and commerce, the means of production. Marxists believe in a fairer society committed to taking care of the needy. Marxist political ideals are also called socialism, although on the left there are varying degrees or shades of belief, ranging from those committed to revolution by whatever means to organisations like the British Labour Party, committed to bringing about change through parliamentary democracy. Left-wing politics are often criticised for stifling individual initiative and creating an unwieldy bureaucracy.

Right-wing politics are represented by a commitment to free market economics. People should be free to make their own way in the world and if they gain wealth at the expense of others, this is their reward for enterprise and initiative. Supporters of this system, such as the Conservative Party, argue that individual endeavour and the willingness to risk capital are essential to creating wealth in a society. Social inequality has to be accepted as an inevitable by-product of such a system. At its extreme, right-wing parties are nationalistic and racist, for example European Fascist parties, the successors of Hitler's Nazism.

In Western democracies most of the major political parties vie for the centre ground of politics, advocating a mixed economy in which capitalism generates wealth which can be used for providing social services such as education and health care. 'New Labour' in fact talks of this as 'the third way'.

Intertextuality is another tool in the analytical toolkit that can help in an exploration of wider contexts. One of the qualities of postmodern media is their capacity to feed off themselves. The capacity for media to reference themselves in terms of other media seems almost without limit. Examples of one form of media commenting on or

criticising another form provide an interesting opportunity to explore wider contexts. Some of the criticism in the press of the issues discussed on previous pages in relation to reality television or sport, for example, can offer a wider perspective on these topics. Another example is the marketing of new films or television programmes where the stars are frequently featured in listings and specialist magazines as well as in newspapers and on radio and television.

Of course the Internet is not the only source of information open to you. Books and libraries still remain a key source of information for anyone undertaking serious research. Before you use a library, though, it is always a good idea to have a clear sense of precisely what it is you are looking for. If you have managed to distil what you want into a couple of relevant questions, you will find library staff not only able to help you but more than willing to do so. If you approach them with some vague unformed notion of what you want, they will be less inclined to offer their time. In a library, very often the simplest places are the best starting point. Encyclopaedias offer easily digested and relevant information to get you started as well as suggestions for places to go for more detailed material. So the reference section of your library may be a good starting point. This will also contain more specialist materials such as the *Guardian Media Directory* and *Benn's Media Directory*, invaluable sources of information about the media in the United Kingdom.

In the section of this book titled 'Resources' we give a list of institutions that you might find useful when exploring wider contexts. But one especially useful source that you can easily overlook is other people. As we have pointed out, the media constitute a prime mechanism for the transmission of culture in our society. It does this to a large degree through the way in which people choose to use them and the impact they have on them. By talking to people, especially those of a different generation to your own, you can gain a valuable insight into the media as well as those wider contexts that are so important for your study at this level. Of course, this is potentially the most subjective information of all, so you need to be selective and discriminating about how you use it. Remember, the more shades of opinion you have available the better. So don't be afraid to go and ask people for the information that you want, but remember it is a matter of courtesy to listen to their reply, even if it is not really what you were looking for.

FURTHER READING

Hollows, J. and Jancovich, M. (1995) *Approaches to Popular Film*, Manchester University Press.
www.theory.org.uk

Storey, J. (1997) *Cultural Theory and Popular Culture: A Reader*, Prentice Hall.

Storey, J. (2000) *Cultural Theory and Popular Culture: An Introduction*, Prentice Hall.

Strinati, D. (2004) *An Introduction to Theories of Popular Culture*, Routledge.

▼ 2 INDEPENDENT STUDY/RESEARCH

In this chapter we look at methods of approaching coursework essays including:

- ■ research techniques
- ■ getting started
- ■ formulating a title
- ■ structure and presentation
- ■ bibliography and references.

Most Media courses offer you the opportunity to undertake some type of sustained independent study or research into a topic of your own choice. This may vary from a dissertation of some 10,000 words to a coursework essay where the word limit may be significantly less. Whatever the parameters in which you are required to work, this is an opportunity for you to pursue a particular interest or idea that you may have developed during your course. Clearly one of the objectives behind this exercise is to assess your ability to work independently and to prepare you for opportunities to undertake more complex and sustained research briefs, either academic or industrial, later in your career. As with all types of assessment, it provides a means of assessing your grasp of theoretical perspectives in Media Studies and your capacity to apply these to debates, issues and texts that you find interesting.

Before undertaking any kind of study, though, it is important that you make absolutely certain of the precise terms of reference under which you are being asked to work. You need to check out:

- ■ restrictions on the subject matter you can tackle
- ■ any word limits you must observe
- ■ the deadline for completion
- ■ the need for/availability of illustrations
- ■ presentation guidelines
- ■ how and by whom your study will be assessed.

The AQA GCE Media Studies Unit 5 offers a typical opportunity for students to undertake an independent study into a topic of their own choosing. Central to this study is the requirement that students focus primarily on a contemporary topic. Indeed, 'contemporary' is carefully defined in the specification as 'two years previous to the start of the GCE course'. Students are limited to texts 'first released' during this period. This prevents a prime focus on older texts that may have been newly released on DVD or retransmitted on satellite channels.

You are not, however, limited to using only contemporary texts as defined above. Historical texts can be used but these should serve as 'a point of comparative analysis'. This means in effect that reference to non-contemporary texts should only be made where these can shed some light on the contemporary texts and issues that are the main focus of your study.

It is always important to ensure that you know how you are going to be assessed before you make a start on any study of this type. One way to do this is to ask your tutor to spell out to you just what s/he is expecting and, more importantly, how it will be marked. All coursework for public examinations such as GCE has to be assessed against published criteria. The task that you are set should also match with published Assessment Objectives. Assessment Objectives, or AOs, define precisely what skills and knowledge you are being tested against. For example, in the AQA independent study unit one of the main assessment objectives is that you:

■ Demonstrate the ability to use appropriate investigative and research techniques in carrying out an independent study of a media text, topic or issue.

ACTIVITY . . .

What do you think is meant by the word 'appropriate' in relation to investigative and research techniques? Here are some possible sources. Explain how each one might be used appropriately:

■ texts
■ books
■ specialist magazines
■ the Web.

You might find it interesting to consider the assessment criteria against which your work will be marked. You can check these in detail for yourself on the AQA website (www.aqa.org.uk) but it is worth considering a bullet point from the top level of the marking scheme; which reads:

Detailed, thorough and well-illustrated research with clear and accurate identification and referencing of sources used.

This bullet point implies that the student must engage thoroughly with different research sources, primary and secondary, and make use of these by carefully selecting

and evaluating them. You then need to illustrate your research with textual evidence that you have uncovered in exploring your topic. Notice too that you are asked to identify your research sources clearly and accurately so that you can reference them (see p. 34).

(see p. 34).

NOTEBOX

Research can be divided into two different types. Research from primary sources requires you to engage first hand in order to get information, for example by interviewing people or considering a specific media text itself. Secondary research is likely to consist mainly of articles, for example, in journals and textbooks. These will have previously explored the issue you are researching. For example, if you are looking into the issue of the audience appeal of soap opera, you may well want to find out what a writer such as Sonia Livingstone has to say in her book *Making Sense of Television* (1990). Both sources of information, primary and secondary, are equally valid but one type of source may be more appropriate than another according to the information you are seeking or the nature of the research you are undertaking.

The AQA independent study seeks to assess two other elements. The first is what is known as your synoptic ability. 'Synoptic' is defined as 'presenting a summary or general view of a whole', which implies that your study should attempt to tie together the many strands of what you have learned on the course as a whole, for example through the key concepts, primarily, media language, representation, audience, institution, values and ideology. The second element is your ability to demonstrate your critical autonomy. This is defined as 'the ability to apply critical ideas and principles to new situations'.

If you consider these two priorities, it becomes clear why there is such an emphasis on exploring contemporary media texts. What you are being asked to do is to apply the many concepts and critical ideas you have been introduced to on the course to new situations – in this case contemporary media texts, which will presumably not have been considered already in textbooks and other sources.

Finally you will need to be aware of the issue of 'wider contexts' which you may also have met elsewhere on your course. In order to ensure you meet the demand to look at these wider contexts, make sure that your study focuses well beyond the texts themselves onto a consideration of them as a reflection of the context in which they are both produced and consumed. At a very basic level you need to relate the texts you are considering to the social, historical, political, cultural and economic background that led to their existence. No small order, you are probably thinking. Make sure you have read Chapter 1, 'Wider contexts'. Exploring wider contexts will involve you in background research into how and why the texts you are considering are like they are. For example, suppose you are looking

continued

at some aspect of reality television. The wider context might lead you to think about why there has been a sudden growth in the number of shows of this genre being screened. (This issue is explored more fully in the Introduction.) You would need to consider looking at some of the following areas:

- digital television and the increase in air time to be filled
- technology and audience interaction
- audience participation
- surveillance cameras
- the Web and new media.

MAKING A START

Getting started is very often the hardest part of any independent work, not least because it puts responsibility on you to come up with ideas rather than relying on a tutor to tell you what to do. Devising ideas that are going to work is a high-level media skill, so don't be daunted if you find it hard at first. There are a number of ways in which you can help yourself get started in order to arrive at a workable title.

Remember it is always better to have far too many ideas than far too few. Your tutor will always be able to help you decide which of several ideas is the best one to pursue. He or she will find it a lot more difficult, if not downright frustrating, should you be unable to come up with any. It is always good to write down any ideas you have in a notebook or somewhere on your computer for future reference. So try to take a run at choosing a topic and jot down ideas for later consideration. Think also about areas that have interested you on the course. There is likely to be at least one topic that you feel you would like more opportunity to get involved in. Consider how it might make the focus of your independent study. Similarly, consider some of your personal or leisure-time interests. An interest in Hollywood cinema, celebrity magazines or even a particular genre of music might all be the focus of a good piece of coursework. It might even be a topic that you feel strongly about – the dumbing down of television or coverage of a particular issue or event in the press, for example. It might even be a political issue, or something connected with sport or a similar interest. You will find the work much more rewarding if it is something you feel you want to engage with rather than a task that will become a chore about which you feel nothing but resentment.

However you find an appropriate area of study, it is of paramount importance that you hone down your initial interest to a title which is workable, focused and able to be realised within the parameters you have been set, specifically word limits and time allowed. It may be that you start with quite a broad area of interest. For example, you may think that writing about the topic 'Women in the Media' would fit the bill. Obviously such a topic has much to recommend it; representations of women are a well-rehearsed debate within Media Studies, so finding material for your secondary research would be straightforward. Similarly women, and specifically images of women, are to be found on a daily basis on television and billboards, in newspapers and magazines, and on the Web, so there would be no shortage of raw material. The topic would also lend itself to engaging with the key concepts outlined earlier and to an exploration of the wider contexts that influence how women represent themselves and are represented in the media. The problem about making this your title, however, is that it is far too wide ranging. There is enough material in a topic like that for at least a textbook the size of this one, if not several textbooks.

Let us consider how we might take this topic and reduce it in a couple of stages to a focused and workable title. As we have indicated, part of the problem is the breadth of the topic. Any attempt to cover this area is likely to result in at best a superficial response with no real detailed engagement. Simply by reducing this breadth to one particular media form or genre will help bring it into the realms of possibility. 'Women in Celebrity Magazines' or 'Women in Sitcoms' are potentially more manageable titles, though both could benefit by being more sharply focused. Another interesting approach might be to look at a sub-category of women, perhaps in terms of age, ethnicity or class. So, for example, teenage girls or working-class women would be a more focused group to consider.

Suppose you decide to base your study on television advertising as this allows you plenty of access to contemporary texts as well as a lot of background material from books and on the Web to help frame the debate about gender representation in this genre. Now consider taking this a stage further and producing a topic that would be tightly focused. For example, you might look at a specific group of products that either target or use women. This might lead you to such potential areas as:

- the marketing of cars to a female audience
- images of women in advertising for men's toiletries
- women and domestic cleaning products.

You should be able to see that what started as a vast and potentially unmanageable topic area has now been slimmed down to a specific focus for which there should be plenty of both textual examples and theoretical concepts to explore. Having found this tight focus, your next job is to devise a title which will ensure you maintain a consistent approach to the topic. One popular way to do this is to frame a hypothesis. A hypothesis is a theory or idea which you intend to test out. In this context, a hypothesis would be a media-related proposition or idea which you would then seek to test by examining textual examples and applying media theory. It doesn't really matter whether you end up proving or disproving your hypothesis. It may be that you find some evidence in support of your proposition and some which is contradictory.

For example, we might take the first topic on our list, 'the marketing of cars to a female audience', and turn this into a hypothesis by applying some critical thinking. You may have noticed that women in contemporary advertisements for cars are often portrayed as being active, for example being seen to drive the car, feisty, challenging the role of men as the 'experts' on all things automotive, and emancipated, as seen in their independence in both choosing and using the car. You may also be aware that such representations have not always been the norm. You may even wonder if there are any social, cultural, political and above all economic reasons why women are being depicted and addressed in this different way. So you might wish to frame a hypothesis to explore why this is so. You might then come up with a title along the following lines: 'Contemporary car advertising is rejecting traditional patriarchal values and aspirations in order to target female consumers'.

Note that although the chosen title invites a contemporary take on the issues it also needs to be informed by some sense of non-contemporary representations. You would, for example, find it fruitful to look back at advertisements from a previous era to identify some of the ways in which women were addressed when similar products were being promoted.

TITLE

A good title will ensure that your study is focused. To be effective, therefore, a title must limit you to a precise topic area which you can cover, rather than leaving you with an open field which would lead to a sprawling and unfocused essay.

NOTEBOX

Stuck for ideas? Remember that the world is full of media texts, each a potential source for exploring a range of issues and debates. The hard bit should be deciding what you are not going to do rather than finding something to write about. If you are having problems finding a topic or simply feel fazed by the difficulties of getting started, then here are some suggestions that might help.

■ Have a sift through some recent back issues of the media sections in the broadsheets, e.g. the *Guardian* Media Section published on Mondays.
■ Have a look in the library at any media textbooks that you have found interesting and accessible.
■ Similarly, visit a few academic media websites that might inspire you to come up with a topic. The one in Figure 2.1 would make a good starting point.
■ Specialist film and media magazines and their related websites can be a source of ideas.
■ The tabloid press often contains stories about controversial issues that may provide a good focus for your research.
■ Look out for television and radio programmes that deal with media-related issues.

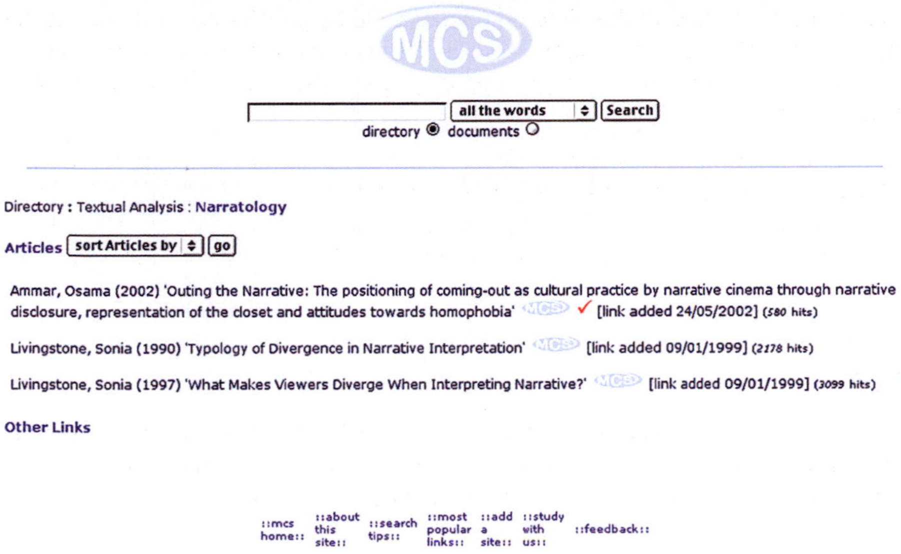

Figure 2.1 *MCS site. Hosted by the University of Wales, Aberystwyth. Source: http://www.aber.ac.uk/media.*

ACTIVITY . . .

Take one of the following topics and decide how you might hone it down into the title of a topic suitable for a 3,000-word study. Try using the approach discussed in previous pages to help crystallise your idea:

- reality TV
- disability
- marketing films
- segmentation
- the effects debate
- censorship
- lads' mags
- downloading music from the Internet.

Once you have formulated your title, you will have defined for yourself the area that you are going to explore. The challenge now is to get started on this exploration. A good place to start with any enquiry into media issues is the text itself, so make sure that you have ready access to any examples of media texts that you need. Where necessary, you may have to make copies of the texts that you are going to use. If you don't have this ready access, it is probably best to give up and do something else. It is also a good idea to limit the amount of textual material you are going to look at. Avoid getting bogged down in viewing hours of videotape or scanning pages of press cuttings.

Remember to keep a note of the source of all the materials you are using. You will need this later for referencing (see p. 34).

Be aware that the text is not an end in itself. You may be tempted to produce a virtuoso piece of textual analysis, but it is likely that what is expected is that you relate the texts to the wider contexts that influence their production and consumption. If you are looking, as we have suggested, at representations of women in car advertising, comparative textual analysis might lead you to the conclusion that women in contemporary examples are portrayed as more independent, assertive and in control of their own lives than their counterparts of ten years ago. While this is an interesting conclusion in itself, you also need to pursue the issue of why it is so. Some explanation of economic, political, historical, social and cultural factors might help to reveal that the increased economic power of women and the declining emphasis on their child-rearing roles have led to their having a disposable income that car manufacturers want them to spend on buying cars. This ability to introduce wider contexts into your study of the texts is clearly very important if you are to demonstrate your grasp of the underlying social factors that are at play when texts are produced.

This is also an appropriate point at which to consider the theoretical perspectives that you might need to apply. In our Introduction we looked at the nature of media theory and considered how it might be applicable to your course of study. Academic study must always take account of previous research into any topic or field that the researcher seeks to explore. So with your study you must acknowledge that you are working within an academic tradition. For example, if you choose the topic outlined above, you will not be the first person to look at the role of women in advertising. In 1982 for example, Gillian Dyer published *Advertising as Communication*, an important book that laid down a lot of the ground rules for exploring advertising in its wider cultural context. It is important that you make a point of seeking out such a publication and similar academic studies to see what has already been said on the topic. You might find a good starting point is the companion volume to this book, *Media Studies: The Essential Resource* (Rayner *et al.* 2004). For example, if you are exploring ideas about audience segmentation and niche marketing, Shaun Moores's article (Rayner *et al.* 2004: 105) might be an accessible starting point.

The trick to writing a convincing essay of this sort is to be precise and confident with the theory that you choose to apply. If you are going to use a theoretical concept or even just a technical term, make sure that you understand fully what it means and how you should use it. Half-understood theoretical perspectives or misused jargon do little to enhance your credibility and must be avoided at all costs.

A Level Media Studies specifications put a lot of emphasis on the concept of synopticity, which can be defined as the drawing together of different strands of the course you have followed to demonstrate that you have an overview of the subject area. You are expected to demonstrate this synoptic ability in your independent study. The key concepts are of paramount importance in helping you to do this, as they form the basis of the toolkit you have developed to help you explore texts, issues and debates in an independent and autonomous fashion.

Taking the title 'Contemporary car advertising is rejecting traditional patriarchal values and aspirations in order to target female consumers', work out how this topic might be tackled by exploring some of the ideas that might be thrown up by focusing on each of the key concepts.

- Media language: How are the advertisements constructed? How do they relate to similar advertisements in the genre?
- Representation: How are the genders represented in these advertisements? How far do these depart from established stereotypes of gender in TV advertisements?
- Audience: What is the target audience for these advertisements? How is it being addressed?
- Institution: What context are the advertisements shown in? For example, at what time and before or during what sort of programmes?
- Ideology: How far are these advertisements a response to a shifting power balance between the genders?

As you can see from this activity, some of the key concepts are going to be more significant than others, depending on the title you are working on. In this case the major emphasis might well be focused on representation and ideology, although clearly the other concepts will be relevant to the study.

AQA independent study

The logic to the emphasis placed on the contemporary should now be a little more apparent. Historical studies are inevitably prone to the rehashing of existing materials culled from secondary sources. A study of *Citizen Kane* (1941) is almost certain to get bogged down in the many critical theories surrounding Orson Welles's film. By insisting on contemporary insight, it is intended that students will apply their critical under-standing and insight to texts and issues that have not already been heavily explored.

Here are some of the places that you will need to visit to develop ideas about how to approach your study. Not all of them will be appropriate to every study, so don't use this as a checklist of things to do. It is intended more as a list of suggestions of sources that you may find helpful.

- The texts themselves: as we have mentioned previously, a good study is likely to start with a detailed look at the texts you have chosen or, to be more precise, a detailed look at those elements of the texts that are most appropriate. For example, if you are exploring the representation of young people in the soap operas *Coronation Street* and *EastEnders*, then your focus needs to be on those segments of the narrative which involve young people.
- Theoretical perspectives: you may find it useful to choose a particular perspective from which to look at issues. For example, a feminist perspective, a Marxist one and a postmodern one provide very different insights into an issue.
- Existing textbook materials: general reading on how an issue has been pursued in the past will not only provide you with useful background but also help to suggest ways in which to frame your own approach.
- Websites: these need to be used judiciously with careful referencing. The way to get the best from the Web is to approach everything from a position of scepticism. Always have an eye to the credentials of the people behind the website. Some websites are unashamedly attempts to promote the people who control them. Consider carefully what authority the originators might have before you give them too much respect.
- Wider contexts: you will probably find you need to spend time looking at some of the social, political, cultural and economic circumstances which have influenced the production of the texts. For example, if you are looking at young people in soaps you may like to think about how some of their storylines have come about. What are the factors in society at large that have persuaded the writers of the soap to look at these particular issues through a fictional narrative?
- It would be a good idea when you come to look at this important area of wider contexts that you revisit Chapter 1, which covers this important topic (pp. 4–18). It is there that you will find some useful suggestions for how best to research some of these background issues that will help place the texts you have chosen into a wider context.

It is important that you understand how to make use of some of the sources mentioned above. Probably the best approach is to make notes from these sources so that you begin the process of writing material in your own words. In cases where you want to use material taken directly from a source, then you will need to make an accurate copy of it. In all cases, whether you are taking notes or copying directly, you must record details of what source materials you have used including, where you intend to quote directly, the page number. The reasons for doing this will be explained more fully in the section on referencing later in this chapter.

This is an appropriate moment to look at an issue of great concern to exam boards and universities throughout the world – plagiarism. Plagiarism is copying someone else's work and passing it off as one's own. The problem has become so extensive that staff in universities now use special software to detect plagiarism in work that has been handed in for assessment by students. Some plagiarism is deliberate cheating, for example where students download pre-prepared essays from the Internet and pass them off as their own work. Bear in mind that this rarely helps students since such pre-prepared materials tend not to fit at all precisely the brief or title to which they are working. Such materials are aimed at students who are either too lazy or too far behind with their studies to do a proper job or those who should be on another course.

In many cases, certainly that of AQA Unit 5 Independent Study, you will be required to sign a statement that the work you have submitted is yours and yours alone. If you lie about this it may have implications beyond simply being disqualified from one exam or one qualification, so do be careful. In fairness, a lot of plagiarism is unintentional. It is committed by students who may not have fully understood the complex business of how to use secondary sources. The very simple answer is to make sure that you attribute everything that you borrow from any sources other than your own head. Not only does this make sure you do not fall foul of the plagiarism issue, it also means you will write an essay which demonstrates your engagement with media issues.

Perhaps the greatest pitfall is where you decide to use source material published on the Internet. The temptation to cut and paste material into a bricolage essay can be too great for some students. What they end up with is a collage of different voices forming a mosaic study that is clearly not their own unaided work. The Internet is too valuable a source to ignore, but do make sure that you use it in just the same way as you might a book or other printed source. Details of how to reference Internet material is given in the section on referencing (p. 34), but do make sure that for each site from which you choose to use material, you make a careful note of the key details.

Also try to make sure that you build on any secondary source you use by providing your own commentary. Either use it to support your argument or to put a counter-position to the one you have adopted yourself. Finally, try to apply the ideas to new texts other than the one used in the original. For example, if a commentator is writing about soaps, the texts referred to will have been broadcast some time ago even if the book is newly published. If you want to refer to or comment on the ideas put forward, then do so in relation to some more contemporary examples of the sort of texts already considered.

Remember that you need to be critical about the secondary sources you use. Just because someone is a well-known writer on Media Studies issues, it does not mean that what s/he says is necessarily right. Part of your job as a student is to weigh up and evaluate what commentators say and decide both its value and its relevance of it to your own exploration of media issues. As Noel Williams points out in his book *How to Get a 2:1 in Media, Communication and Cultural Studies*:

> MCCS [Media, Communication and Cultural Studies] students need to develop a healthily critical attitude to every idea they come across. Everything you hear and read is based on certain attitudes, conventions and traditions. Much of it is based on vested interest, misperceptions, ideological bias, research limitations, cultural prejudice, and so on. Even a text like the one you are reading now is not a 'neutral' guide on how to be the best student you could be. It is written by a

particular author, with particular expertise, a particular cultural and personal background, a particular set of views on what is good and bad in MCCS, and so on. All of my perceptions and preconceptions mean that this text will probably have a particular slant, particular strengths and weaknesses, which I am (by definition) unlikely to recognize. It's up to someone else, you, the reader, to take a critical attitude to this text; to decide what is worthwhile and what less so; to determine what can be used, and what should be regarded with a slightly sceptical air.

Williams 2004: 26

NOTEBOX

The AQA specification requires that texts used are contemporary. This is carefully defined in the specification to include only those texts first released no more than two years prior to the start of your course. For most GCE students this will mean around three or four years prior to the time when they are working on their independent study. For example, if you start working on your independent study in January 2006, it is likely you started your GCE course in September 2004. So you can look at texts released any time after September 2002. Note that the words are 'produced or released'. This means that texts that are rereleased, or released on a new format such as DVD, are not eligible. *Citizen Kane*, for example, is often shown on terrestrial and satellite channels, but that does not change the fact that it was released cinematically in 1941. Of course you can refer to such an important film as background detail but it should not be the prime focus of your study. It can be quite informative, particularly if you are looking at the development of a genre, to use historical texts as a contrast to the contemporary texts that are your prime concern. If you need to check the first release date of a film, The Internet Movie Database (http://www.imdb.com/) is a reliable source. Checking the dates on which television programmes were first broadcast can be a little more complicated, so you need to be careful.

Once you have completed your research, you are likely to end up with some considerable detail about the texts themselves, the wider contexts in which they are produced and consumed, a theoretical perspective and probably some contrast with historical texts. In other words, you are likely to have far more material than the word limit for the essay is likely to provide. Clearly you are going to have to select your material to fit the parameters you have been given. One way in which you can do this is to prioritise the information, which means that you decide what is most important and what is least important. This is much easier to achieve if you have thought through how you are going to give your essay a structure.

STRUCTURE

There are a number of factors you need to take into account when deciding on a structure, but you must always bear your reader in mind. In most instances this will be your tutor. There may also be other secondary audiences. These include:

- external examiners whose job it is to check the marking of your tutors and ensure it is in line with national standards
- fellow students from whom you might seek support and criticism
- a wider audience, if your work is particularly good and is used for exemplar purposes, say on the Web or by an exam board at teacher training days.

So how are you going to make your work user-friendly to this potential wide and diverse readership? Well, one way is to make sure that you have a structure that will guide readers through the essay from start to finish without their having to do any unnecessary work by guessing what your argument is or which bit belongs where. You need to create a narrative which will carry the reader through the essay in a convincing and coherent manner. Even an accomplished reader will find 3,000 words quite a lot to absorb, so one of your tasks is to break up this narrative into digestible portions in the form of self-contained sections which are linked closely to each other. You also need to think about how you are going to signpost these individual sections in order to create a pathway through the essay. Consider the following as a possible way of creating a user-friendly structure.

- Title: a precise title explaining clearly but concisely what the essay will deal with.
- Introduction: it is at this point that you have the opportunity to tell your reader why you chose the topic and what you are setting out to demonstrate. You should then develop the title by explaining to the reader what approach to the topic you are planning to take, identifying the texts you will be focusing on, and outlining what methodologies you have used to find information. Remember one function of your introduction is to get your reader interested in much the same way as the 'intro' to a news story.
- Development: a survey of the existing situation in terms of study that has been made into this topic and what theoretical perspectives have been brought to bear by previous researchers.
- Findings: this is likely to be the main focus of your essay. This is the section where you expand and develop your ideas and offer the evidence that you have collected to support your arguments.
- Conclusion: explain what ideas you have ended up with and what further research might be undertaken to explore the topic further. Just as your introduction should make an impression on the reader, so your conclusion should leave him or her with a firm sense that your study has been worthwhile and meaningful, even if there is more research to be done before a full conclusion can be reached.
- Bibliography: list of sources used.

Such a shape is not going to be appropriate for every single attempt at independent research but it does provide you with a template or format that can be modified readily to suit different situations and demands. Notice that each of the sections would lend itself to being given an appropriate heading. This will allow you to use some typographical devices to further help the process of signposting. The use of different point sizes and bold and italic typefaces will all serve as useful ways of differentiating the sections of your essay.

A desktop publishing package like Word can take a lot of the hard work out of organising material into a logical structure through typographical signposting. It is worth spending some time getting used to this, or similar software, in order to access the useful formatting tools such as auto-text and auto-formatting. The essence of producing an attractive reader-friendly document is to be consistent in the use of the typographical devices that will signal, say, the start of each section. This will, of course, require some pre-planning so that you can decide which are main headings and which are sub-headings, for example. Remember too that devices such as numbering and bullet points break up dense texts and make them more accessible. Think also about what typeface it is best to use. Every typeface carries with it different connotations, some suggesting more seriousness and authority than others. Be prepared to experiment on your computer with different layouts and typefaces until you find the ones you feel best match the content of your essay.

This book has mainly been set in a typeface called Novarese. What do you think this typeface communicates about the book? Do you think this is what the publisher hoped would be communicated?

Perhaps the most important tool in presenting any material is the paragraph. The paragraph is defined in dictionaries as a group of sentences that deal with one specific point or topic. Try to make your paragraphs exactly this: focused, single-topic units of syntax that ask the reader to deal with one idea or point at a time. If you find yourself writing fewer than three paragraphs to a side of A4 then it is very likely you are overloading them with too many points. So you need to go back and check them. See the paragraph as the basic building block of your essay, each a unit in its own right but linked to and supporting its neighbour.

Looking at the issue of using paragraphs in a way that helps the reader brings us neatly to a consideration of writing style. You may have noticed that as you explore the world of Media Studies, different commentators and critics speak with rather different voices. There have probably been a number of occasions when you have picked up what you hoped would be an accessible book on a particular topic, only to find it written in a style and with a vocabulary that are barely recognisable as English. On other occasions you may have sought out an article and found it particularly easy to grasp the ideas and argument being put forward. You might like to consider why the latter proved more accessible than the former in order to make your own work as convincing as possible. When you are writing your essay, it is a good idea to assume that your reader is an intelligent, educated person with some knowledge of the subject area. If you have this sort of person in mind you should avoid the extremes of patronising on the one hand and writing above the reader's head on the other. Some of the points it will help you to take on board are the following.

■ Register: your use of language should be as direct as possible with careful use of specialist terminology. If you are not sure that a reader will have come across a specialist term before, be prepared to offer a brief definition or explanation.

- Tone or mode of address: try to avoid overuse of the first person (e.g. 'I think this' or 'I want to show that') and write your essay in a tone that is appropriate to the importance and seriousness of your subject matter. You are looking to put forward a reasoned argument intended to convince your reader of the validity of your case. You should aim for a style which is fairly detached and unemotional without being pompous. If you disagree with a theory or an opinion it is usually much more effective to use precise and surgical techniques of analysis rather than the blunt weapons of sarcasm or insults.
- Syntax: try to keep your sentence construction fairly straightforward. That is, don't overload your sentences with too much information.
- Use paragraphs as building blocks to help organise the flow of information (see p. 32).

NOTEBOX

Giving the study some theoretical clout

In the first chapter we looked at the role of theory in Media Studies and considered how it can most appropriately be used by students undertaking study into areas of the media. It is probably worth reiterating some of the points here to help you decide just how you are going to use theory in your independent study. Here are some points to bear in mind.

- Don't try to reinvent the wheel. Realise that a lot of the ideas you want to explore have at least been touched upon before by media theorists.
- Make sure you dig around for any existing research before you proceed.
- Summarise existing research rather than copying it wholesale.
- Consider your own position in relation to existing research. Do you agree or disagree with the position it takes?
- Set out your own case, giving evidence from sources such as contemporary texts.
- Don't use theory where it does not fit or, worse still, if you don't really understand it.

Always remember that it is important to take a critical stance in the work that you produce. It is easy to be overawed by work that has been published, either in print or on the Web. While it is important to respect the work of people who may have dedicated their lives to exploring and writing about cultural issues, it does not mean that you have to assume they are right. As we point out in the Introduction, a theory that once held true may now be quite out of date and no longer relevant, given changes that have taken place. So do be prepared at all times to question the wisdom that comes from such sources and always be prepared to test the ideas against the evidence that you have amassed in the process of undertaking your study. Indeed you may well make questioning the validity of an existing theory or concept the starting point for your study, perhaps for example testing the value of some aspect of genre theory in the light of the shifting perspectives of genre in a contemporary medium.

BIBLIOGRAPHY AND REFERENCES

As we have explained, if you are to avoid being accused of plagiarism, it is important that you acknowledge other people's ideas when you produce work for your independent study. Of course, in a complex area such as Media Studies there is a huge amount of published material that you may wish to refer to. It is a good idea to learn the art of referencing and acknowledging source material as this is an important issue whatever level of academic study you are engaged in. What proper referencing enables readers to do is to check back to the source you have quoted. By doing so they are able to ensure that you have accurately represented what that original author said. It may be that you have interpreted material in a specific way. A reader may feel that the material you have quoted is open to other interpretations and that you have chosen one that particularly suits your own argument.

The Harvard system of referencing is the most frequently used in academic works and Media Studies is no exception. Below you'll find examples of how you should refer to your sources using the Harvard system. This follows a well-established protocol. It is important that when you write your own bibliographies or references, you observe the correct punctuation and type style, right down to the use of the comma, the colon and the full stop. This formula for citing the work of an authority can be quite a complex one, especially if you are dealing with such works as conference papers and academic journals. The three most common sources, however, are books, newspapers and electronic sources, so here is a brief guide to citing these.

If you refer to a book by a single author then any reference should be accompanied by the name of the author and the date of the publication:

> McNair (1994, p. 110) points out that commercial television 'continues to be committed to quality journalism at peak time'.

This style of including the quotation as part of the text is acceptable up to a maximum of two lines.

In cases where there are two authors, you should cite both:

> Bolter and Grusin (2000, p. 226) explain how amusements parks can be seen as hypermediated:
>
>> An amusement park like Disney World is hypermediated; it offers sensory overload and places side by side a series of visible remediations of film and television. Like television and the World Wide Web, the amusement park insists on the reality of the media: at Disney World the cartoon characters are larger than life-size and walk around the park hugging the children.

When you are quoting from a book written by three or more authors then you just give the name of the first author and use the phrase *et al*. to indicate the others.

Beck *et al.* (2002, p. 1) suggest 'we use the mass media as a source of messages that offer us both information and entertainment'.

If you want to reduce the length of an extract by cutting out irrelevant material, you can do this by using three full stops to replace the missing section. This is called ellipsis:

Bennett *et al.* (2005, p. 253) point out that:

British television cop shows of the 1970s were noticeably influenced by domestic political concerns . . . The period was characterised by social and industrial unrest and successive moral panics about crime waves. A more aggressive and confrontational approach to law and order displaced the emphasis on crime as a social problem.

At the end of your essay, you will be expected to expand on all these references by means of a bibliography. A bibliography is a list of sources, usually books, that you have cited or referred to in an essay. Whenever you produce a written piece of work, it is essential that you give such a list at the end. The books cited above and on the previous page would appear in alphabetical order of first author as follows:

Beck, A., Bennett, P. and Wall, P. (2002) *Communication Studies: The Essential Introduction*, Routledge.
Bennett, P., Slater, J. and Wall, P. (2005) A2 *Media Studies: The Essential Introduction*, Routledge.
Bolter, J. and Grusin, R. (2000) *Remediation: Understanding New Media*, The MIT Press.
McNair, B. (1994) *News and Journalism in the UK: A Textbook*, Routledge.

If you wish to refer to a newspaper article then the Harvard reference should be as follows:

Greenslade, R. (2004) 'Red tops plunge into freefall as their message gets lost', *Media Guardian*, Monday 15 November 2004, p. 13.

A website can be cited in this way:

Taylor & Francis, http://www.mediastudiesarena.com/mediastudiesarena/about. html (accessed 9 April 2004).

Finally if you want to refer to a film or television programme this is the style to adopt:

Neighbours (2004) BBC 1, 21 April.

PRESENTATION

It is also important to think about the presentation of your independent study. We have looked at some suggestions for making your study user-friendly, for example by using some of the formatting devices available on word-processing packages, to ensure that readers are guided and supported on their way through the essay. There are some other issues that you need to take account of in deciding on the final presentation of your study. These include producing a title page (and list of contents, if appropriate) which sets out clearly the title of the study, who wrote it and why it has been produced.

Don't forget to use the facility on the word-processing programme for numbering pages. This is particularly helpful to anyone who is required to mark your work.

You may be wondering whether to include illustrations in the body of the text or to make them part of an appendix, or simply to avoid the use of illustration altogether. The best answer is that illustration should only be used if it genuinely adds to the reader's understanding of the work. Decorative pictures, such as film or television stills, really have no place in your essay. Of course there are possible exceptions such as where you are offering a detailed analysis of a magazine cover or a still from a film. On the other hand tables and charts, perhaps showing the breakdown of audience figures, may well serve to make an important and valuable point much more succinctly than you could in continuous prose.

SOME MORE ON AQA UNIT 5

If you are undertaking this unit, it is probably worth getting hold of the AQA specification to ensure that you are meeting the requirements laid down. You can either ask your teacher for a copy or you can download it from the Internet yourself. One important point to bear in mind is that the study should be text-based. This means that it is inappropriate to debate a media issue, no matter how important, without close reference to specific media texts. For example, if you want to write about the need for stricter regulation of the tabloid press you must do so by referring to specific stories or issues raised in these newspapers and then develop your argument from the evidence provided by these texts.

The specification also suggests that the work for this unit could usefully develop work already undertaken in Unit 4 Texts and Contexts in the Media. Although this is not a requirement, it is good advice for most students as it will allow you to develop in much greater depth a topic you have prepared for your Unit 4 exam. It also means that you will have the opportunity to develop your own independent research which can be used as part of your response to the Unit 4 exam questions.

One final word of caution: do not turn your study into a number-crunching exercise. The specification warns explicitly that 'the Independent Study is not intended as an exercise which will involve the collection of large quantities of empirical data'. By all means devise a short questionnaire if you feel this is an appropriate means of obtaining information about an audience, but don't spend the whole of your 3,000 words analysing it. Remember this is about using texts as a jumping-off point to explore some contemporary media issues.

FURTHER READING

Williams, N. (2004) *How to Get a 2:1 in Media, Communication and Cultural Studies*, Sage.

▼ 3 GENRE

In this chapter we consider the importance of ideas about genre from a number of perspectives and in a number of contexts. We:

- provide broad definitions of genre
- explore the ways in which ideas about genre are useful to different groups of people: actors, writers, directors, consumers, producers/owners
- look in some detail at the functions of genre as an idea
- lay foundations for your own genre studies
- look at hybridity as a tendency in genre study
- provide flexible and useful case studies to demonstrate all of the above.

GENRE: CODES AND CONVENTIONS

Genre is an important tool in supporting our understanding of the nature of media texts, how they are produced and how they are consumed. At its simplest, genre is a means of categorising texts that share similar features. So we have genres across all media forms such as soap operas, musicals, celebrity magazines and radio comedy. Of course none of these categories can ever be watertight and there are examples, as you will see later, of texts that exhibit features of more than one genre. However, genre study by its nature encourages us to deal in broad generalisations rather than in detailed and specific textual features.

Genre is probably best viewed through three of its key functions. Firstly, it has an important role in our understanding of how texts are produced. Media production is a sophisticated industrial process. Media entrepreneurs invest large sums of money in plant and equipment in the form of studios and printing presses, for example, and in networks for distributing media products to audiences. They make this investment in order to make a return on their capital through the sale of media products in just the same way that the owner of a baked bean canning factory would expect a return on a similar capital investment. In order to ensure a profit, it is necessary to market products, be they baked beans or lifestyle magazines, that will find favour with consumers. Genre formulas provide a recipe for proven success which producers hope will guarantee future popularity in the market place. Also producers will build up expertise and contacts in making products in a specific genre, rendering work in this field significantly easier than in one where they have little expertise. Look, for example, at the success of Endemol in the production of reality TV shows or see how many names, of both actors and crew, recur on the credits of different sitcoms.

Success is of course never that simple. Producers see audiences as fickle in their tastes and they have to try to be one step ahead of these whims. So often you will find subtle changes within genre formulas which maintain familiarity but at the same time seek to avoid being too predictable.

ACTIVITY...

Consider the development of reality TV programmes from *Big Brother One* (summer 2000) to the present day. Make a list of the generic features that have remained constant and those that have changed during this time. How do you account for some of the changes? What would you see as the defining moments in the development of the genre?

Secondly, genre offers a useful insight into some of the ways in which audiences consume and use media texts. Genre acts as a signal to audiences to arouse their expectations. It says in essence: 'You liked that, now try this'. So confronted by an overwhelming choice of media texts at the end of the satellite remote control or on the shelves of a newsagent or video rental shop, audiences will often reach for familiar formulas on which they know they can depend. They do this not only because they know they will like what they are getting but also because genre can offer a shortcut to audience pleasure. Familiarity with a genre means we know how it works; we can find our way around the text without too much difficulty. We know the conventions, so we don't have to learn a new code. Consider how tabloid newspapers and women's magazines share similar formats. At a more sophisticated level of audience pleasure is the subverting of genre conventions. A film or television programme which subverts genre conventions can give audiences a great deal of pleasure.

Thirdly, genre is an especially useful tool when media texts are considered from an academic perspective. Media texts generally form part of popular or low culture. They are created to be consumed and discarded, unlike elite or high culture texts like operas and novels that invite repeated study. The latter are often subjected to immense critical debate aimed at revealing the complexities of their construction. Few texts that belong to popular culture are considered worthy of such investigation. However, by using genre study to lump them together we are able to draw significant conclusions about their role and function within our society. Through genre study we can begin to understand some of those wider contexts we spoke about in Chapter 1. By looking at texts as a group we can learn a lot about the social, political and economic circumstances in which they are produced and consumed. For example, a study of soap opera would reveal to us a whole raft of social concerns that society has dealt with, from the early days of *Coronation Street* and its fixation on working-class angst through to Todd's gay love affair in 2004. The popularity of a genre can reflect the interests and neuroses of an age.

Genre study has its origins in Film Studies research, much of which took place in the 1960s and 1970s in the United Kingdom. Much of the work revolved around the western, which lends itself readily to genre study. Some commentators, however, would question the value of genre study in broader media terms. They would argue that it does not work so well with other genres and that a media form like television mutates so rapidly into hybrid forms that genre study finds it hard to keep pace. It is interesting to note, though, that the digital age has brought with it themed channels dedicated to scheduling programmes all of the same genre.

Genre is also important in that it provides a mechanism for limiting the meanings that are available within a text. As film theorist Tom Ryall points out, genre supervises both the construction and the consumption of a text. So we can see a genre text in terms of an equation of familiar elements or signs taken from familiar sign sets or paradigms. The finale of a teen slasher movie might predictably break down to: attractive teen female + darkness + frantic music + active camera + knife + mask.

Wes Craven's *Scream* (1996) was of course even more revealing than this:

> MAN ON PHONE: You should never say 'who's there', don't you watch scary movies? It's a death wish. You might as well come out here to investigate a strange noise or something.

PARADIGM A set of signs from which discrete choices must be made. These signs are part of the genre's iconography or range of signs such as costumes, props or settings that form a visual motif or imagery that places the text within a specific genre.

ACTIVITY

What are the signs which form the iconography of the following: soap opera; men's magazine cover; road movie; TV ad for cleaning products?

PINNING DOWN THE IDENTITIES AND MEANINGS OF GENRE

Any Media Studies book worth its salt can provide a working definition of genre. Fewer are able to pursue the essential character of this system of classification. Genre is not a science; it is rather an instrument or a tool. We use 'genre' with intent, we can't avoid this. It is a theory which unites the key components of the communication process: gratifying audiences, reassuring senders, organising texts and producing contexts. It contains assumptions and generates expectations, much like the subjects of its analysis.

KEY TERM

GENRE The term used for the classification of media texts into groups with similar characteristics.

ACTIVITY...

For each of the genres below, describe what you expect in terms of the following:

- content (be specific, e.g. 'more men than women', 'guns will feature significantly')
- style (how it looks, sounds, impacts)
- form (how it is structured).

Genres:

- prime-time television game show
- teen horror film
- computer magazine
- romantic fiction (Mills & Boon style)
- local radio news
- daytime television game show.

Genre study proposes there is an important relationship between any given text and those texts that share traits or characteristics with it.

KEY TERM

MODE OF ADDRESS The way in which a particular text addresses or speaks to its audience.

The functions of genre

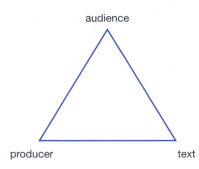

Figure 3.1 *The audience–producer–text triangle of dependency.*

Genre has different functions for its different 'users' at different times when you are classifying and understanding texts with different purposes. It is an important critical tool. It is equally useful when you are scrutinising the relationships between audiences and texts and the media industries (see Figure 3.1).

Genre is about creating expectations and then both satisfying and developing them. It gives an audience a sense of security which pleases the media institutions because it helps to consolidate a core audience for a 'brand'; 'those who like horror' are relatively easier to 'hit' than 'those who might like a quirky drama about growing up'. The presence of generic elements in the 'offer' a media product is making goes some way to guaranteeing that the price we are paying is going to give us some kind of return. This is why 'action' and 'horror' are such solidly successful film genres – they both make offers of simple experiences as part of their generic package which will usually be delivered even when the overall product is neither successful nor satisfying: few horror films fail to offer some level of excitement or surprise; what action film doesn't offer at least a couple of set-piece chases and/or shoot-outs? In some ways this is a version of what Paul Klein of NBC dubbed the 'least objectionable programme theory' in the days of terrestrial TV scheduling competition. Klein suggested that when faced with no strong positive choice the mass audience tend to choose those products that offend them least, in the sense of offering them fewest surprises/discomforts. At the contemporary multiplex perhaps it is a matter of 'least risk'.

Given the massive investment of all kinds which is made in the production and promotion of a new media product, it is easy to see why most media products are consciously genred or at least make reference to one or more identifiable genres in their structure and style.

Genre is a practical rather than a theoretical tool. It influences our behaviour as media consumers: it is a factor in how you spend your £5.50 on a Friday night (in or out). This is an activity to do and discuss with others (at least one!). Imagine you have decided to rent a video with a friend (friends). Rate the following real/imaginary films:

- a gory horror show
- an action film about fast cars and their drivers
- a British gangster film
- a 'grossout' teen comedy
- a buddy-buddy cop film
- an intelligent drama about bereavement.

Academic genre studies have been largely done in relation to film, where once-and-for-all decisions have to be made against often massive financial outlays. This makes film a very conservative medium, one which changes very slowly so genre as an idea is entrenched and 'useful'. It also allows for a genuinely historical dimension and the history of Hollywood film is largely a history of the great genres. The American auteur director Martin Scorsese identifies the western, the musical and the gangster as the primary American genres; each has enjoyed its period of dominance and all are now arguably in decline. Not surprisingly, this is where the academic writing is concentrated, a good way from our contemporary context in which genre is much less clear than it once was. Nevertheless few films at the local multiplex escape easy classification: most display their generic identity like a badge from the film poster onwards (see Figure 3.2). Expectation is the name of the game.

Other media have more leeway because they have the advantage of timescale. The generic identity of a television series, a new soap opera for instance, can be adapted and negotiated over a period of time to the responses of its audience and usually the significant starting costs can be salvaged. A notable exception to this was the BBC's ill-fated 'Brits in Spain' soap *El Dorado* which never recovered from a very poor start and sank without trace after only a year on air (*Coronation Street* is more than forty years old and counting!).

In the same way a new glossy magazine will at least have a limited period in which to find its place within the generic paradigm (in this case a set that measures how tightly the product seeks a specific identity and audience). A film is a discrete product in the way that these others are relatively continuous and as such has less time (and space) to make its play and enter into negotiations with its audiences. This goes a long way to explaining the specific character of contemporary Hollywood film.

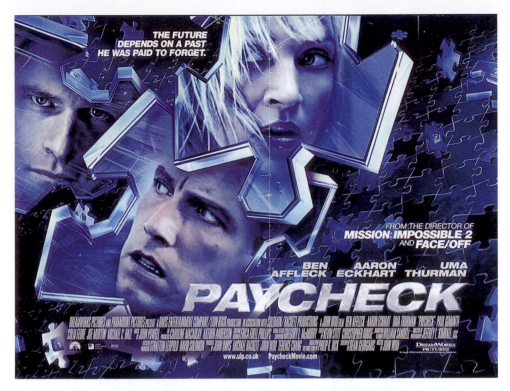

Figure 3.2 Poster for Paycheck (2003). How much of what is on offer can be deduced from this film poster? Aside from generic elements, what else is being communicated? Source: Dreamworks Pictures.

GENRE STUDIES

The structuralist critic Tzvetan Todorov argues that it is as important to have a theory of 'genre' (he calls it 'a grammar') as it is to have a theory of narrative (and Todorov's most important work is a theory of narrative). All media production takes place in the light of other media production and represents partly a response to the pre-existing world of production. Each new product presents itself not only in relation to the generic norms but also as an influence on them.

Since the definition of individual genres cannot be fixed, genre becomes for Todorov 'a continual coming and going between the description of facts and the abstraction of theory': between what is happening in individual texts and the theoretical models we have of the genres they inhabit.

One of the dimensions of this 'coming and going' is the historical dimension. Some genres may superficially appear to have changed little; for example, the gangster genre's use of urban settings, violence and certain kinds of women might be the same in films made in both the 1930s and now. However, as meaning systems, genres will necessarily

Figure 3.3 *Moore's paraphernalia in* Watchmen.
Source: Watchmen *No. 5, c. 1987, DC Comics. All rights Reserved. Used with permission.*

reflect their own historical and social contexts. If, as Jonathan Culler suggests, genre offers a 'norm or expectation to guide the reader in his encounter with the text' (Culler 1975, p. 136), it must be true to say that those norms and expectations will shift in time.

It is argued that each new text in a genre is not only generated by pre-existing notions of what, for example, a horror film is but is itself adapting that notion and modifying it. Some texts like Alan Moore's pioneering graphic novel *Watchmen* (2004) make this process explicit (see Figure 3.3). Moore and artist Dave Gibbons redefined the comic book genre in a comic that systematically yet implicitly provided a potted history of the genre complete with explicit paraphernalia: mock essays and real ones, the various evidence of research. All the classic comic book elements are there – caped crusaders, special powers, a threat to the world – but they are very firmly contextualised by Moore's obvious interest in and knowledge of the genre. In this way, as in the films of film buff Quentin Tarantino, the genre (and medium) becomes both the subject and technique of the piece.

In a completely different way the recent 'Best British Sitcom' competition, run in the format of the 'Greatest Britons', offers an interesting overview. The top ten shows tell their own story, if we are willing to listen, while also asking further questions about the usefulness of genre as a tool. The list in Figure 3.4 does at least cover much of the limited history of television comedy or at least the last thirty years of it. It also stands as an interesting statement about the opportunities and limitations offered by genre.

Figure 3.4 *Top ten sitcoms. Source: BBC.*

ACTIVITY...

What we have in Figure 3.4 is a classic set of indexes. These 'emblems' were constructed to represent the essence of each of these programmes, the bit we would all recognise. What do you notice about them? According to these images what does situation comedy, at its best, boil down to? What are the factors that bind them together?

Genre 'tags' programme our readings of texts, thus reducing their complexity as unknown/unseen. This collection of items read as 'comedy' involves different expectations from reading something as tragedy. Looking at the collage previously anchored by 'best' and 'comedies' it is easy to smile for a number of different reasons. Perhaps you are remembering reruns of John Cleese doing Hitler's 'funny walk' to startled German guests or of David Jason's alter ego Del Boy falling through the counter at a posh London wine bar. Perhaps your smile suggests that you yourself have got many of your own personal favourites in the top ten and are congratulating yourself or the public on your/their taste. However, your most pronounced response might be a Victor Meldrewish 'I don't believe it!' kind of smile at others of the programmes' claims to be comedy of any variety.

Comedy more than any other genre requires its representatives to 'qualify'. Whereas soap operas may want communities and shared locations, situation comedies need affect and impact: without these there's just no 'delivery'. Comedy is an example of what Roman Jakobson called 'conative' communication, communication that depends heavily on the receiver for its character, even for its existence. If *The Vicar of Dibley* fails to provide connotations for its audience, it cannot deserve the title 'comedy', whoever the writer is. As such comedy opens up the widest gap imaginable, in Todorov's terms between 'description of facts' and 'abstraction of theory'. There has to be an absurdity in applying a generic checklist to a text that fails to meet the first and most important criterion (that 'comedy' by implication makes us laugh). If we are not careful (or vigilant) we retreat to the citadel of bad criticism, wherein the unworthy (a polite word for 'rubbish') are subjected to analysis on the dubious grounds that they share superficial qualities with the worthy. This is a useful reminder of the need for critical discrimination which should be aided by available tools like genre, not paralysed by them.

Genre study is at its most useful when it focuses our attention on certain aspects of the process through which a text communicates with its audiences. These might fruitfully include the following.

The status of the sender and their intentions/purposes

Frustratingly, 'genre' work is often given less status than other work in the given medium. It is seen as the antithesis of art, the very individuality and uniqueness of which constitute a powerful reproach to the supposedly formulaic and standardised genre text. Its intentions are also downplayed, reduced to their most banal level: the stimulation of a set of 'pat' responses which are little more than largely emotional reflexes. In situation comedy the intention, of course, is simply to make us laugh, as if this in itself precluded any other more 'serious' effects. Given that the representative sample of 'sitcoms' pictured (Figure 3.4) have very different textures and depths, there at least seems room to challenge these assumptions and ask some questions. How far do the specific generic codes produce this quality and deviation? Is not *Fawlty Towers* made great by its adherence to and negotiation of extremely restrictive generic conventions: the 'static' situation, the 'battle of the sexes', the juxtaposition of home and work (those binary oppositions that drive all narratives perhaps). In direct contrast is the success of something like *Blackadder*, dynamic, verbal and open-ended.

The nature and range of audiences and their likely readings

Given that genre is, according to Terence Hawkes, by implication a reflection of all our experiences, it is interesting to examine the degree to which genre audiences segment as general issues give way to particular ones. The massive audiences constructed by significant media genres like soap opera and situation comedy on television or by lifestyle and celebrity magazines conceal significant segmentation on a text-by-text basis. The demographic of *Hollyoaks* is very different from that of *Coronation Street*; likewise *Blackadder* and *The Vicar of Dibley* (despite a common writer). There is therefore much potential for exploring the gaps between the general and the particular, between the audience for Nu-metal and that for Marilyn Manson, which may be broader or narrower.

Part of this argument concerns the character of audience adherence to a genre, sub-genre or generic text. Genre as a concept has a multidimensional appeal, as do generic texts. This means they have range but also 'depth'. Some texts have a broad appeal because they offer gratification in return for a relatively small investment (of time perhaps, or concentration and commitment). Other texts demand rather more in terms of attitudes, lifestyle, even appearance, and will therefore usually create a smaller but more committed audience.

This is the point at which it becomes relevant to talk about fandom, which is a sort of degree of audience commitment. Stereotypically, fandom is most readily used to describe the behaviour of those who like such genres as science fiction or horror or, in music, heavy metal. For example, 'Trekkies', fans of the *Star Trek* 'family' of products, will hold conventions, dress in costumes from the original series, even write dictionaries of the Klingon language or research the scientific feasibility of the *Enterprise*'s Antimatter drive. By contrast 'fans' of 'Britain's Favourite Sitcom' *Only Fools and Horses* will do little more than watch old episodes on TV and buy the occasional Christmas special on DVD or video.

Thus identifying the best of any genre from an audience perspective, even when using a crude device like 'best-loved', remains problematic. Do we mean 'loved by most' or 'most loved'? This is perhaps why the now popular open Internet poll, even a Txt/telephone poll, is more interesting than reliable. For some results it is clear we are measuring commitment (registered by the number of votes cast by any given 'fan') alongside the discrete number of people who are actually voting. This is partly why the massive votes cast that we have had in recent years for reality TV shows are strictly just that: massive numbers of votes cast does not equate to massive numbers of people. Thus headline statistics like those which claimed that more people voted in the first *I'm a Celebrity Get Me Out of Here* than in the last Australian general election were only on safe ground if they used the term 'votes cast'.

This is surely why the BBC's most requested show of the 1980s and early 1990s was a low-budget sci-fi epic called *Blake's Seven*. When it was on air its audience could not support a further series but its cult status has generated an army of acolytes, who continue to lobby for its return and support this demand by continuing to exchange new scripts in specialist fanzines and on 'shrine' websites. Ironically *Blake's Seven*, written by Dalek creator Terry Nation, was originally commissioned to fill the *Dr Who* slot. First broadcast the day after President John F. Kennedy was assassinated in November 1963, *Dr Who* is another cult show, which has survived seven time-travelling doctors and a ten-year absence from our screens, and, as we go to press, is screened in its regular Saturday slot with Christopher Eccleston as the ninth doctor. It too has a fanatical following ('Whoies') and Doctor Four, Tom Baker, reports his alarm when at an American Who convention he was confronted by a sea of desperate fans muttering (without irony) 'Take us with you, Doctor, take us with you'.

The function of generic codes as mechanisms for the communication of ideological values

Television, claimed De Fleur, 'communicates social values not social reality' (De Fleur and Ball-Rokeach 1989). Genres as formulas which govern the shape and character of communication inevitably contain coded information about the society that created them. Moreover, this 'blueprint' will then colour every individual text within that generic development: Todorov talks about 'every work' telling 'the story of its own creation'. Genres as constructs are always going to be value-laden for they are meaning systems, encoded instructions about how texts will be conventionally constructed, styled and received. They are systems of representation: of men, of women, of families, of truths. Their encoded information makes or at least influences the decisions the text is allowed about such matters as costume, settings and props. In doing this it inevitably unloads its ideological agenda. After all 'a system of representation' is also how Althusser (2003) defined ideology. The ways in which genre texts 'hail' their audiences ideologically is always of interest to us as Media students.

ACTIVITY . . .

ARE YOU A GENRE FAN?

Which of the following describes you?

    I largely watch films from the same genre.

    I buy magazines to support my interest in genre.

    I have book tie-ins.

    I have been to a convention at which my interest was represented.

    I collect film/TV/music memorabilia.

    I wear 'theme' clothing (T-shirts to Freddie Kruger mask).

    I can recite lines from the book/film/programme.

    I can speak Klingon or Elvish.

Which genres from film, television and popular music/rock are most prone to this kind of promotion and fandom?

Chiefly genres suggest 'off the peg' ways in which people and their issues can and will be addressed and treated. Pretentiously speaking, they are disguises which we get 'the human condition' to wear in order that it might be persuaded to expose itself to us. Genres are a set of patterns which remind us of the kind of things there are and the kind of things we like. Genre is a ready-made set of answers to a number of stock questions.

What ought to interest us, apart from the fact that in each mass medium there are comparatively few genuinely powerful genres, is what the semantic implications might be of texts obeying or addressing a common set of directives. If we look beyond the paraphernalia and character types, is anything else shared by genre texts, anything more profound? Are, for example, generic texts implicitly more sensitive to popular prejudice and dominant ideology? Despite the apparent variety of the sitcom top ten, this is a very much more restrictive designation of genre than, say, the novel, where the variety is more or less endless. This in itself serves to undermine and devalue genre as a useful term and to set up genre work in opposition to that which is 'serious'. It may also lead us to argue that the 'best stuff' denies generic classification: that when genre work is good it is so because it's not really a genre piece. Yet to some extent no work escapes generic classification, it's just where in the respective paradigms the evidence decides a work should go.

Only by making a systematic and wide-ranging analysis of a specific genre will we really get to grips with the underlying characteristics, messages and meanings. Looking across a significant number of genre texts should allow us to distil the essence of that genre, whatever its superficial qualities. The aforementioned sitcom top ten offers ample opportunities to explore the foundations of that genre and avoid some of the pitfalls of having to find a representative sample. In Figure 3.4 situation comedies have been selected by their single most relevant quality: their ability to be popular with audiences. At a glance these programmes seem decisively different, with 'comedy' as the singular, and sometimes elusive, 'theme'. However, begin to ask these shows some awkward questions and a different story can be told.

Take, for example, three simple elements: the identity of the central character, the situation and the location; then take one issue of representation, like the position and role of women. when these are tabulated, as in Figure 3.5, patterns do start to emerge.

ACTIVITY....

Consider Figure 3.5 when answering the following questions.

- What kinds of titles do sitcoms have?
- Who are the central characters?
- What do women do in sitcoms?
- What are sitcoms about?
- What kind of 'situations' do they use?

continued

Now answer the same set of questions for another significant television genre like soap opera or game shows or even news or sports programmes. What differences do you notice?

Perhaps the most interesting observation we can make on the sitcoms in Figure 3.5 is how superficially 'serious' they all appear to be and how easily they could all be turned into serious drama. Take, for example, a more realistic Peckham than that containing Nelson Mandela House (Peckham was after all the place in which schoolboy Damilola Taylor was stabbed to death).

At one level then, sitcoms simply tell the 'old story' about being human and alive albeit in a humorous and upbeat way. This is one of the discoveries perhaps, that decoding one often gives up the rest. Uncontroversially describing the content of *The Good Life* as 'the struggle to be self-sufficient' somewhat surprisingly allows us to unlock the other nine (and an important ideological message if we want it). And so the process develops for a while as you match the particular self-sufficiencies: 'in a small business sense', 'as a woman' and so on.

HYBRIDS

The top ten of any recognisible television or film genre are quite likely to be safely mainstream, although to some extent the tag 'mainstream' is itself subject to 'historical' context. Look beyond the top twenty, however, and you're likely to find items that are stretching the genre in one way or another. In the case of situation comedies, our current example, it is possible to identify a number of these ways from a quick survey of the whole chart (http://www.bbc.co.uk/sitcom/winner.shtml). Three groups are of particular interest: let's call them the 'regressives', the 'progressives' and the 'mavericks'. In any 'living' genre these are the signs of life.

Regressives

These represent the genre's past, their 'stretching' is inactive: they simply point to what and where the genre has been. They may have lost their purchase on an audience because of seemingly old-fashioned and in some cases unfashionable ideological attitudes towards, for example, minority groups like the disabled or black people. Examples from the recent survey of sitcoms (Figure 3.5) would be *Love Thy Neighbour*, a very popular 1970s take on immigration and race relations, or *Mind Your Language*, a sort of 'Carry on Language School' which featured a rather contrived group of national stereotypes.

Progressives

These represent the vanguard of the genre: they indicate where the genre may go next. They are often contemporary shows which have chosen to site themselves within a

Title/source	Central character	Context/location	Narrative	Female roles
Only Fools and Horses	Male, w/c, middle-aged, white	Peckham, London	Struggle to get on	Dead mum, wives (later)
Blackadder	Male, u/c, 30ish, white	Various, historical	Struggle to get on	Queen, 'Bob', minors
The Vicar of Dibley	Female, m/c, middle-aged, white	Vicarage, church, village	Struggle to be accepted (like a man)	Central character, village stereotypes
Dad's Army	Retired male, m/c, white	Church hall, seaside resort	Struggle to be a team	Mrs Pike, Mrs Fox, marginal
Fawlty Towers	Male, m/c, middle-aged, white	Hotel	Struggle to get on	Sibyl, Polly
Yes, Minister	Male, m/c, middle-aged, white	Parliament, government	Struggle to get on	Annie Hacker
Porridge	Male, w/c, middle-aged, white	Prison	Struggle to get on	Pin-ups on cell wall
Open All Hours	Male, ageing, w/c, white	Corner shop	Struggle to get on	Nurse Gladys, customers
The Good Life	Male, m/c, middle-aged, white	Suburbia	Struggle to be a team	Barbara and Margot (types)
One Foot in the Grave	Retired male, w/c, white	Home	Struggle to get on	Wife, Mrs Warboys

Note: these are to some degree arbitrary descriptions: most of the narratives could equally have been 'the struggle to be self-sufficient' or 'the struggle to survive'. The social class designations (u/c (upper class), m/c (middle class), w/c (working class)) are deliberately crude. Basil Bernstein has suggested that socialisation makes people 'safe': comedy to some extent is about having the confidence to be funny (which often in practice means 'unattractive'). Social class in this country is still one of the principal things that makes people 'safe' by which Bernstein means unlikely to have to make compromises in order to live the life they want.

Figure 3.5 *The top ten British sitcoms as voted by the great British public. Source: BBC.*

genre to use its conventions for their own purposes. They are interested in exploring the boundaries of the genre, particularly where it interacts with other generic identities. British comedy writing has been particularly blessed in the early years of the new century and it is the work of young writers like Ricky Gervais and Steven Merchant, of Peter Kaye and the *League of Gentlemen* team which is most significantly representing the progressive strain in the recent chart.

In what might be described as a postmodern mood, much of this work is exploring issues of generic identity and hybridity, not so much as a way of engendering ever more 'bastard' genres but rather as an artistic uncertainty principle. In contrast to the comfort provided by the traditional sitcom, much of the new is edgy and problematic, both formally and thematically. To a postmodernist this is predictably the way things go when even the artifice of genre itself has itself become insecure. In a world of simulacra (simulations) even the forms are faked. Pastiche is the order of the day and paradox the central philosophical principle. *The Office* cleverly turns 'fly-on-the-wall' into a sitcom with the unexpected pay-off provided by its pathos: rarely on TV has Henry David Thoreau's claims about most men leading 'lives of quiet desperation' been so powerfully examined. Audiences may be uncertain about voting the David Brent experience Britain's best sitcom but no one doubts its quality, merely its identity.

Similarly *Phoenix Nights* might have the texture of a film drama and the multi-casting of a sketch show but its real appeal is closer to what you might get if Roy Clarke were suddenly to write some jokes into *Last of the Summer Wine*. Take *The League of Gentlemen* or before that *The Fast Show* and you have the essence of situation comedy (memorable characters and situations) in a sketch show format. Hybridity is here again an artistic principle rather than a generic blueprint: an experiment rather than a proposal.

Mavericks

Mavericks are those items that fall between 'then' and 'now', those one-off shows that continue to deny classification and end up in the 'best fit' slot. Was *The Young Ones* really a situation comedy or a sketch show? Is *The Bill* a soap opera? What about *Mr Bean* and *Auf Wiedersehen, Pet*? Both make us laugh at behaviour in particular contexts, so why do we hesitate? The difference here is that the relationships to ideas about genre are less conscious: they are not so much playing with conventions as ploughing their own furrow.

NOTEBOX

One place where hybridity has always been a factor, and is increasingly so, is the music business. When folk singer Bob Dylan plugged in his electric guitar for the second half of his gig at the Manchester Free Trade Hall in 1965, an audience member screamed 'Judas!' because he was seen to be symbolically leaving (pure) folk for a hybrid (electric folk or folk rock). Contemporary dance music often uses the term 'fusion' to suggest the interaction of different styles. In music, of course, genre has particular significance because we are as likely to describe our tastes in terms of genre as of artists, and sub-cultures based on music are the staple divisions of the teenage audience. Musical 'taste' can in this way significantly define your identity.

These principles are not of course limited to television and film, though predictably more attention is directed towards the 'docu-soap' and the 'sci-fi comedy' because of the central position of moving image media in our society. A trip to any largish newsagent will convince you that hybridity is also a recognisible strategy or tendency in the print media. Here genre is a visible and visual division: a statement and an attitude. From 'top shelf' magazines, through the seemingly hundreds of magazines aimed at different kinds of women down to children's comics and crossword and puzzle magazines, genre is on display as a system of classification. Here genres come 'mobhanded': the twenty-five computer magazines demand attention collectively and to some extent co-operatively.

Magazine production is the epitome of niche marketing, with each viable title defining its own demographic, its specific audience. Specificity is taken to its ultimate here, where the audience of say PC *Format* may be exactly that untouched by PC *Gamer* and, given patterns of ownership in magazine publishing, it would not be unusual to find that two such magazines were published by the same group. This is a vast paradigm wherein the more specific your needs the more specifically they will be addressed: hence the infinite number of 'guest' publications available for ironic inclusion in that other hybrid, the satirical sketch show cum current affairs quiz show *Have I Got News for You*.

The very look of 250 titles arranged in a grid tells of security rather than competition. The fact that more than 50 per cent of this array feature (rather blandly) smiling women and/or girls is, the first time you recognise the fact, simply startling: from *Men Only*, through FHM via *Cosmopolitan*, *Woman's Own*, *Sugar* and *Barbie Magazine* to *Practical Photography*, PC *Format* and *The Puzzler*.

The 'normal' cover shows a healthy female smile somewhere between medium close-up and close-up. Moreover, given the entirely different functions and audiences of magazines as diverse as *Playboy* and *My Weekly*, it is equally startling to note that the similarities between these representations of the female are far more prevalent than the differences. What this amounts to, aside from the obvious issue of representation (where men are the lookers and women the 'looked at'), is a certain blandness, an otherwise inoffensive uniformity which stresses once again the generic at the expense of the discrete.

> Do some follow-up on the idea that most magazines have cover girls. For which genres of magazines is this especially true? What messages are being sent to audiences (a) generally, (b) specifically? What messages are being sent to (a) men, (b) women? Which genres of magazine have pictures of non-famous men on them?

However, the undercurrents beneath the tranquil surface are significantly more animated. With some 8,000–10,000 magazine titles available (and one-third of these consumer and lifestyle magazines), the competition for a place in the market is necessarily fierce. The balancing act, then, for all but the most established, is between maintaining a traditional (built-up) identity and responding to perceived trends in both publishing and society. The preferred model is 'evolution', the reality is too often 'reaction'. To some extent, over the last twenty years hybridity as a strategy has functioned as a kind of half-way house. Rather than strike out completely alone in the hope of consolidating or even increasing market share, look instead for a successful 'adjacent' genre and seemingly halve the risk.

The boom in 'lads' mags' in the late 1990s was just such an example. Until the advent of *Loaded* and FHM, men, who statistically have always bought fewer magazines than women, were offered two extreme choices: on the one hand, the social stigma of porn-ography and, on the other, a tired selection of hobby, music and sports magazines. Crudely the 'lads' mag' is a hybrid of these genres: a collection of film, sport, gadgets and tastefully half-naked, semi-famous, beautiful women. Or the list is reversed, depending on which end of the paradigm you stand at, though presently everything seems to be heading girl-wards. What started with a sharp new look has quickly become the softest soft porn, 'classic films' replaced by 'lingerie specials'. It may be of course that a drawback of the hybrid is that it does have the potential to decompose in this way back to its component parts.

Another example of hybridity in print media concerns TV listings magazines. Prior to the loosening of the monopoly on the right to print TV listings in 1991, there were two highly successful, some might say indispensable, TV listings magazines: TV *Times* which gave details of the schedules for Independent television and, at that time Britain's most popular magazine, the *Radio Times*, which published television and radio schedules for the BBC. The legislation had seemed incongruous for a while though it is partly representative of the way in which the mass media have traditionally been regulated on a 'make it up as you go along' basis. Just as once television had not been allowed to broadcast news after 6pm (to prevent competition with newspapers) so the schedules of the two public service broadcasters remained an industry-protected 'secret' to all but those who bought the company magazine.

The scramble for this substantial market was predictable and many titles came and went in the battle over cost and quality. In itself this is an interesting case study in genre and audience, particularly the ways in which audience expectation engendered by two familiar and traditional titles responded to the clutch of 'cheap and cheerful' competitors. On balance the need for more than basic information won out and we now have a fairly stable 'new' market, wherein old stagers like the *Radio Times* mix with the more resourceful of the first wave of replacements (like TV *Quick*) alongside specialist satellite stuff and other interlopers which periodically make their plays in this still lucrative market place. In a stable context competition is largely about redefining market share, and hybridity has become a key strategy in this respect.

ACTIVITY . . .

It has been argued that successful genres have specific functions or answer specific needs. Given that all newspapers (and some magazines) have often substantial daily and weekly TV listings, what are the 'special' functions of a TV listings magazine? Use the following questions as a starting point for your discussion.

■ Where do you, your friends and your family get information about TV programmes?
■ What kind of 'information' do you need?
■ What kinds of programmes do you seek information on? Are these genre programmes?

What it boils down to in this case is what is to be added to the central lure, the weekly TV listings. Traditionally, the *Radio Times* and TV *Times* supplied background information: features on new series, interviews with the stars, celebrations of milestones like the thousandth episode of *Last of the Summer Wine*. These are still components of the genre but sometimes a broader definition is made of what is meant by 'background'. In fact, this genre is another that has been subject to, or has responded to, the increased interest in and exposure of the idea of 'celebrity' in all media contexts. There is an even greater tendency for TV listings magazines to explore and exploit, both in content and format, the sources of what have become called 'celebrity lifestyle' magazines. At the same time it is now normal for these 'celebrity' magazines, like H*ello* and H*eat*, to include TV listings. In this way hybridity can be seen as an active, dynamic element in contemporary media contexts.

Hybridity in practice then is not so much about the creation of new genres, or even sub-genres. Rather it is an essentially responsive and proactive means of generic evolution, rejuvenation and ultimately survival. By being sensitive to its audience's needs and the prevailing media context, producers of genre texts can stay 'relevant' and 'in the game'. By grafting on something generically 'local' and reliable or relevant, media producers are able to maintain that vital quality of 'momentum' in a title, particularly when the market is stable or static. In simple terms, hybridity is about maintenance and the desire for organic innovation and improvement.

CASE STUDY: CELEBRITY LIFESTYLE MAGAZINES

Examining a genre in any medium in detail is like taking a cross-section of that medium itself: it is an essential act of media study. Genres are important codes through which the media communicate and to understand the components of these codes is to go some way to understanding the medium in which and through which they operate. What follows is just such an analysis of a largely contemporary print genre, the 'celebrity lifestyle' magazine, presented in a question/prompt–response format to promote clarity and reduce equivocation.

What is this genre called? What does it call itself?

These are celebrity lifestyle magazines: the essence is in the combination of 'celebrity' and 'lifestyle'. The paradigm runs from lifestyle magazines with a significant number of celebrity stories to magazines about celebrities with lifestyle features.

What are its 'members' called and how are their names significant?

The old 'wave' are called *Hello* and OK. The new 'wave' are called *Heat* and *Now*.

The movement from old to new is significant though from here nobody can really say how (long term). The original celebrity magazine *Hello* set the rules and others have followed. Its name is unashamedly banal, a simple piece of phatic communication. It says 'Here I am' or 'Look over here' and then bombards its readers with lush and lovely photographs of the famous, anchored by gushing, celebratory copy.

The second wave has equally phatic 'handles' with just a hint of where the genre is going. *Heat* and *Now* are merely (and marginally) 'hotter' and 'more happening' versions of *Hello* and OK. When we delve beneath the surface we get a variation on the generic themes: a similar format of colour pictures of the beautiful (if less famous) presented in a set of imitative typefaces with distinctly more tabloidised texts. There is also a new relationship to the idea of 'news': *Heat*, for example, describes itself as 'this week's hottest celebrity news' whereas *Hello* and OK rely on the fact that their celebrity 'exclusives' are well chosen. The Beckham wedding, for example, famously spawned an extra news value because of the battle fought by *Hello* and OK over the right to publish

Figure 3.6 *Chris Tarrant and his family taking a well-deserved holiday. Source:* Hello *magazine.*

the official images or rather (and more importantly) the right to prevent others printing theirs. This is the closest the celebrity lifestyle magazine gets to 'real' news: the medium is very much the message.

ACTIVITY . . .

The essence of any cover is to provide a sort of sophisticated 'hide and seek': it covers what is inside and then provides an illustrated 'menu', full colour pictures of the tastiest dishes. We all know that this is a kind of game, that this 'invitation to treat' is not a guarantee of satisfaction (we've all seen film trailers that contained all the best bits of the film) but that is part of the pleasure for both sender and receiver.

Hopefully, as advanced students of media, we will be able to understand that the offered agenda will work in a number of ways: formally, stylistically, thematically, in terms of intention, in terms of effect, even ideologically. Samuel Johnson, the compiler of the first English dictionary, reckoned that people were best judged by what and how they spoke: 'Speak that I might see you' was his best version. Texts are best judged in this way too. *Hello* is a well-known, even notorious, title but what can you establish about it from concrete evidence (see Figure 3.6)? Respond to the following prompts:

- impact
- audience
- layout

- illustrations
- messages
- qualities.

How does the genre 'look'? What are its costumes/liveries/ uniforms, its key props, its formats, its 'paraphernalia'?

ACTIVITY . . .

The cover headline is 'WE'RE FALLING IN LOVE' (see Figure 3.7) and for obvious reasons that's the tack that the magazine would like to impose, but what is the evidence? Self-presentation guru Erving Goffman suggested that our performances of ourselves ranged between the 'cynical' and the 'sincere'. Make two lists based on Figure 3.7 headed 'YES THEY ARE' (in love) and 'NO THEY'RE NOT'.

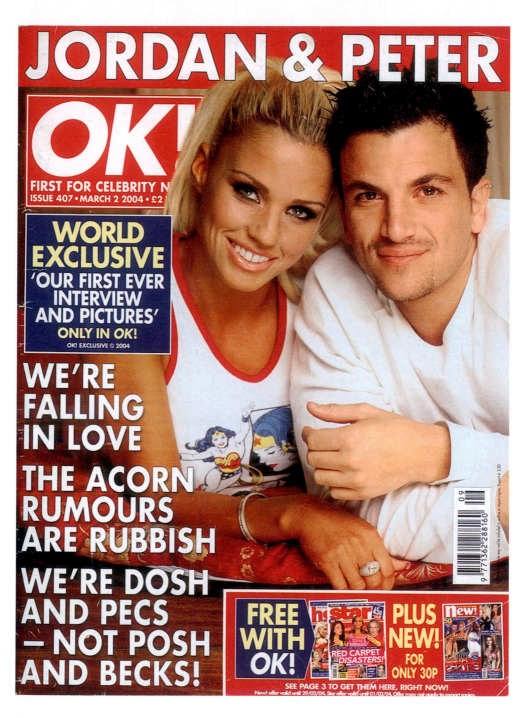

Figure 3.7 *Jordan and Peter Andre. Source:* OK *magazine, 2 March 2004.*

Essentially, it has a distinctive look and works most significantly in a visual way. Deconstructing the key elements might reveal the following active paradigms.

- **Production values**: these are full-on glossy magazines because 'what you see is what you get' is both a promise and a philosophy.
- **Size**: the traditional version has a distinctive size which is 'coffee table' rather than 'public transport-friendly'. At some subliminal level this probably connotes a certain kind of class just as broadsheet newspapers still carry a certain kind of 'aura' (though recently the spell has been broken by tabloid versions). The newer versions have returned to the conventional size of lifestyle magazines (a generous and convenient A4), which indicates the shift that is taking place from one conception of the genre (as a niche market) to another (as part of the hybridisation of the lifestyle magazine as a generic format).
- **Colour/lighting**: the world of the celebrity magazine is a world of high-key lighting, where everything is evenly, consistently and therefore unrealistically lit. It is a bright, colourful and some would say bland world: a world of surface rather than depth. This reality cannot exist in black and white.
- **Cover design**: as we have seen, a visual and verbal menu is created whereby this week's celebrities are introduced to us. There is a staged formality to this that makes it distinctive, partly because these pictures are properly posed. It is almost as if the celebrities are involved in some kind of elaborate chat show: having waved to the audience at the start of the show, they await their turn.
- **Iconography**: a magazine like *Hello* actually works across an extremely limited range of 'shots' and 'stagings' so that a house style emerges which binds the whole endeavour together. It defines and describes 'celebrity' in terms of its own meaning system; in other words, in terms of: its relationships with significant others (partners and children); its possessions (especially an obscenely large house whose every room must be 'christened' with a photograph); its beauty/presentability (understood in terms of a world of make-overs and skilful lighting); and its sense of satisfaction (page after page of endless smiles). *Heat* does the same thing as *Hello* with a tabloid disrespect and a 'feet of clay' philosophy. If you were cynical you might think that lacking the money to pay 'guests' enough in the current market they have chosen instead to undermine them. This comes down to preferring 'Kylie's wind problem' (the wind 'captured' blowing up her flimsy dress) to 'Penelope Cruz and Tom Cruise dazzle in London and Rome'. Which do you prefer – studied respect or studied disrespect?
- **Mode of address**: again there is a good range across the genre: from the stagey formality/late Victorian opacity of *Hello* ('controversial "wildlife warrior" Steve Irwin introduces baby son Bob and talks of the joys of fatherhood') to the equally stagey tabloidese of *Heat* ('How Kylie makes sure her boys bulge'). This genre is primarily a visual one so the text does little more than gee us along, not so much anchorage as atmosphere. In the context of large, glossy, highly motivated images the text is often redundant and tautological, and this creates a tension against which fluency will always battle. The essence of the celebrity lifestyle magazine is the non-story: 'Look at Demi Moore's wrinkly knees'; 'Chris Tarrant goes on holiday'; 'See the people arrive at the Coroner's court for the Diana inquest'. Many a full page comes

from a single quote from an unnamed (close friend of) or well-paid (the actual celebrity) source. Jennifer Lopez's apparent dislike of boyfriend Ben Affleck's goatee became a full-page story with three glossy pictures despite consisting, newswise, of: 'One friend told *Scandal*! [the inside *Heat* section: 'The pages the stars dread'], "Jen says it's not really that pleasant to kiss at all. I think she's probably worried about getting a rash around her mouth."'

■ **Ideology**: 'Ideology', claimed the French Marxist Louis Althusser (2003), 'is indeed a system of representation'. In other words, it is an influence on the way the world is seen and shown, and how meanings are made. The world represented in celebrity lifestyle magazines may be many things but it is certainly wittingly (if sometimes witlessly) constructed in a mode redolent with ideology. If, as the liberal economist J.K. Galbraith (1969) suggested, 'Advertising is a relentless propaganda on behalf of goods in general', then celebrity lifestyle magazines surely qualify as essentially advertisements for the acquisition of 'things' and the attainment of the almost sacred 'celebrity status'. Survey the whole paradigm and one feels overfed not with celebrities but with attitude, a straining fawning fascination that contains massive ideological assumptions. *Hello* and OK again lead the way in this, with royalty rubbing shoulders with millionaires and the occasional soap star.

ACTIVITY . . .

Examine the ways in which the selection, sizing and positioning of the images in Figure 3.8 create meaning in this layout. What other messages could these three images send (be creative here)?

This is largely beyond aspirational: *Heat* and *Now* might have Jodie Marsh and Jordan, *Hello* has Prince Edward and Formula One team boss Flavio Briatore. Briatore's desire to have 'a little cabin in the sun' spawned 'The Lion in the Sun', a 12-acre African retreat which took five years and $5 million to build in 1989. We see it in its awesome or awful glory across eight pages (*Architectural Digest* called it 'one of the most beautiful houses in the world'). To witness this second (or, worse, third or fourth) home is to be reminded of the worst excesses of other times: the last days of Rome, the court of Louis XIV, the doomed magnificence of a Victorian country estate. This is an orgy, aesthetic and material: the indulgence of excess or rather the uncritical presentation of it.

ACTIVITY . . .

Examine the ideological meanings of the sophisticated composition in Figure 3.9. You may find it interesting to look, for example, at the representation of:

■ the man
■ the idea of 'home'

■ Africa
■ celebrity.

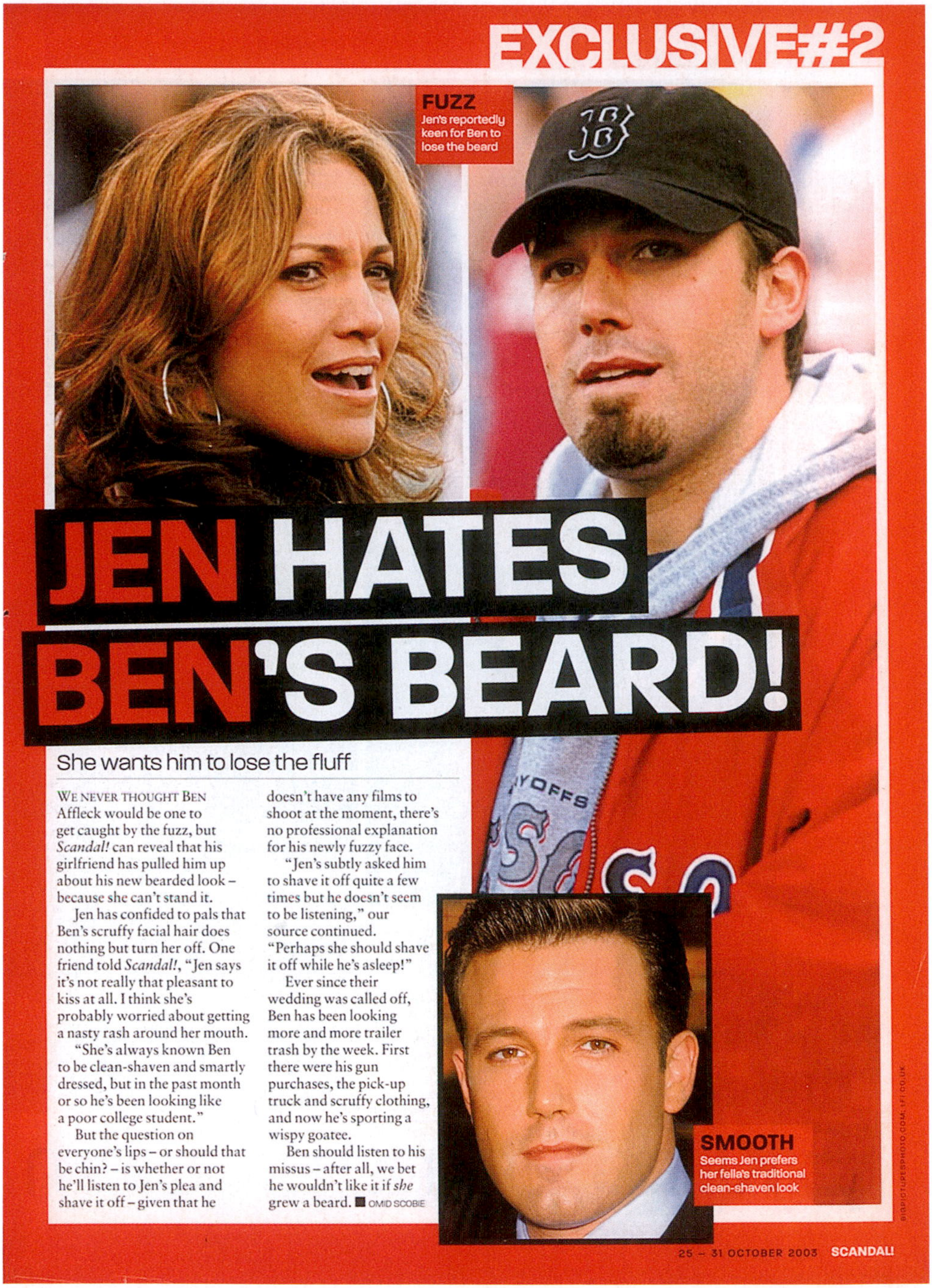

EXCLUSIVE#2

FUZZ
Jen's reportedly keen for Ben to lose the beard

JEN HATES BEN'S BEARD!

She wants him to lose the fluff

WE NEVER THOUGHT BEN Affleck would be one to get caught by the fuzz, but *Scandal!* can reveal that his girlfriend has pulled him up about his new bearded look – because she can't stand it.

Jen has confided to pals that Ben's scruffy facial hair does nothing but turn her off. One friend told *Scandal!*, "Jen says it's not really that pleasant to kiss at all. I think she's probably worried about getting a nasty rash around her mouth.

"She's always known Ben to be clean-shaven and smartly dressed, but in the past month or so he's been looking like a poor college student."

But the question on everyone's lips – or should that be chin? – is whether or not he'll listen to Jen's plea and shave it off – given that he doesn't have any films to shoot at the moment, there's no professional explanation for his newly fuzzy face.

"Jen's subtly asked him to shave it off quite a few times but he doesn't seem to be listening," our source continued. "Perhaps she should shave it off while he's asleep!"

Ever since their wedding was called off, Ben has been looking more and more trailer trash by the week. First there were his gun purchases, the pick-up truck and scruffy clothing, and now he's sporting a wispy goatee.

Ben should listen to his missus – after all, we bet he wouldn't like it if *she* grew a beard. ■ OMID SCOBIE

SMOOTH
Seems Jen prefers her fella's traditional clean-shaven look

BIGPICTURESPHOTO.COM; LFI.CO.UK

25 – 31 OCTOBER 2003 SCANDAL!

Figure 3.8 *Ben Affleck and Jennifer Lopez. Source:* Heat *magazine, 31 October 2003.*

FORMULA ONE BOSS FLAVIO BRIATORE

INVITES US INTO THE BREATHTAKING KENYAN HIDEAWAY WHERE HE ESCAPES THE PRESSURES OF HIS HIGH-OCTANE LIFESTYLE

5 ▶

Figure 3.9 *Flavio Briatore in the sun. Source:* Hello *magazine.*

In this sense *Hello* and OK are reminiscent, not to mention resonant, of those eighteenth-century English paintings of aristocratic families pictured within the grounds of their estates to validate their social status. Where once they'd call Gainsborough, now they call a commissioning editor. These magazines validate 'celebrity', establishing claims in the way that Debrett's might authorise the right to bear arms (of the heraldic variety). They also grade celebrity and reward the A-listers by endorsing their need to be 'happy' and have 'normal' relationships by including them in a world of simple unproblematic 'love'. When former model Nina (once dubbed 'The Body') Carter is pictured embracing 'her hope for the future' in various rooms of her house and alone on the beach, she is entering a paradigm which has the 'real' Royal Family above her and the sordid truth about the padded genitals of Kylie's dancers way below her and out of sight.

CASE STUDY: BRITISH TELEVISION CRIME FICTION

This extended case study of the British TV crime series is designed to help you to understand the relationships between two key concepts: genre and representation. Also, it will develop ideas about this particular genre with economic, social, political and cultural contexts. After reading this case study and working your way through the activities you will be able to:

- analyse texts in terms of their generic conventions
- discuss representations of law and order
- explain the development of a genre in terms of social and cultural changes
- develop your research skills.

Of course a genre like television crime fiction also provides a historical context or dimension, an overview of which is provided in Chapter 10, 'Crime fiction'. The fact that it stands as a resource maintains a proper relationship between your engagement with contemporary texts and the various contexts which are shaping both these texts and your responses to them. The resource provides a series of wider contexts but it is always up to you to be selective: depth beats breadth every time.

Before undertaking the activities you will need, individually or as a group, to identify a current television crime series which can be used for analysis, discussion and comparison. As well as viewing an episode from a contemporary crime series you will need to do some basic research, most of which can be done on the Internet using search engines, newspaper and media sites such as *Guardian Unlimited* and bbc.co.uk. After working through each of the activities you will be able to compare your discussion notes and conclusions with our own observations on the 2004 BBC series *55 Degrees North*. You will also find it helpful to view some episodes or extracts from the following texts: *Dixon of Dock Green*; *Z-Cars*; *The Sweeney*; *The Gentle Touch*; *Prime Suspect*; *Cracker*; *Inspector Morse*; *The Bill*; *Cops*; *Blue Murder*.

Contexts and the crime series

How and why are *contexts* helpful for the understanding of a genre such as the British TV crime series? At one level, we could argue that television drama reflects contemporary concerns, beliefs and attitudes at the time of its first broadcast. In this sense, television is reactive and provides us with a set of texts to illustrate social history. At another level, we may detect a more complex relationship between the genre and wider society. On some occasions, for example, fictional television series have helped to promote public debates about the role of the police and the causes of crime. Many series show the police in a very sympathetic and positive light but sometimes, as the case studies in this chapter show, the police have reacted angrily to their portrayal on the screen.

As you would expect, many of the wider contexts used in this chapter relate directly to law and order: representations of morality, right and wrong, justifiable punishment, the reasons why crime happens and the behaviour of the police and other law-enforcing professionals. However, genre television of this sort also relates to broader areas of social concern. Looking at crime series made over the last fifty years or so, we are able to track and understand changing approaches to class, ethnicity, gender, work and interpersonal relationships as well as dominant political philosophies. In this sense, television drama can be seen to be proactive as well as reactive. Programmes do not just hold up a mirror to social reality, they can operate more as an experimental laboratory of social and cultural change.

ACTIVITY . . .

Compile brief notes on the following aspects of your chosen crime series:

- institutional background
- production company, scheduling issues, ratings
- critical reception, e.g. reviews in newspapers and magazines or on the Internet
- main characters with character profiles.

55 Degrees North

This six-part police drama series was broadcast on BBC1 in summer 2004. It was made by Zenith Productions for BBC Scotland.

Although originally planned for transmission at 8pm on Sundays, the series eventually went out at 9pm on Tuesdays after schedulers realised that one of the episodes dealt with the theme of prostitution in a way which could not be broadcast before the watershed. The main character is Nicky Cole, a detective

continued

sergeant recently relocated from London to Newcastle. Other principal characters include Cole's unconventional 'family' (his nephew and uncle) and his working colleagues, most of whom view him with mistrust or outright hostility. The critical reaction to the first episode was lukewarm, with several reviewers referring to the predictability of the narrative. However, press comment was more favourable by the end of the series, a reaction paralleled by an improvement in ratings. The first episode was watched by 4.7 million; by the last in the series this had risen to 6 million and the BBC was sufficiently encouraged to commission a second series.

In broad cultural terms it could be said that crime fiction is an important way in which members of society can explore, reinforce and, occasionally, challenge our shared values in such areas as right and wrong, justice, punishment and the use of violence. This ideological aspect of the crime fiction genre may also be linked to some of the audience pleasures available. Cop shows enable us to dabble in the world of forbidden behaviour. We take vicarious pleasure in the transgressions of criminals (and sometimes the police as well) as order is disrupted before being triumphantly restored in the last act. Alongside these more visceral rewards of both breaking and then enforcing the rules are the more cerebral delights of solving clues and unravelling puzzles.

NOTEBOX

Pleasure

A principal reason for viewing television crime series (or any other media entertainment) is that we hope it will be an enjoyable and rewarding experience. Although the different types of enjoyment are liable to overlap, we can still identify various categories of pleasure available to viewers as follows.

- *Aesthetic pleasure*: the appreciation of something that is beautiful or exquisite. This could be satisfaction with the visual information on the screen or cerebral (intellectual) gratification derived from the perfect construction of the narrative: a beautifully told story.
- *Visceral pleasures*: these are the pleasures felt at a physical rather than an intellectual level; the sort of pleasure that can make you want to express yourself by shouting out loud, laughing, crying or punching the air. Retribution, revenge, 'come-uppance', violence and sex all provide opportunities for visceral pleasure.
- *Voyeuristic pleasure*: this is the satisfaction gained from spying, prying and knowing something unknown to others. Often a television drama will *position* the audience as voyeurs – unseen observers of a crime or a sex scene, for example.

- *Disruptive pleasure*: this is the delight to be had in throwing away the rules and being out of control. In life, this is the pleasure of behaving without inhibition or prohibition, but in the entertainment media, it is likely to be a vicarious pleasure.
- *Vicarious pleasure*: this is pleasure enjoyed remotely through the experience of others. In drama, we can identify with characters and take a vicarious pleasure in their triumphs or even their tragedies. In the case of tragedies and disasters we can enjoy the consoling thought that 'at least this isn't happening to me!'

At the level of genre recognition the television crime series offers us familiar iconography: the blue lamp and the flashing lights of police cars, uniforms denoting a range of ranks, badges, batons, guns, fingerprint charts and so on. Viewers are familiar with some staple examples of the *mise-en-scène* which have remained fairly static throughout the decades: the incident room where briefings take place with photos of victims and suspects, maps, dates and times prominently displayed in the background, the crime scene with flashing lights and photographers, the chalk outline of the body and barriers or tapes to keep back members of the public. Naturally new elements have found their way into these familiar locations to reflect the use of contemporary technology by the police. Computers are now a ubiquitous presence in the incident room and the white sterile suits and paraphernalia of forensic science have been added to the stock elements of the crime scene. Some series have dealt almost exclusively with forensic pathology, e.g. *Silent Witness* and CSI.

55 Degrees North

One of the most important settings of 55 *Degrees North* is police headquarters and here we find much of the familiar iconography of the police genre. The boss (DI Dennis Carter) has a glass-walled office to the side of the main workroom where the detectives have their desks. Other sets include the interview room, the desk sergeant's reception desk and the cells. In outside scenes we see police cars, flashing blue lights, uniformed officers, scene of crime tapes and CID identity cards. There are a number of action and chase sequences.

Stock characters include the tough no-nonsense boss (DI Carter), the traditional uniformed copper (Sgt Astel) and the naïve young PC and sidekick (PC Clark).

In terms of expectation we are rewarded with recognisable characters, familiar plots and predictable narrative patterns, all of which give us the opportunity to participate in the investigation and derive satisfaction if we guess 'whodunit' first. As with all examples of genre programmes, however, it would be a mistake to over-emphasise the degree of predictability in the television crime series. Each new series draws on the established conventions of the genre but at the same time it must establish its own identity and individuality. This is the creative challenge which faces the makers of all genre-based texts: follow the conventions too closely and the audience will soon be bored by the stale application of a familiar formula, but stray too far from the conventions and you run the risk of bewildering or even angering the audience. Additionally, each episode in the series can exploit the creative potential of genre conventions. Without throwing the 'rule-book' out of the window, one or two of the rules can be selectively broken to provide each episode with its own 'twist' or distinctive character.

ACTIVITY . . .

In the crime programme you have viewed what narrative devices are used to move the story forward? How do these devices 'break the rules' or twist the conventions of the genre?

55 Degrees North

Each episode of 55 *Degrees North* is self-contained in the sense that new crimes are committed (enigma) and we follow Nicky's efforts (often hampered by unhelpful colleagues) to bring the perpetrators to justice (resolution). Sub-plots, often involving Nicky's family, help to reinforce the juxtaposition between work life and home life. The theme of parenthood is explored from different angles in a number of episodes. From Episode Two onwards, though, it becomes clear that there are plotlines which are being developed from episode to episode. These plots, involving the underlying themes of police corruption, institutional racism and Nicky's relationships with other law enforcers, become increasingly significant as the series progresses, reaching a denouement in the sixth and final episode. In this sense, 55 *Degrees North* is something of a hybrid form with elements of both the self-contained episodic series and the extended plotlines of the serial.

In some senses, DS Cole is a classic example of a familiar character in the police genre: the loner maverick/outsider. Not only is he black, he is also a Londoner and a known whistleblower. This makes for a frosty reception from his new colleagues in Newcastle. Unlike most mavericks, though, Nicky is supported by his unconventional family, in particular his uncle and mentor Errol Hill (played by George Carter). This relationship, unusual in a crime series, helps to provide Nicky with the moral and emotional ballast needed to confront the dilemmas of his working life. As Carter says of his character:

> He's balanced. Errol is a Trinidadian guy who is very sage like, he is also a very decent, straight and upright person. . . . He's a man, that's what he is, and a new kind of father figure. He's a patriarchal type, but he tends to help by helping you find the light within yourself.
>
> (http://www.bbc.co.uk/pressoffice/pressreleases/stories/
> 2004/06_june/11/55degrees_harris.shtml)

The genre also works on an ideological level, offering comfort and reassurance that, in a world where the threat of crime seems to be continually on the increase, the baddies will always be caught, justice will be served and the men and women of the police force are there as a barrier between us and the forces of lawlessness. It is worth bearing in mind, at this stage, that our perceptions of crime are generally very different to the realities of crime (at least so far as those realities are recorded by criminal statistics). For example, we perceive ourselves to be most at risk of assault out of doors and on the streets at night time, yet most assaults take place in domestic environments. The elderly have a heightened fear of being physically attacked but in fact it is young adults who are most likely to be both victims and perpetrators of assaults. Fictional crime genres tend to deal more with the kinds of crimes and the kinds of risks which we *perceive* to be the most significant rather than those which actually occur most frequently. Even though some doubts may be cast over the interpretation of criminal statistics and the measurement of police effectiveness, most real police forces would surely envy the almost perfect clear-up rates of their fictional counterparts.

Representations of crime types and social classes also tend to be skewed. Assault, robbery and murder are drastically over-represented in the crime series. The perpetrators of crime are very likely to be young, urban, working-class males and the victims are likely to be middle-aged middle-class men and women. So-called white-collar crimes such as fraud, embezzlement, tax evasion and insider trading receive very little attention in crime dramas compared with street crime and violence.

Location, too, is treated in a rather schematic way in the sense that it is consciously designed to provide an interesting set of contexts for characters and 'capers'. Location is often an element in the programme's problematic, its special set of circumstances and problems. Locations may appear to be 'unsuited' to crime, particularly violent crime, or they may be unusual places to which 'crimefighters' return at the end of the day. They are always an important part of the conversation the programme is about: what is real and what is 'interesting'. Location is also an idea as general as the Holland of *Van der Valk* (the classic 1970s crime series with Barry Foster as the Dutch detective) and as specific as Inspector Morse's Mark 2 Jaguar, the site of many a Morse/Lewis culture clash.

ACTIVITY ...

REPRESENTATION OF PLACE

What is the location of the contemporary series you have chosen to study? How are the place (city, town or rural environment) and its population represented in the series?

55 Degrees North

55 Degrees North is set in Newcastle on Tyne. Many exterior scenes include shots of the city's icons, particularly the Tyne bridges. Depictions of Newcastle itself are fairly even handed, with shots of a busy and thriving centre, yuppie apartments and affluent suburbs as well as more run-down areas. Nicky Cole and his family live close to the city in a healthy and attractive seaside setting which further enhances the generally positive representation of Newcastle and its environs.

The representation of local people, though, is more controversial. In an earlier cop show set in the North-East, *Spender* (1991–3), most of the main characters were sympathetically drawn Geordies, with out-of-towners usually playing villainous roles. In *55 Degrees North*, however, Nicky and his family are Londoners and the show's female lead is Irish. As one critic put it:

In conclusion, then, it is difficult to find even one component that is an essential ingredient of the television crime fiction genre. Our examples here and in Chapter 10 have shown this genre to be fluid and dynamic, evolving under pressure from institutions and audiences, developing in the context of social, political and economic changes. Certainly there is ideological work being carried out by the cop show. This may take the form of a powerful endorsement of the establishment, reinforcing our faith in the police, the judicial and penal systems and their underlying values. However, it would be a mistake to see this or any other genre as a compliant instrument of dominant ideology. Just as individual texts and series can challenge the conventions of the genre, so the genre itself can be used progressively, to challenge and subvert the received wisdom and 'common sense' of dominant ideology.

ACTIVITY . . .

In common with many genres the crime series exploits the tensions between various sets of binary oppositions. Often these oppositions become familiar to viewers who can then enjoy a new version of an old refrain. Below are some of the oppositions that are often found in the television crime series. For each pair, try to think of examples of how this tension has been explored in the crime series you have chosen to study. If you can't think of an example, suggest ways in which the binary opposition could be used in a crime series you know of.

High tech	vs	Traditional policing
Intuitive methods	vs	Rules and regulations
Individual	vs	The team
Amateur	vs	Professional
Male policing	vs	Female policing
Youth	vs	Experience
Justice	vs	The law
Uniform	vs	CID

IDEAS FOR EXPLORING GENRE

Genre study above all requires discipline, in order to pass from the mundane and superficial (clothes, cars and guns) to the meaningful and enlightening (narrative, register, mode of address, ideology). One way to approach this problem is via comparative study: take two genres aimed at the same audience like 'teen comedy' and 'teen horror'. You need to decide how you are going to analyse them by identifying some areas of investigation. Genre study works best if systematically based on a set of pre-determined prompts. One set might be:

- What is the genre called?
- What are some examples of this genre?
- What kind of titles are these?
- Conventionally, who is the central character (gender, age, ethnicity, personality, other)?
- What do they do in the story?
- Who helps them?
- Who hinders them?
- What happens in the end?
- What is valued by and in this story/these stories?
- What is condemned/feared by and in this story/these stories?

In a similar way, a systematic analysis of more than one text from a chosen genre can be very revealing of the underlying patterns. Perhaps a comparison of texts from different periods will be useful. It may then be helpful to see the genre as a broad paradigm and establish a critical order so that you can choose from different parts of that paradigm. A critical order is just a theory about what might be an interesting way to look at some texts. In the historical studies, the critical order is 'chronology' and the selection will cover the 'origins', 'development' and 'contemporary practice' of the genre, but the range of orders and examinations is practically limitless. You may wish to identify gender orientation as a critical order for, say, situation comedy or 'franchising'/intertextuality for a study of children's comics. Genres of popular music might be approached in terms of their use of different combinations of instruments or 'plugged' and 'unplugged', or via the significance of their lyrical content or their countries of origin.

In a sense, the critical order is a kind of hypothesis, an assumption, an admission of where you are starting from. We are identifying areas of enquiry which might be profitable while at the same time recognising the degree to which our informal inter-pretations always inform, or at least precede, our formal interpretations. To put this another way, we are once again reminding ourselves that genre is in itself a critical order, an element of media output advertising its own significance. And that, of course, is where we came in.

Is the concept of genre still a useful critical tool given the hybrid nature of contemporary texts? Provide examples throughout your answer. AQA January 2004

Outline the recent significant developments in one genre of your choice. Illustrate your answer with examples. AQA January 2003

'Parody aims to mock in a critical way.' Fredric Jameson. How has parody been used in contemporary media? AQA June 2003

For further reading see p. 261.

▼ 4 REPRESENTATION

In this chapter we consider the importance of ideas about representation as a key concept in the study of media texts and meanings.

- We provide definitions of representation.
- We explore the relationship between representation and mediation as key principle and key process.
- We look in some detail at the implications of a widely mediated reality.
- We examine stereotyping in the representation of minority and other groups.
- We explore the relationship between representation and ideology.
- We provide flexible and useful case studies to demonstrate all of the above.
- We offer guidelines so that you can make your own case studies.

WHAT IS REPRESENTATION?

Consider for a moment what you have learned about sign systems in the media. You will know for example that visual media rely heavily on the use of iconic signs to represent the world. Iconic signs are signs which work by their similarity to the real-life objects they represent. When you switch on your TV, the images are largely iconic; they look like the images that you see when you look through your window at the world outside. Indeed TV is often described as 'a window on the world', which suggests that what we see on our screens is in fact the world outside. However, television is not a 'window', nor could it ever be. Every televised image is the product of many decisions about how reality should be transformed. For this reason, television cannot simply show reality, it can only offer versions of reality influenced by the decision-making processes of media producers and the technical constraints of the medium. This is what we mean by the construction of reality by the media. Because all media messages are constructed in this sense, everything contained within them is a representation. Of course, representation does not just concern pictures; it concerns every aspect of communication. Newspaper journalists, for example, may talk about 'telling it like it really is' or 'transparent reporting'. The implication is that they convey 'reality' exactly as it is to their readers.

Much of the nature of the construction of television programmes and films is designed to make them appear as natural and as realistic as possible. Continuity editing, for example, creates the illusion that programmes have a natural flow, that they are put together without seams. With television's technical ability to produce slow-motion action replays and use multiple camera angles, a sporting event viewed on TV has a reality beyond that of spectating at a live event. In a sense, the television experience becomes 'more real than real'. Inherent in this are obvious consequences to the individual. The postmodernist commentator Jean Baudrillard talks of distinctions between the real and the unreal collapsing, so that TV no longer *represents* the world, it *is* the world. We are overloaded with information and images to such an extent that we no longer differentiate between the real world and media constructions of the world: a condition which Baudrillard describes as hyperreality.

Representation, then, is not solely confined to the mass media. It is an integral part of all human communication. It is simply the term we use to describe all the ways in which we encode the world in order to be able to share our versions of it with other people. Whenever we use language we are involved in representation, because language is just one of the codes we use in which to share this information. Because this sharing is an essential part of communication, it is necessary for the users of a code to have an agreed understanding of how the code works. This agreed understanding links together members of a culture, but it also means that we will probably not understand the codes of a different culture. As we shall see, systems of representation are culture-specific codes.

Consider the communication of primitive men and women, be it drawings on cave walls, non-verbal behaviour or even the rudiments of language. As we try to decode these 'primitive' representations, perhaps those found on the walls of certain French caves, we are caught somewhere between our objective reality, the marks themselves and the system of representation, now lost, that was used to create them. There is no set of rules, no handbook we can use to reconstruct the meaning of these signs and have absolute confidence that we can understand the intentions of their creators. We can speculate more confidently, though, that these marks demonstrate an ancient and deep-seated desire to make signs which represent reality. In a sense, the mass media are a modern version of the burnt sticks used to decorate the walls of caves. If pioneering media theorist Marshall McLuhan is to be believed they do this by extending the relationships we already have as individuals with reality: 'the mass media', he claimed, 'are an extension of our senses'. The whole list is interesting:

- The book is an extension of the eye.
- The wheel is an extension of the foot.
- Clothing is an extension of the skin.
- Electronic circuitry is an extension of the central nervous system.

(McLuhan 1964: 3)

If McLuhan is right and we are able in this way to 'see' further, what will be the implications for what we see and how we see it? Our relationship with reality is changed fundamentally by the experience of media consumption simply because of the enormous volume of information that is brought to us. The comparison with the cave painter could not be more stark. For him or her, almost all experience was *direct* but, for us, the great majority of our experience of the external world is *indirect*: it is brought to us by the mass media. The process by which the media represent the external world for us is called 'mediation'.

MEDIATION AS A PROCESS

When a medium (such as radio or film) carries a message, it is mediating it, simply carrying it from one place to another. Mediation is the act of 'going between', in this case between 'an audience' and 'the world', but this simple process has some very complex implications. Inevitably, the relationship between the world and the audience is changed by the process of mediation. When you sit down and think about it you might come to the conclusion that most of what you know and most of your experiences are 'merely' mediated: since the encounters have been second rather than first hand. Think of what you really know about Africa or GM foods, let alone the war in Iraq or al-Qaeda, then subtract all you received on the subjects from 'mediators'. What is left? At best, perhaps, your holiday in Tunisia or the Gambia.

It is a primary function of communication to bridge this gap between our experiences of reality and the experiences of other people. However, mediation is always an 'interested' activity. There are technical considerations which mean that reality can never be 'captured' in its entirety and there are also social, economic and political factors weighing on those who have to make decisions in the mediating process. Numerous decisions are made in this process, for example: the selection of material, the type of language, the framing and composition of shots, the style of presentation. The people making these decisions may be influenced by their own personal beliefs and values, they may be influenced by the corporate agenda of the organisation they work for or they may be influenced by the government of their country. There may be all sorts of other considerations influencing their choices and decisions. What is certain is that something or someone will be influencing the mediation process in one way or another. This is what we mean when we describe mediation as an 'interested activity': we are using 'interested' in the sense of 'vested interests', rather than 'fascinated'.

ACTIVITY...

Think of some of the ways in which mediation could be described as an 'interested activity'. Bear in mind that mediation does not necessarily imply deliberate distortion or cynical manipulation of audiences (though both of these can occur). Consider such texts as:

- newspapers and news bulletins
- soap operas and sitcoms
- Hollywood films
- men's magazines
- rap music.

In representing the world on our behalf the media are involved in two distinct processes:

- **perception:** 'seeing' the world and in doing so selecting those elements that are significant and comprehensible
- **communication:** fashioning texts through which these perceptions might be 'voiced' and in doing so making another series of selections.

When Marshall McLuhan dubbed the mass media 'an extension of our senses', he meant that the sheer speed of contemporary media channels reflects the speed of our senses in face-to-face communication. The media rarely 'see' by accident and never without interest, although it is often at pains to 'cover its tracks' by allowing reportage and 'realism' to be casually confused with reality. Writing specifically about television realism, Abercrombie (1996: 27) identified three aspects of realism (which affects a particular kind of mediation).

- Realism offers a 'window on the world'; an apparently unmediated experience.
- Realism employs a narrative which has rationally ordered connections between events and characters.
- Realism attempts to conceal the production process.

The paradox here is that so much that appears natural, from the live outside broadcast to the painstakingly researched film drama, is in fact the result of a complex industrial process. What is 'real' is defined in terms of what is realistic. Neil Postman (1985) has claimed that 'TV reality is *the* reality', suggesting that the mediated world has become a blueprint for the unmediated version.

The mediated world

What De Fleur says of television is a relevant comment on all agencies of mediation, that they represent 'social values, not social reality' (De Fleur and Ball-Rokeach 1989). The mediated world is a world seen by some on behalf of others and it is therefore a constructed reality which will necessarily invite comparisons with our own experiences. In some contexts, in most film and television genres for example, it has to pass the 'common sense' test: we are not that easy to fool. If this reality is 'idealised' it is done so in a proportion that makes it at least believable but the fact that it is 'idealised' is perhaps best evidenced by the disappointment often felt by people who meet TV stars or visit the set of The Rovers' Return (the pub at the corner of Coronation Street). In other genres, like cartoon, from *The Simpsons* to *Finding Nemo* (2003), the text creates a self-referenced 'world' and in doing so constructs reality without attempting to resemble it.

This situation is one that was clearly aggravated in the second half of the twentieth century by the proliferation of those things we call 'the mass media'. The implication of this proliferation is that we simply have more access to and experience of the mediated world. Postmodernists would argue that we have entered a debate about what is real, stemming from this context. As long ago as the 1970s Neil Postman was claiming that 'You have to watch TV to be American.' Even earlier McLuhan was warning

that 'we shape the tools and they in turn shape us'. More recently, Todd Gitlin has argued that the most significant thing about the contemporary media is not their content or effect, but their sheer volume. In this view, we, as audience members, no longer even expect the media to deliver us representations of the external world. We want the media to be a part of our own personal and selfish reality: a source of cheap thrills.

> We aim, through media, to indulge and serve our hungers by inviting images and sounds into our lives, making them come and go with ease in a never-ending quest for stimulus and sensation. Our prevailing business is the business not of information but of satisfaction, the feeling of feelings.
>
> (Gitlin 2002: 5)

In a 1974 essay entitled 'Drama in a Dramatised Society', Raymond Williams attempted to tease out some of the more important implications of media proliferation. He examined and refined McLuhan's 'extension of the senses' argument by firstly dismissing it in its simplest form. Clearly, he said, television (for example) has done much more than simply extend the audience for 'quality' drama: it has, rather, made us all more involved in drama at all levels. The media provide us with representations of the world with all the boring bits left out, to such an extent that we have become hooked on exciting and dramatic representations. Williams went on:

> Till the eyes tire, millions of us watch the shadows of shadows and find them substance; watch scenes, situations, actions, exchanges, crises. The slice of life, once a project of naturalist drama, is now a voluntary, habitual, internal rhythm; the flow of action and acting, of representation and performance, raised to a new convention, that of a basic need.
>
> (Williams 1989)

What Williams, as a teacher of Drama as Literature, was saying is that we have been witnessing for a while a new place and perhaps a new function for drama. Drama began in temples as ritual and progressed to theatres as rituals of a different kind: special-occasion stuff where a community or class group might meet to examine or confirm its values. For fifty years or so we have been living with a new context for drama which has been made possible by electronic media. We live in a world where dramatic representations are commonplace and where they increasingly provide us with ways of understanding how things are. In this way life moves from being potentially dramatic to being, at least at the level of perception, 'dramatised'. The conventions of film and television drama become unwittingly the tests of truth and substance and we potentially get hooked on representations rather than reality. What Williams would have made of reality TV no one can say but in one sense it both powerfully confirms his initial hypothesis and takes it to another level.

STEREOTYPES AND MINORITIES

The 'slice of life' which Williams referred to is certainly a staple part of our media diet. Reality TV offers us 'real people' in 'real situations'. Magazines help us to deal with 'real problems' and the popular press deals with the 'real lives' of 'ordinary people' (as well as celebrities, of course). Soap operas give us an opportunity to share the lives of 'realistic characters' in lifelike settings. But is any of this reality-obsessed entertainment actually real? Of course not. As we have already seen, these fictional and non-fictional texts have no alternative but to provide mediated versions of the world. Some commentators have argued, though, that we as audience members may be organising and understanding our own lives in the terms provided by this mediated version of reality. In other words, there is a link between media representations and the identities of audience members. Representations of 'people like us' suggest to us who we are, what we can become and how we should evaluate ourselves. As Woodward puts it:

> Discourses and systems of representation construct places from which individuals can position themselves and from which they can speak. . . . The media can be seen as providing us with the information which tells us what it feels like to occupy a particular subject-position – the streetwise teenager, the upwardly mobile worker or the caring parent.
>
> (Woodward 1997: 14)

Logically, the impact on identity is felt particularly strongly by members of groups which are negatively represented in the mainstream media. In a study of black minority television viewers, Karen Ross found that most of her respondents were critical of British television's representations of ethnic groups and the relations between them. In the following extract, Ross makes it clear that the representation of places as well as groups can have an important impact on feelings about identity and self-worth.

> The lack of positive role models and the way in which black minority characters are routinely stereotyped contribute to feelings of low self-esteem and failure, especially among black minority children. . . . Because most black minority children in Britain were born in the country, their knowledge of 'home' is very limited, gleaned from what their relatives tell them and, of course, from television. Viewers reported sadness at the reactions of their children to their homelands of Africa, India or Pakistan which, because the media's slant on the developing world tends to be negative, is one of shame at the 'backwardness' of their country of origin.
>
> (Ross 2000: 145)

You will remember that Barthes characterised the relationship between signifier and signified (between what a sign is and what it means) in terms of three tendencies:

- the iconic: resemblance (the *Mona Lisa* is the iconic representation of a woman)
- the indexical: existence (the *Mona Lisa* is an index of art, the Renaissance and Leonardo da Vinci)
- the symbolic negotiation (the *Mona Lisa* is a piece of language, consisting of eight letters, the meaning of which is dependent on knowledge of one or more linguistic codes).

The supremacy of our visual media rests on the predominance of the icon in a society where 'seeing is believing'. In the easy realism of much media representation 'reality' is dressed up, manufactured out of local colour and half-truths. The Oxford of *Morse* or

the Greater Manchester which contextualises *Coronation Street* are rendered out of fairly superficial local details and then recast for impact.

ACTIVITY . . .

What are the significant details that define the following as 'realistic':

- *Eastenders*
- *The Bill*
- *Buffy the Vampire Slayer*

- *The Simpsons*
- *Ibiza Uncovered*
- (etc.)

Representation, the construction of versions of reality to stand in for reality, does indeed take place at all levels of the (technical and creative) media process: in the writing, direction, camerawork and action. However, as Abercrombie points out, it is one of the abiding characteristics of realism that 'the illusion of transparency is preserved': he goes on to clarify this when he writes, 'The form conspires to convince us that we are not viewing something that has been constructed.'

The representation, for example, of minority groups often founders at a simple level. We fall for the one about the neutrality of the media, the plausibility of 'the camera never lies', and we confuse 'resembles' with 'represents'. The former is an implication, the latter an active process. If we wish to represent a multicultural society or one in which women are challenging the traditional roles allocated to them, we must do so. It is disingenuous of media professionals to act as if the ideological meanings of a text are a mystery, unknown even to its makers and even beyond its makers' influence. Although it may be true that ideology operates at the level of the unconscious, this is not to say that ideological issues are invisible.

ACTIVITY . . .

Imagine that the next two days of your life are being filmed as an innovative 'total drama' project, with the working title *Yet Another 48 Hours*. For forty-eight hours cameras will unobtrusively track your every move and interactive viewers will be able to monitor your 'actions'.

You are called in at the end of the project to discuss the production of an edited ninety-minute version. You are asked for your opinion on two issues.

1   What would be the differences between a film of your life for two days and a conventional film or television 'drama'?
2   What principles would you suggest on which to model a ninety-minute version of the recording?

The representation of minority groups often amounts to a failure to be proactive, as any amount of content research will prove. People with disabilities, for example, seem

to have dropped 'beyond the frame' of the mediated world as if they were always just out of shot. This is what Barthes (1977) called 'absent presence', the fact that the very invisibility of some groups becomes an almost palpable issue. If we consider the representation of minority ethnic groups in the British media, the world of television situation comedy or game shows will furnish fruitful examples of absent presence. Conversely a consideration of human interest stories and accompanying photographs in local or national newspapers might be relevant.

It would be easy to see 'absent presence' in mainstream soap operas like *Coronation Street* and even *EastEnders* as a pressure that has progressively made programme-makers address this issue. However, we must not succumb to a crude oversimplification of the issue and merely see the problem in terms of a journey from 'none of them' to 'more of them', whomsoever 'they' may be. This is not a numbers but a meanings game: it is not about quotas but about questions.

Without appropriate questions we all too easily move from 'absent presence' to 'present absence', the empty representations which we call stereotypes (groups are represented but there's nothing going on). Stereotypes are moulds into which reality can be poured, or at least part of it. A stereotype is a shorthand form and as such a reduction of the complexity of the reality represented. Stereotypes do not normally try to open debates about, for example, gender representations; they actually paper over them or 'skirt' around them.

The idea of stereotyping is often used with negative connotations, as if the removal of all stereotypes would make media representations fair and unbiased. However, a brief examination of the concept reveals that stereotypes are a necessary component of all mediated communication. There is never the time or space to do justice to the complexity of human beings. The variety of our environments and the sheer diversity of individuals make it inevitable that shortcuts are taken in the telling of stories and the reporting of events. Furthermore, in an influential essay on stereotypes, Tessa Perkins (1997) made the point that we tend to make assumptions about stereotypes which can in themselves be misleading. For example, we sometimes assume that stereotypes are always wrong and always negative; but this is not necessarily the case. Nor is it necessarily true that stereotypes always concern minority or oppressed groups or that they are simple and unchanging. On the other hand, it is possible for contradictory stereotypes to be held of the same group (see Perkins 1997: 75).

Perkins goes on to reinforce the point that stereotypes are essentially *ideological* because they are predominantly evaluative beliefs expressed about groups and by groups. As with any ideological effect, the repetition of stereotypes and the absence of plausible alternatives means that the values wrapped up in the stereotype come to appear as 'common sense'. The stereotype does more than simply *describe* characteristics assigned to a particular group, it also carries value judgements. Andy Medhurst illustrates this principle in relation to stereotypes of gay men:

> [T]he image of the screaming queen does not just mean 'all gay men are like that', it means 'all gay men are like that and aren't they awful', which in turn means 'and they are awful because they are not like us'.
>
> (Medhurst 1998: 285)

In terms of the representations of minority groups stereotyping is often a double handicap as even the range of stereotypes is often limited.

Stereotypes are clearly useful in the sense that any shorthand is: they allow us to take a quick look and know what we're being given since we only need the 'gist': that he's French, she's a bimbo and he's Irish, for example. However what we're also doing is undermining the integrity of the world we are 'viewing', unless we are also given the chance to address or challenge these crude assumptions.

Self-reflection is a feature of more sophisticated texts and sometimes unwittingly of cruder ones. Part of the power of, for example, a film like *American Beauty* (1999) lies in its ability to construct recognisibly stereotypical elements – the dysfunctional family, the teenage temptress, the frustrated middle-aged man, the crazy teen, the lonely teen – and then create a narrative that both exploits and deconstructs them. Similarly something like TV's *Auf Wiedersehen, Pet* may start from a default of working-class regional accents but it delivers a maturing drama about masculinity and mortality with wit and warmth.

Perhaps the most miraculous of all is the popular love song: a tightly controlled and contrived blend of stereotypical elements still capable of great tenderness and power for all or any of us. Consider, for example, these 'lyrics':

This Romeo is bleeding
But you can't see his blood
It's nothing but some feelings
That this old dog kicked up.

It's been raining since you left me
Now I'm drowning in the flood.
You see I've always been a fighter
But without you I give up.

Now I can't sing a love song
Like the way it's meant to be.
Well, I guess I'm not that good anymore
But baby, that's just me.

('Always': Bon Jovi)

Candle light and soul forever
A dream of you and me together,
Say you believe it, say you believe it.
Free your mind of doubt and danger,
Be for real don't be a stranger,
We can achieve it, we can achieve it.
Come a little bit closer baby, get it on, get it on,
'Cause tonight is the night when two become one.

('2 Become 1': Spice Girls)

ACTIVITY . . .

Consider love songs that are meaningful or moving for you both personally and 'objectively' and those that you consider 'corny', 'cheesy' or otherwise un-convincing.

- What do these two 'types' share?
- What are the elements that make a difference?

ALTERNATIVE REPRESENTATIONS

As noted above, the ideological effect of stereotyping is most pronounced when stereotypes are reinforced by repetition and an absence of alternatives. However, it would be a mistake to see all media representation working in this way. There are many justifiable concerns about negativity and bias in media representation, but it is worth bearing in mind some of the following.

- There are alternatives to the mainstream media.
- The mainstream media often provide space for alternative representations.
- Many groups have intervened successfully to take more control over representation.
- 'Dominant' representations can change with great speed.
- The media provide many positive role models.
- Campaigns against biased and negative stereotypes have succeeded in changing industry practices, voluntary codes of conduct and statutory controls (laws).
- Media-literate audiences have a sophisticated understanding of the techniques and devices used to 're-present' reality.

An excellent case study for the alternative take on representation is provided by Matt Groening's *The Simpsons* which has been inhabiting its own heightened reality since 1989 in the most conservative TV environment in the world. Here the cartoon form is used to animate all kinds of debates about how the world is and how it can be. The show targets cant and hypocrisy wherever it finds it from the exploitative manipulation of mass advertising to the crusading mock respect of political correctness. In one episode, Apu, the Hindu manager of the 'Kwik-e-Mart' (a large corner shop!), reveals to Homer his shrine to Ganesha, the elephant-headed god. Homer is certainly challenging in his

response: 'Wow. You must have been out having a wazz when they were giving out the gods.'

On the other hand if you want a summary of dominant stereotypes of gender, ethnicity or social class where better to go than to the films of the Farrelly Brothers or that dubious British classic 'brand', the *Carry On . . .* series of films? Here the stereotypes are so crude and so crudely humorous that they unconsciously provide a platform for their discussion or at least an exposure of their limitations. The same may be true of *Footballers' Wives* or *Sunday Sport* or rap music videos or even *Hello* magazine (see p. 63).

TYPES OF REALISM

Realism, or how art can realistically replicate the world, has been an issue for the artist and writer for many centuries. It is interesting that the birth of photography and later moving image technology provided an opportunity to advance this ongoing search for the accurate depiction of reality.

The earliest films are works in what we would now call 'documentary': *Employees Leaving the Lumière Factory*; *Baby's Breakfast* (both 1895); a wall being demolished. Crowds flocked to see reality recorded and a relationship was struck up between moving image technology and the mass audience that largely persists. Moreover, this moment sums up much about the nature of our experience of both film and television, which is always a strange mixture of the natural (or lifelike) and artificial (in this case technological). As the experience develops we are confronted by two coincidental elements: the 'wow' factor of effectiveness, the verisimilitude (the closeness to life); and the realisation that it is to some extent trickery, the 'how on earth do they do that?' factor. In other words, at the moment of greatest impact, of maximum 'realism', we are also most aware that all effects are caused.

Whether it be the underwater sequence in Buster Keaton's 1922 film *The Navigator* (which appears to us simply to be a man filmed in a large tank wrestling a rubber swordfish) or Leonardo Di Caprio and Kate Winslet standing on the prow of a computer-generated SS *Titanic*, we have all experienced these 'miracle' moments, which in turn remind us that realism begins in the relationship between individual texts and their audiences.

ACTIVITY . . .

What are your 'miracle' moments, times when you were amazed at the seeming reality of moving images (film, television, computer graphics)? How do 'amazing' film sequences compare to 'amazing' things you have seen in nature/real life?

What we have called 'the discourse of realism' is negotiated afresh with each new text and audience but the context is always the particular norms and standards, codes and conventions of the individual context: *Star Trek: The Next Generation* will have a different starting point to *Tonight with Trevor McDonald* or a feature in *Hello* magazine on the

Beckhams or the latest reality TV programme. Media producers bring us their take on reality through their take on realism and we are free to 'buy' these or not on a text-by-text basis. This is sometimes called a 'modality judgement' and is the result of the media product, say a film, establishing its approach and the audience debating whether it is plausible. It reminds us that more often than not the realism of the modern media is a kind of technologically aided naturalism, a sleight of hand in which the obviously composed and constructed takes on the appearance of the natural.

KEY TERM

NATURALISM A significant movement in late nineteenth-century drama, championed by Constantin Stanislavsky. He was the first to put on the plays of Anton Chekhov and he did so in a way that stressed that the audience was eavesdropping through an invisible 'fourth wall' on a fully realised reality. Naturalism is about reducing to nothing the differences between what is on stage and what is not. In naturalism 'getting it right' is about being true to life. Much television and film drama of the twentieth century has settled into a largely naturalistic mode of address, encouraged by the ease with which the technology can get the look right (as in 'convincing').

The danger of naturalism is that it appears to be transparent, almost formless, and by implication neutral, even 'truthful.' Naturalism only tells its truths as far as it can and as far as it wants to. Its original motivation for showing things as they really are was not aesthetic (artistic) but rather social and political. In its purest form it is a model that has continued as a strand in both television and film drama in the work of, for example, Mike Leigh and Ken Loach. It is also the version of realism that dominated the drama of Communist Eastern Europe, where it became socialist realism. This history lesson only serves to demonstrate that all versions of realism are interested ones, that even the desire to present the world accurately presupposes opinions on what that might be like. This is where we came in with a recognition of how difficult it is to say simply if and how a text is realistic. Perhaps we now need some places to start.

ACTIVITY...

Before you read any further, compile your own list: what is it that makes us label a text or sequence within it realistic?

- **Surface naturalism**: Val Pope calls this 'making it look real' (www.litnotes.co.uk). It's about crudely matching external reality and the text's representations; it's about locations and costumes and props; it's about authentic Welsh accents and no wristwatches in historical drama.

- **Realism of content**: much media work records reality in a journalistic or documentary fashion which then functions as either the subject of a text or its backdrop. While not unmediated, this content does invest its particular context with a certain credibility. News, for example, calls upon verifiable external reality in this way, as does any outside broadcast or 'on-location' drama shoot.
- **Psychological realism**: in a straightforward way the focus of human communication is the human figure, so most texts will need to establish the credibility of characters, which is a difficulty for documentary just as much as for drama. Wherever humans appear (on whatever planet, in whatever situation) we must believe in them, that is, believe they are behaving in a realistic way.
- **Realism of narrative**: this is about telling credible stories in a way that seems plausible. Whether this is *The Lord of the Rings* or a new short story in *Cosmopolitan* magazine, the rules are the same: it must at least make us want to read/hear/see the next 'bit'. Barthes sees this as the danger of narratives: they deliver ideological values effectively because we are chasing the next 'bit'.
- **The technical conventions of realism**: ironically perhaps 'the discourse of realism' extensively uses the technical conventions of a range of media to support its negotiations. For example, it has become a convention of film realism to expect non-diegetic sound (especially music) and a certain style of editing (which stresses narrative rather than naturalism). Film that doesn't follow these conventions might initially be described as unrealistic or artificial (and 'arty'). One of the principal uses of advanced technology is to recreate the appearance of live performance: rather than recording in one take, bands spend large amounts of time and money making it sound as if they have.

Technology is, of course, a significant element in what postmodernists would see as the struggle between different versions of reality: on the one hand, that inhabited by us and, on the other, that provided by the mass media. Baudrillard coined the term 'hyperreality' to describe the latter and suggest its impact and character. The question this prompts is: does a hyperreality require a hyperrealism? If it does, it probably already exists in the cranked-up, ultra-enhanced experience of computer and console games where a highly sensitised and accelerated reality is created compared to which your own day-to-day experience sometimes seems mundane. A multimillion-pound leisure industry has been created out of this fact, and like the mobile phone phenomenon it has happened 'recently'. In the early 1980s there was no equivalent experience: we were coming to terms with a fourth terrestrial TV channel and struggling with the rubber keys of the ZX SPECTRUM. Now we can place ourselves into fully realised representations of the streets of ancient Rome, F1 race tracks or even the mountains of the moon, and seemingly 'look around' at our leisure, always amazed by how realistic everything looks. And yet our experience helps us out here for the more realistic it manages to appear the more profoundly we know that it is not real. This is why we often, after long sessions of gaming, feel strangely unfulfilled, however engaging the game: we are aware somehow that much time has been spent to little avail. This too is part of what Jean-François Lyotard (1984) called 'the postmodern condition'. As we tear down the old standards and embrace the new reality we are sometimes given a glimpse of how little is left. 'We live in a cultural Disneyland', Lyotard insisted, 'where everything is parody and nothing is better or worse'.

However, as we have seen and shall see, values are never far away and remain central to the issues of representation. All types of realism share one significant quality: they are interested, one might say 'biased', versions.

IDEOLOGY AND REPRESENTATION

Representation is an act of making choices from largely available 'sets': semiotics would talk about creating syntagms (sign chains) from socially generated paradigms (sign sets or 'menus'). It is important to acknowledge that these signs are rarely newly coined, it's in the infinite combinations that we seek originality. The problem is that 'used' signs are stained by their use, by the contexts in which they operate and by the dominant values of these contexts. Ideology, which Althusser described as 'a system of representation', colours the way signs are chosen, delivered and understood. We can only communicate with society's tools, with languages suffused with the dominant assumptions.

It takes little work to find the values that colour much of our available language: a quick trip to 'male' and 'female' in a standard dictionary or to 'black' and 'white' in a reputable thesaurus will remind us that the tools of representation are not exactly clean.

Main Entry: [1]**black**

Pronunciation: 'bl|a|k

Function: *adjective*

1 a : of the color black **b** (1) : very dark in color <his face was *black* with rage> (2) : having a very deep or low register <a bass with a *black voice*> (3) : **HEAVY**, **SERIOUS** <the play was a *black* intrigue>

2 a : having dark skin, hair, and eyes : **SWARTHY** <the *black* Irish> **b** (1) *often capitalized* : of or relating to any of various population groups having dark pigmentation of the skin <*black* Americans> (2) : of or relating to the Afro-American people or their culture <*black* literature> <a *black* college> <*black* pride> <*black* studies> (3) : typical or representative of the most readily attended parts of black culture <tried to play *blacker* jazz>

3 : dressed in black

4 : **DIRTY**, **SOILED** <hands *black* with grime>

5 a : characterized by the absence of light <a *black* night> **b** : reflecting or transmitting little or no light <*black* water> **c** : served without milk or cream <*black* coffee>

6 a : thoroughly sinister or evil : **WICKED** <a *black* deed> **b** : indicative of condemnation or discredit <got a *black* mark for being late>

7 : connected with or invoking the supernatural and especially the devil <*black* magic>

8 a : very sad, gloomy, or calamitous <*black* despair> **b** : marked by the occurrence of disaster <*black* Friday>

9 : characterized by hostility or angry discontent : **SULLEN** <*black* resentment filled his heart>

(Merriam-Webster Online Dictionary)

Main Entry: ¹**white**

Pronunciation: ˈhwɪt, ˈwɪt

Function: *adjective*

1 a : free from color **b** : of the color of new snow or milk; *specifically* : of the color white **c** : light or pallid in color <*white* hair> <lips *white* with fear> **d** : lustrous pale gray : **SILVERY**; *also* : made of silver

2 a : being a member of a group or race characterized by light pigmentation of the skin **b** : of, relating to, characteristic of, or consisting of white people or their culture **c** |from the former stereotypical association of good character with northern European descent| : marked by upright fairness <that's mighty *white* of you>

3 : free from spot or blemish: as **a** (1) : free from moral impurity : **INNOCENT** (2) : marked by the wearing of white by the woman as a symbol of purity <a *white* wedding> **b** : unmarked by writing or printing **c** : not intended to cause harm <a *white* lie> <*white* magic> **d** : **FAVORABLE**, **FORTUNATE** <one of the *white* days of his life – Sir Walter Scott>

4 a : wearing or habited in white **b** : marked by the presence of snow : **SNOWY** <a *white* Christmas>

5 a : heated to the point of whiteness **b** : notably ardent : **PASSIONATE** <*white* fury>

(Merriam-Webster Online Dictionary)

Of course ideology is also about the relationship between representation and power, which is why representations of the powerless are always more significant than representations of the powerful. We are surely right to be more concerned with negative representations of ethnic minorities and women than those of middle-aged white men merely because the dominant ideology is, according to Fiske (1989), 'white, patriarchal capitalism'.

NOTEBOX . . .

> This is what is particularly interesting about a debate in 2004 involving deaf sign language which was featured in all the prominent news media and even made Jonathan Ross's Friday night TV chat show. Users of British Sign Language, which despite having more users than Welsh or Gaelic was not recognised as a language

until 2003, were called upon to 'renew' (for renew read 'clean up') some of the signs they used to represent certain minority groups: chiefly the sign for gays/homosexuals and the sign for Orientals. These were thought to promote stereotypes in a negative way: they were both highly iconic signs, a limp wrist and pulled eyes respectively.

In fact further investigation produced an even more interesting demonstration of the issues since the 'story' was some ten to fifteen years old, which tells us something first of all about the media news agenda. It also provides a context in which these issues of representation can be examined and debated. When called on to respond to this (outdated) charge, representatives of the deaf (themselves a significant minority 'interest') argued that these attacks were themselves prejudicial to their sense of identity which, as with national groups, is enshrined in their language. In other words, they argued that the tools of their representation of the world contained more than simply a set of counters which might be used in place of, for example, the idea 'homosexual'. It was in fact an index of their intrinsic values, which is also of course what their opponents were arguing (and that these values were prejudicial).

Cath Smith, a widely published author of sign books including sign dictionaries, has suggested that these issues are at the heart of many of the problems faced by the deaf community. The very fact that BSL was so recently acknowledged by the government is an indication of a situation where often those who can hear and vocalise spoken language make decisions for those who cannot. Smith acknowledges that even at the time that the signs were being recorded there was a tendency for those recording them to have a greater sensitivity to issues of offence than those using the signs, and in many cases new signs were 'proposed' to replace the more insensitive (blunt) ones.

'Gay' and 'Oriental' are two cases in point. The former has transformed itself from the camp limp wrist to the version in Figure 4.1 with no significant protest.

Cath Smith compares those who still use the 'limp wrist' to those who persist in using verbal terms like 'poof' and 'poofter' rather than the generally acceptable and uncontroversial 'gay'. The Oriental revision, however, was rejected out of hand and the pulled eye remains the conventional sign in a victory for practice over theory. Incidentally, the Oriental deaf sign for Europeans similarly traces the eye shape, only this time with a circular motion.

Fiske uses the example of women who wear high heels perpetuating ideas about women which are essentially constructed out of the male gaze and male desire. He points out that it is not only by wearing the items that the ideological practice is enacted but also in the simple act of accepting that these images of 'woman' apply to them. The feminist writer Angela Carter, after all, argued that any woman who wears high heels is letting the side down. Fiske also suggests that men are interpellated by images of women in

Figure 4.1 *Gay deaf sign.*
Source: Let's Sign
Dictionary,
www.deafsign.com.

high heels, but in this case they are installed as 'watcher' and therefore empowered. In the case of the 'limp wrist' sign similar roles might be seen to apply: not only are male homosexuals being asked to accept this representation of themselves but at the same time 'straight' men are having something confirmed about themselves.

In the most basic sense we are seeing that a key message of any representation is 'this is what the represented subject is like'. At a simple level this is why iconic representations (where the sign simply looks like its subject) are relatively unproblematic. A photograph of your parents taken in acceptable light with a decent camera will probably address the first layer of the statement, 'this is what my parents are like'. However, beyond this, all is difficult, particularly if the language changes slightly to 'this is what parents are like'. Ideology is forever raising the stakes and leading us into the temptation of ready-made ideas: stereotypes which draw the personal always in the direction of the general and, with a little luck, the universal.

In a society bombarded with images of women in high heels and lingerie or both, we are constantly challenged by the assumption, 'this is what women are like'. We are also provided with a set of reasons why this should be so, which at their most persuasive are described as 'common sense' (perhaps the most powerful form of ideological communication). This is the battleground of what Gramsci calls hegemony, the aggressive negotiation of meaning in which the dominant ideology must engage to keep itself 'healthy' and perpetuate itself. In simple terms ideology has become an active ingredient in society, embedding itself within social institutions like education and the media. We find social values everywhere, disguised yet actively persuading us in every aspect of our lives (work and leisure) that society's dominant opinions are indisputable.

Take a look at the picture of Graham Norton in Figure 4.2 and see how easy it is to employ the anchor 'this is what gays are like' and how almost impossible it is to imagine 'this is what men are like'. In fact Norton's preferred word would probably be 'queer', a classic piece of appropriation by the gay community of a favourite form of homophobic abuse. The TV drama *Queer as Folk* took this to the limits and still stands as a byword for courageous and controversial programming. It is deliberately provocative to the 'straight' community which may have settled for the rather more coy representations of 'gay'. In the same way that rap group NWA helped to reclaim the word 'nigger' to the discomfort of liberal whites particularly, so 'queer' is a mite more powerful than the limp wrist 'salute'. Graham Norton is a flamboyant role model and pioneer, but he is also 'professionally gay'. What we see is a persona, performance and a good deal of staging: something constructed inside and outside the terms of his sexuality.

Figure 4.2 *Graham Norton.*
Source: Andrew Williams.

Identify the elements that make up the Graham Norton 'phenomenon' as presented in Figure 4.2. Which of these elements are also components of his perceived sexuality?

INTRODUCTION TO CASE STUDIES

The issues of representation are most often addressed when we consider the ideological implications of disadvantageous representations of minority groups or those lacking in economic or political influence. An inordinate amount of time is spent deconstructing the really quite obvious liberties taken by the media in their representations of, for example, women, particularly in terms of objectivisation and sexual exploitation. This is not to say that these issues are unimportant but it has two rather unfortunate implications. On the one hand, the familiarity we have with a narrow range of representation issues breeds a proverbial contempt: we begin to lack the appetite for yet another deconstruction of the cover of a computer magazine featuring a girl in a gratuitous bikini or posed on an over-sized mouse with 'FUN-SIZE' emblazoned across her. More significantly, though, we begin to think that there are specific issues of representation, that this narrow agenda is all we need to address or even worry about. This includes the unspoken emphasis on images, as if words are somehow not the focus. We must understand that the representation of the world that we label 'news' is just as squarely in the centre of this section on representation as, ironically, are worries about the implications of Barbie and Ken dolls.

A good example of how ideology can work on a level that is, as Gramsci suggests, profoundly unconscious is the way we were made to believe in the terrorist threat of the 'dirty bomb', supposedly made from radioactive material. It was later revealed that creating such a bomb is a scientific impossibility, given the speed with which radioactive dust disperses. If ideology can do its work unnoticed or camouflaged as common sense, human nature or objectivity, all the better. If representation is associated largely with the ways certain groups are depicted then there is a whole world of values going unchallenged. The more we appreciate the ways in which we are responsible for the world we live in semantically (at the level at which it has meaning), the better we will be able at least at that level to challenge and change it. Marx [1886] may have argued that 'the philosophers have variously interpreted the world, the point however is to change it', but it is arguable whether the difference between 'interpreting' and 'changing' is so great. Raymond Williams (1962) was surely closer to the mark when he pointed out the deficiencies in thinking that reality and representation can be so easily separated. 'My own view is that we have been wrong in taking communication as secondary. Many people seem to assume as a matter of course that there is, first, reality, and then, second, communication about it.'

In the 2003 film *Bruce Almighty*, Jim Carrey's Bruce gets a chance to play God for a while courtesy of a black God, played by Morgan Freeman. In 1989 Madonna brought down

the wrath of American Christianity when she featured a black Christ in a video to promote her single 'Like a Prayer', despite numerous precedents in European shrines. Representation is then always about the negotiation of the meaning of the world we inhabit with those inhabited by others. The issue of God is perhaps as broad and timeless as the concept itself but it is always an issue of representation and in a Western context its 'default' is still an old white man with a beard. All representations, comic or serious, must then address this anachronistic version in the same way that representations of 'pirates' have to address eye-patches and parrots and wooden legs. In Althusser's terms they 'hail' us because they contain ideological information: crudely, that God is like us and pirates are not.

ACTIVITY...

Consider the common representations and assumptions about the following items and ideas.

1	Travellers	4	Terrorism
2	Christmas	5	Michael Jackson
3	Democracy	6	Angels

There is, therefore, an awful lot invested in representation at a personal and social level. Psychologically it very often operates as a form of what psychoanalyst Sigmund Freud called 'projection': we invest negative representations with our fears and insecurities while using positive ones to self-handicap our hopes.

The case studies that follow investigate some of the issues that are involved in our creation of and participation in a mediated reality. At the same time they hope to remind all of us that representation is the broadest and most significant media issue. In considering the representation of 'place' we are trying to dispel the impression that something as multidimensional and organic as a site of human settlement, a village, a town, even a country, might be semantically neutral. The fact that we don't think too much about the meaning of our towns, cities, even country is an issue in itself. Places are significantly represented across the media in both casual and detailed ways, from the offhand things that people write and say to the fully fledged 're-creations' that are modern British soap operas.

CASE STUDY: 'IN A BIG COUNTRY': THE MEANINGS OF SCOTLAND

In a big country,
Dreams stay with you
Like a lover's voice fires a mountain side . . .

('In a Big Country': Big Country)

Barthes suggested that the way in which signs represent their subjects has two tendencies which he labelled 'motivation' and 'convention'. Motivation in simple terms is the tendency of a sign to be iconic, to work in the relationship of resemblance, to 'look' (or sound or smell, I suppose) more and more like its subject. It is the tendency of the signifier to take its form from the form of the signified. A lifesize model then is a highly motivated sign because it takes its shape and size directly from what it is representing.

In the other direction is the tendency towards convention. Conventional signs tend towards the symbolic, to work in the relationship of agreement. Symbols have meaning only by our understanding the codes in which they are operating. Convention as a concept usefully allows us to assess the degree to which other information is required for the deciphering of a sign. In this context an index might usefully be seen as a halfway house on the journey from motivation to convention (see diagram).

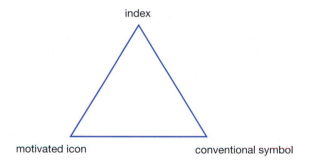

If the word sign 'AUSTRALIA' is to represent a particular area of the world, it needs our consent. As an indigenous Aboriginal weapon, a boomerang represents the same area because of an objective association, a real connection which registers the actual existence of the signifier in the 'region' of the signified. In the same way the kangaroo has become a significant index of Australian life, simply because this animal is actually a part of it. While Australia is also represented iconically it is much more difficult to represent 'big' ideas as highly motivated icons, so icons of an idea like Australia are also likely to function as indexes (that is, need a degree of extra information) or to be very clearly anchored. The Sydney Opera House and Ayers Rock, for example, are common visual representations of Australia but they have meaning not as pure icons, more as significant indexes.

In the same way, as the Big Country lyric suggests, Scotland is both a big idea and a charged context, a place where people live, to which they commit and by which they define themselves. The fact that 'Dreams stay with you' makes this a semantic night-mare, a place that can only be and must always be negotiated. As outsiders, we can only reach sensitively in the direction of conventions.

ACTIVITY . . .

You're making a collage of SCOTLAND: what ten items/images do you include for an English audience? How might this differ if the audience were (a) Scottish, (b) North American or Far Eastern?

It is quite likely that among the ten items you have selected for your collage of Scotland at least one bears the mark of what film critic Colin MacArthur calls 'tartanry'. This is the sanitised and tidy version of Scottishness that was originally derived by the Victorians from a far less sanitary past wherein the plaid (literally the cloth that served as all-purpose clothing, not unlike a coarse sari) was a sign of clan identity. After the battle of Culloden in 1746 where the Highland clans, fighting – ironically – for an Italian-born pretender to the English throne, were brutally suppressed by a modern English army, the wearing of the plaid was outlawed. This was one of a series of draconian measures introduced to bring the Highlands to order, which would see them within a hundred years emptied of people and filled with sheep. It was then safe to reinvent the Scots and do ideologically what had been done militarily.

The new Scot was a version of 'the noble savage': wild and undisciplined but capable of great loyalty and courage if treated well. Queen Victoria herself had a loyal Scottish retainer, John Brown, who, bekilted, accompanied her on her visits to Scotland. This is surely not all that far from the tendency of European monarchs of the sixteenth and seventeenth centuries to keep 'pet' dwarves. The reinvented Scot was really little more than an Englishman in a kilt, which itself had been reinvented as a skirt for men. Even the stories about what real Scotsmen wear beneath their kilts seem mainly designed to dispel thoughts of effeminacy and transvestism, and you can protest too much.

ACTIVITY . . .

What is Scotland according to the familiar image in Figure 4.3? Be precise. Isolate the most significant details.

The approach of Figure 4.3 is to create what Gillian Dyer would identify as a figure of accumulation. This is a rhetorical device (a technique of persuasive communication) by which we are persuaded to the text's point of view by being offered a number of similar objects or arguments. In this case we are persuaded to a view of Scotland through the argument that these biscuits are essentially Scottish, a context that the text has created for itself.

Figure 4.3
Scottish
shortbread.
Source: Duncan's
of Deeside.

The producer of the text is consciously creating an equation of meaning or a 'syntagm', a chain of signs for us to resolve. The Scottishness is found not only in the details but also in the overview. It will be for some a very comfortable image and an attractive one: the very essence of Scotland. To others it is irredeemably bland, the reduction of a culture and a tradition to an insipid veneer: the meaningless masquerading as the meaningful.

ACTIVITY . . .

Imagine you are designing a promotional advertisement for a product from your own town or region. What would be its stereotypical equivalent? Which images would sum up your area and its people? How does this compare with the Scottish version? (Is it funnier, more ludicrous, cooler, more realistic?)

The danger on both sides is to imagine that such obvious images indicate a lack of meaning or even a neutrality. In creating an equation of highly conventional elements, what has been done is an act of omission (or more precisely acts of omission). Absent are any 'signs' (pun intended) of the problematic nature of representing Scotland: of the often fraught relations, for example, between Scotland and England or the social problems of Scotland's large cities. These cities are largely missing from much of 'promotional' Scotland, losing out to lochs and castles and heather. The two 'cultures' were juxtaposed famously in Danny Boyle's film *Trainspotting* in which a group of young Edinburgh heroin addicts go on a nature walk.

Figure 4.4 *Scene from the film* Trainspotting *(1996).*
Source: The Kobal Collection.

ACTIVITY...

> What differences are there between the versions of Scotland in Figures 4.3 and 4.4? Consider particularly the relationship to people and their environment.

What we are doing is reminding ourselves that representation is almost infinitely variable, that the permutations are endless. In the same way that putting heroin addicts instead of pipers in a motivated Highland landscape makes a significant shift in meaning, so any aspect of the sign choices which is altered changes our view. The heroin addicts cannot stand for Scotland, save indirectly, since their conventionality comes only from their cultural relevance, as components of the 1996 film *Trainspotting*. To represent their country they'd have to be more contrived. In other words, they stand as indexes of the film and to function beyond this as merely or essentially Scots would require some work.

Duncan's are trying to address the essence of Scottishness in one way (critics might call it 'anglicised') but the negotiation (in a semiotic sense) is ongoing and as time goes on even the essential becomes a stereotype. These attempts to sum up or distil the idea 'Scotland' are in effect simple techniques to find a way between two poles: the archetypical and the stereotypical. The former represents success, a sense that you have for a moment had the last word (captured something of the essence, the truth), the latter that you have succumbed to other people's generalities, given in to the surface. Stereotypes prevent, in the same way that archetypes allow, analysis, understanding, appreciation. In concrete terms it is the difference in action heroes between Arnold Schwarzenegger and Steven Seagal, or in female sex symbols between Marilyn Monroe and Pamela Anderson (the former being the archetype in each case). And for Scotland and the Scots? Well, which of these is distilled/concentrated?

ACTIVITY

Which of the three images in Figures 4.5–7 has the greatest motivation? Examine the particular claims of each 'candidate'. For which image do you need to bring most information/background? Which image gives you most?

The common visual theme is 'slightly wild and unkempt: all northern and a little primitive and out of control'. Clearly this is only partly useful to those whose job it is to sell Scotland as a holiday destination or even as a place for commerce and culture. It's as if Hadrian's Wall still existed as a metaphor (or is it an ideological filter?) at least as far as those of us south of it are concerned. What we see seems quite limited in range, a sure sign of misrepresentation. There are a few old stories that seem to be told: 'tartan tales', 'tales of loch and glen', 'tales of honour and blood'. These sell everything from 'ethnic' foodstuffs (shortbread and haggis) to financial services (what makes 'Scottish widows' more secure if not the stereotypical care with which their former husbands provided for them?).

Figure 4.5 *Mel Gibson in* Braveheart *(1995). Source: The Kobal Collection.*

Figure 4.6 *Scottish football fan (painted in the flag of St Andrew). Source: Jeff Gilbert.*

Figure 4.7 *Liam Neeson in* Rob Roy *(1995). Source: Kobal Collection.*

Meanwhile Scotland attempts to enter the twenty-first century semantically at least, with culture and commerce trying to replace claymore and kilt. Scottish nationalism has always to an extent looked to Europe (beyond England) for civilised allies: the EU represents for many a model for independence. However, the image of Scotland as a modern European country is one that has needed considerable help from pan-European models, and critics would argue that this sacrifices national flavour for a superficial and limited elegance. Certainly Scotland, land of culture and commerce, is very different from 'Scotland the Brave'!

Figure 4.8 Gallery of Modern Art, Glasgow. Source: Greater Glasgow & Clyde Tourist Board.

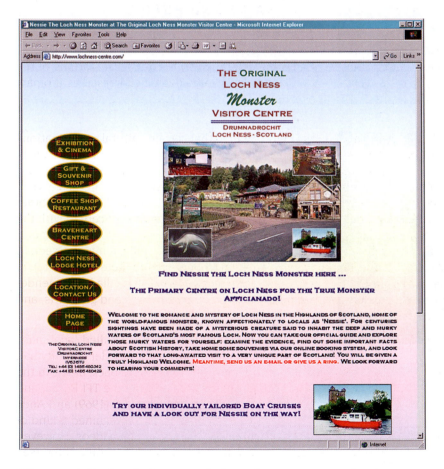

Figure 4.9 Loch Ness website. Source: www.lochness-centre.com.

Where is the idea of Scottish identity in Figures 4.8 and 4.9 and what does this do to the more generic elements?

In Figures 4.8 and 4.9 the notion of manufactured identity is much clearer, with Scotland as a kind of movable feast, what postmodernists would call a bricolage. In fact it can be remade according to taste, or audience need. What Scotland is becomes that which we want or need it to be, as senders or receivers of media messages. In this way ideas that seem concrete and almost objective are revealed as amorphous and problematic as if to remind us that 'where?' is not a simple question but rather one that often elicits the rather aggressive answer, 'who wants to know?'

CASE STUDY: 'SLUGS AND SNAILS AND PUPPY DOGS' TAILS': THE MEANINGS OF MEN

'Straightforward' and 'unproblematic' are not words used often to address issues of gender representation. Gender is an issue embodied by most representations of the human form in any context. Gender is usually to some degree expressed as a binary opposition where being male (for example) is partly understood in terms of not being female.

In her 1990 book *Gender Trouble* Judith Butler argued that certain cultural configurations of gender have gained a 'hegemonic' hold. These are those that stress gender as a binary opposition, one thing or the other. This necessarily disallows views of gender which are more fluid. This division, which tends to leave men powerful, has ironically only been confirmed by feminism, which has unwittingly reinforced the dichotomy. In other words, the issues of gender are never reached because we are too concerned with the particular problems of inequality. Butler claims that the whole issue of gender and sexuality is ideologically manipulated in a context where sex (male, female) is seen to cause gender (masculine, feminine) which is seen to cause desire (heterosexuality). In other words, the assumption of much of what we receive from the media is that gender is somehow fixed. Thus boys will endlessly be stereotypically boys and girls girls, and masculine men will forever consort with feminine women.

This would appear to be the agenda for the new generation of so-called lads' mags which began by claiming they were underlining the progress that gender equality had made by being ironically retro about it. Suddenly 'dolly birds' were back, albeit in the context of Austin Powers movies and the popular 1990s programme TFI *Friday*, and 1960s chic became the trend. Men took their lead from *The Italian Job* (1969) and Andy Williams rereleased 'Music to watch girls by'. Even blaxploitation regained a kind of retro respectability which found itself particularly in hip hop and rap videos. However, it was still a surprise to see the *Observer* Music Monthly playing the ironic game (see Figure 4.10).

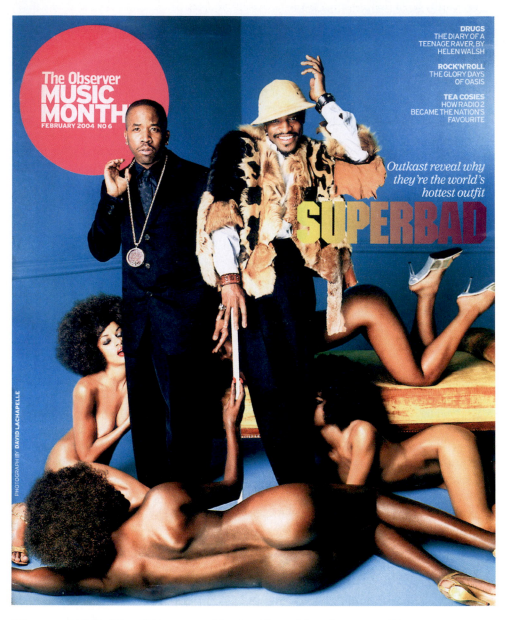

Figure 4.10 *The* Observer *Music Monthly. Source:* Observer.

This shows extreme pictures of men and women as different creatures with different functions. We don't need a term like 'male gaze' to understand how this one works but we may be mistaken if we think it has little to do with gender representation in the mainstream. In abstract terms the women are here reduced to something like 'hair and beauty' whereas the men are those to whom and for whom the woman are beautiful and naked (and bowed).

In the representation of men in the mass media, the primary question 'Who is he?' tends to amount to 'What does he do?' (What role has he achieved?) If the same process is followed for the representation of women the questions tend to be very different. In this case, 'Who is she?' tends to mean 'Who is she related to?', 'Who is she doing that for?' or even 'Whose is she?' This even happens at a metalingual level, at the level of the media code, where men are still much more likely to be the focuses of media texts, the central characters. As a result females and female characters are much more likely to find their roles ascribed. For example, in the most ideologically regressive medium of all, mainstream Hollywood cinema, it is highly likely that at least one of the functions of any female character is to be the wife, partner, mother, sister or 'love interest' to at least one more significant male character. Try this out next time you visit your local multiplex cinema or watch a film on television at home. Women are more often than not defined by their relationships with men. Even when there is good reason to do so, we do not conventionally read men this way.

Figure 4.11 *Scene from* The Godfather *(1972).*
Source: The Kobal Collection.

It is as if men always have a reason to be photographed or otherwise represented which extends beyond their appearance. Well, perhaps it would be truer to say that they seem to need a reason. Left to their own devices, they fall back on attitude as a kind of disguise, either refusing to recognise the presence of the viewer's gaze or confronting it with aggression or posturing. The publicity surrounding rock music offers an interesting example.

The music press has always faced the dilemma that the dynamic ritual that is rock music does not fit easily into the essentially static combination of words and still images. Rock bands have traditionally tended to be groups of men of indeterminate age. Their preferred means of self-presentation is 'on stage', 'live', protected by their 'gear': instruments, microphones, even costumes. They might be carrying their guitars, for instance, anything but merely posing for a photograph, the 'role-less' stone! Only teen idols and boybands, whose audience is 'girls', photograph 'pretty'; in fact only those without credibility even acknowledge the camera save perhaps to scowl or raise a single middle finger. More conventionally they feign or show no interest or affect interest in each other, or look into the distance, faces strained in their devotion to rock. In the absence of the normal channels of engagement (eye contact, body posture, facial expression) we are forced to look for clues, to exercise our peripheral vision or deduce the fantasy narrative that the picture constructs. It is then that we see the significant props: the hair, the shades, the tattoos. We also notice the setting and another aspect of the gender divide: women communicate through images, men communicate in them.

RIDERS ON THE STORM

Death, despair and dining with the Devil – these have been turbulent times for **U2**. In a world exclusive interview they reveal the drama behind the album of their lives... >

WORDS: PAUL REES PHOTOGRAPHER: ANTON CORBIJN

U2: (from left) Bono, Adam Clayton, The Edge, Larry Mullen, Lisbon, Portugal, April 2004.

Figure 4.12 U2 *in* Q *Magazine*. Source: Q Magazine.

ACTIVITY...

What is being constructed in Figure 4.12, a publicity shot for an article on the recording of U2's *How to Dismantle an Atomic Bomb* album in Q *Magazine*? What are the key components in this 'narrative'?

This is, of course, central to Laura Mulvey's arguments in her influential essay 'Visual Pleasure and Narrative Cinema' [1975], which reinforce the idea that women understand what it is to be looked at, to be an object of what she usefully labelled the 'male gaze'. 'Male gaze' is, it seems, the dominant perspective of the mass media: what else could explain the predominance of certain kinds of images of certain kinds of women? Not only is this a patriarchal perspective but it is supported by a hegemonic alliance of common sense and prejudice which suggest that this boys watching girls stuff only works one way. Men look at women in a particular way because of how they're wired, it is argued; women, on the other hand, don't particularly like looking at men in this way.

This may seem to you to be uncontroversial or utterly mistaken but it does explain why the female pin-up is a centuries-old comprehensible format and its male equivalent is pale and unconvincing. Even when the finish and verve of a lads' mag style is employed, J17's 'Tops-Off Totty' (Figure 4.13) seems nothing like the real thing.

Figure 4.13 'Tops-Off Totty' Gary Lucy. *Source:* J17.

What are the significant differences between Figure 4.13 and the conventional 'girlie pic'/topless pin-up?

There are clearly mixed messages here because on the surface the female pin-up is often clearly empowered by nearly everything non-verbal that is going on and in particular by her ability to face or even face down the camera. The young man in Figure 4.13 by comparison seems in all things unconvincing, needlessly topless and hardly revelling in it. In fact, of course, neither is much empowered since it is the gazer who imposes meaning, not the gazed at, and if anything the awkwardness of the young man redeems rather than oppresses him. The confidence of the classic 'girlie pic' on the other hand is no defence for on closer inspection it barely covers an awkwardness which is both widespread and part of the plan. John Berger perhaps summed this up best in his seminal study *Ways of Seeing* (1972): '[M]en look at women. Women watch themselves being looked at. This determines not only most relations between men and women but also the relation of women to themselves.'

In an age of Botox injections and cosmetic surgery this issue is hardly being addressed; 'Because you're worth it' too easily translates for many women into 'because it's all you're worth'. Writing in the *Observer* of 2 May 2004 in a piece with the tagline 'Women who buy into the illusion of youth delude themselves if they think it is an act of emancipation', journalist Yvonne Roberts attacked the ways in which women in particular are persuaded to look younger. She questioned the ways in which women are sold cosmetic improvements as something for themselves. Roberts uncovers the 'social, political and economic inequality' that is the basis of this issue, suggesting that 'females have always been strongly conditioned to believe that beauty is a large part of a woman's worth'. She is most scathing on the beauty industry, revealing 'the most vital of beauty secrets: cash conquers all', but also on what she calls 'the female physical elite' who end up with 'the face of a child, the body of a boy and the neck of a woman heading towards old age'. She also, almost mournfully, quotes sociologist Wendy Chapkis who has pointed out that 'we end up robbing each other of authentic reflections'. In other words, we've lost our perspective on what it is to age.

A new twist was applied by an article in ZOO magazine on Swedish uberbabe Victoria Silvestedt in February 2004 which had the provocative tagline: 'I hope your readers like my boobs'. This is interesting because what the article revealed was that these 'boobs' were, as it were, 'new' (for new read 'enhanced') so there was an even more real sense of their existence as extrapersonal objects. It is as if the process of disempowerment has become even more profound or desperate. Where the traditional pin-up would once say (in effect), 'Look at my lovely boobs which I am lucky enough to have', they are now saying 'Look at my lovely boobs which I have been clever/wealthy/desperate enough to buy'. Despite the significant increase in the popularity of plastic surgery, there are just no semantic equivalents.

Men remain representationally largely free to be what they are (if not what they want to be) and even at times to be who they are. Our tendency in the representation of men is to allocate meaning specifically, to take them one by one. Women are more readily allocated to predetermined 'role' groups wherein their meanings are long established. Once identified, this is a relatively easy process to challenge and there are plenty of examples in all media forms of work that set out to establish interesting and problematic female characters, who require us to apprehend them as individuals rather than types. However, it remains true that part of the power of these progressive pieces is an acknowledgement that the norm is still one that offers us endless variations on the mother/virgin/bitch/whore paradigm.

Moreover, it remains overwhelmingly the case that women are largely excluded from whole swathes of media output by the very nature of this limited range of representations. For example, in a media sense women are not funny (the exceptions prove the rule), perhaps because comedy lives on imperfection and an ugliness that women are not really allowed to have. This is an acid test, where the proof of the pudding lies very much in the eating: ask yourself if this is true (not if it should be). Then ask yourself why, despite the plethora of pretty girl exploitation shots in Media Studies text books, it is also true that representations of men are significantly more interesting than representations of women. The ideology here is multilayered in a world that is flooded with images of a few sorts of women, yet is much more telling in its representation in far fewer images of a more significant range of men.

What do we learn about men from these two advertisements (Figures 4.14 and 4.15)? In what ways are the meanings directed by significant anchors?

Figure 4.14 *NHS careers advertisement. Source: NHS.*

Figure 4.15 *Advertisement for* Queer Eye for the Straight Guy. *Source: Scout Productions.*

REALITY TV

No exploration of the issues of representation and in particular the discourse of realism can ignore the impact that has been made on ideas about realism by reality TV. The label is of course plainly ironic because the reality on and of television has not been significantly altered but the way we think about reality and the media has perhaps been changed for good.

Television has always 'employed' reality as a component in its output. In fact the character of television is to provide for a series of 'levels' of representation which allow us to discriminate between the realistic yet dramatic portrayal of a character in a drama and the performance of a kind of self (a persona if you like) which is the stock in trade of the celebrity singer or chat show host. In short, television has always shown us 'real' people being themselves, often using their own names. They populate a sliding scale (or paradigm if you prefer) which runs from so-called 'stars' to television journalists and weather girls (or, as they're now called, 'the cast' of I'm a Celebrity Get Me Out of Here). And these are themselves our likeliest access to the rawer stuff: vox pops, eye-witness accounts, quiz show contestants, the questioners on Question Time, the complainants on Right to Reply, the audiences of a host of live shows.

What's happened since Big Brother One is that this age-old hierarchy has been disrupted. Acting on a hunch that 'ordinary' people were at least more interesting than B list and C list celebrities, Channel Four unleashed Big Brother and suddenly we were all stars or versions of stars. The show had been a massive hit in Holland, demolishing the argument that 'it could only happen here', and it took Britain by storm. Since then we've had everything from pop star 'trials'/'school' to Celebrity Fit Club. We have at the same time seen a re-emergence of the 'grandfather' of the genre, the fly-on-the-wall documentary. This itself has ranged widely from traditional fare like Airport to hybrids like Club Reps Uncovered or Jamie's Kitchen, which has itself inaugurated its own sub-genre. Professional kitchen-based drama/documentary with a side-order of game show made Jamie Oliver an even bigger television star and then did the same for former Glasgow Rangers footballer turned chef, Gordon Ramsay.

Jamie's Kitchen, in which Oliver tried to turn fifteen disadvantaged young people into chefs competent enough to cook in his new restaurant, 'Fifteen', offered ample opportunities to assess the state of this 'new' genre and consider the issues of TV reality and realism. What unfolded over six weeks was certainly gripping television and what many considered to be significant insights into the hidden world of the chef and the restaurant kitchen. As he battled with a variety of problems the so-called 'Naked Chef' was also revealed as more than the rather cheeky (and to some infuriating) celebrity chef. What the cameras revealed, in a way, was someone far more interesting than his celebrity persona, a man who was hard enough to make difficult decisions, whose language was foul enough to keep the 'beeper' busy all night, and yet whose personal commitment to the principles and practicalities of the project was palpable. The combination was unstoppable and the format interesting in the sense that it rejuvenated fly-on-the-wall with a little 'Big Brother'. While nothing like the phone vote or nomination was attempted, there was nevertheless a sense that we were seeing the 'contestants' whittled down for the most significant prize of all: a future.

This registers a range of questions about the 'reality' of what we see on television, since we are watching people who know they are being watched. To add the tagline 'fighting for their chance for a better future' makes this almost gladiatorial (and therefore unsettling). Moreover, the beauty is that while they're fighting for their 'livelihoods' they soon forget that we're there watching. In *Jamie's Kitchen* there was ample evidence of this as tempers flared and burned across the whole series to the point that a number of Jamie's 'contestants' walked out of both TV fame and a potential career without as much as a backward glance (at the camera): a real result.

However, we are only invited to think about this process in one way: as usual, the vital production contexts are submerged, hidden to preserve the illusion of reality. This is, of course, a paradox since the very essence of reality TV is the admittance of (and admission of the fact of) a television crew to a 'real' context, for example Jamie Oliver's virtual and then actual kitchen. It could in fact be argued that the primary act of 'forgetfulness' is not the way that a group of desperate kids forget they are competing for a future in public. Rather, it is the way that we as an audience are lulled into accepting that what we are watching, one way or another, is 'drama'. The genre, like any other, exists through a series of assumptions and techniques, with the former gradually overpowering the latter or perhaps covering over the traces. As a narrative medium, television naturally succumbs to the power of the story, the 'drama' that we found Raymond Williams explaining earlier in this chapter as 'a voluntary, habitual, internal rhythm'. Oliver and his cast in this way naturally become characters: as a well-established cross between Norman Wisdom and Robbie Williams, Oliver himself has the shortest journey to make. His is the dramatic energy to draw both the engagement of the audience and the participation of the minor characters.

As early as episode two this trick had worked and viewers were more concerned by how X and Y had fared that week than by any reflection on the impact of such a pro-gramme on those involved or the degree to which the presence of a camera crew removed or added to their fears. Most significantly, the quality of the footage displayed across six fifty-minute episodes failed largely to ask us to contemplate how much we didn't get to see. Even if we leave aside the questions 'On whose behalf?' and 'With what intention?' the simple scale of the edit must give us pause for thought. If this is considered, five hours suddenly seems 'a little' rather than 'a lot' and the room to manipulate seems endless. Add to this the need for Jamie Oliver himself to justify his billing, and 'room for manoeuvre' becomes almost redundant. The ability of the programme even to report the events now seems in question and *Jamie's Kitchen* has just edged a little closer to 'The Jamie Oliver Show'. It is as if fly-on-the-wall has had an encounter with *Stars in Their Eyes* ('and tonight Cat, I'm going to cook a pizza'). This is not simply to attack what remains engaging and informative television but rather to attempt to provide it with an appropriate context, which is slightly more modest than the one it gave itself.

By contrast, the real innovation of 'third generation' reality TV is to extend mass com-munication theorist Denis McQuail's surveillance function of mass communication way beyond even his expectations. Digital technology has enabled the co-existence of an arguably less engaging and interesting twenty-four-hour, differently edited, version of

the latest reality shows. This implicitly allows the terminally determined (or desperate) insomniac to challenge the authority of the mainstream edit that appears on terrestrial TV or even potentially to make their own. Just like those DVD film buffs who re-edit from out-takes their own 'director's cuts' (*Bladerunner* is a particular favourite), technology provides a particular kind of empowerment. In practice, it is rather more limited but it might furnish enough evidence to answer *I'm a Celebrity* . . . contestant Mike Read's accusation that he was edited out. The knowing answer of course is to understand exactly why Read was almost certainly right and at the same time woefully naïve.

Certainly the field has been thrown wide open to innovation (or novelty, as it is less seriously known), though more often we are drawn back to the oldest fascination: relationships (particularly romantic/sexual ones). This aspect of human behaviour was perhaps first and most dubiously exploited by *Mr Right*, the show in which many 'eligible' women tracked one 'eligible' bachelor who in the end opted for the show's blonde Swedish hostess. Here was reality biting back and outsmarting the format, though the programme-makers were able to treat 'triumph and disaster . . . just the same'. Everything about this format seemed ideologically dubious from square one: the obvious differences in the meaning of 'eligible' for the women (good-looking and well-groomed) and for the man (sports car and wealth). Watching intelligent and attractive women on triple dates with a man vain enough to bear the legend 'Mr Right' was a puzzling and galling experience but at least by the end most of them had realised that the premise of the show was profoundly wrong. When there were fifteen 'girls' (or women playing at being 'girls'), most were desperate to stay. When there were five or six, most were far less convinced. Ultimately the one he chose would not choose him and Ulrika stepped in to save the show. Reality had the last laugh though, refreshingly, as Ulrika's relationship with 'Mr Right' seems to have proved 'right' and real.

Mr Right to some extent opened the flood-gates and reality-style dating shows quickly became the norm, each vying with the others to push the intimacy–crassness balance. One reran *Mr Right* with a millionaire who wasn't one, as if to paradoxically expose the foolishness of gold-diggers, who were anyway paid by the channel to take part. Equally problematic was the show that had men competing to spend time with the beautiful pre-operative transsexual 'Miriam', where the 'point' was that we knew and they didn't (on paper this doesn't seem very funny, let alone ethical). Ultimately, though, it did make a profound point about media products, since outraged contestants were paid to have their edited (partly on their own terms) 'humiliations' broadcast and everyone was happy (even Miriam?).

The serious issues here are both general and particular: from the abstract philosophical discussions about what constitutes reality to the genuinely fascinating social and psychological insights that are, often unwittingly, being offered in even the crassest reality shows. *Big Brother* was launched with much greater focus on the resident psychologists and sociometrists who reinforced the level at which this was an interesting and reputable social experiment. That factor has waned in proportion with the degree to which the contestants have become less and less our representatives. Thus the responsibility for understanding and interpreting it all has passed from experts

to the audience. The result is neither wholly bad nor good but it is debatable, as are all of these formats. This is part of their appeal: even those who deride them have to engage.

The programme-makers on the whole ignore or even exploit these issues, preferring to make shows more visceral and controversial, rather than better discussed and analysed. This is a debate as old as television: the tension between the potential of the medium to entertain and to inform. The BBC's first director-general Lord Reith was not prepared to compromise the latter with the former, fearing that allowing 'entertainment' to be a defining principle of television production would in the long term do for 'education' altogether. Who can say that Reith was wholly wrong?

EXAM QUESTIONS...

'Media representations of the world can appear so natural that we easily see them as real.' Discuss this quote with reference to one social group or place that you have studied. (AQA January 2004)

Is it inevitable that a social group that is represented as alternative eventually becomes mainstream? Discuss with examples. (AQA January 2003)

How far is it possible for the media to produce fair and accurate representations? Discuss with reference to either social groups or places. (AQA June 2003)

▼ 5 AUDIENCE

In this chapter, we examine the role played by the receivers of media messages: the mass audience. On completing this chapter and its associated activities you should be able to:

- understand the changing and dynamic nature of the media audience
- understand how and why information about the audience is collected by media institutions and by academic researchers
- consider the audience in relation to media institutions and texts
- compare and evaluate different theories of 'passive' and 'active' audience
- discuss the relationship between new technology and media audiences.

INTRODUCTION

An understanding of the audience is right at the heart of Media Studies. After all, it is the audience that defines our subject. An act of communication needs to be witnessed by a large number of people before we can realistically speak of the mass media. It is the presence of a mass audience that allows us to make the distinctions between the mass media and communication on a much smaller scale. Technology, of course, has played a key role in the development of the mass media by allowing communicators to reach more and more people over greater distances. However, it is not the presence of technologically enhanced methods of communication which defines our subject. For all their technical sophistication, videophones or email conferences are not really central to the concerns of Media Studies. It is the presence of or, at least, the capacity to reach a mass audience which defines the field.

THE AUDIENCE; THAT'S US

All of us consume the products of the mass media and we are all therefore members of many audience groups. Think of a film or television programme you have watched recently and consider the following.

- Do you think you were a typical member of the audience?
- Was the text directed specifically at people like you?
- What influenced your decision to watch that particular film or programme?
- Did you interact in any way with the text?
- Did you interact in any way with other members of the audience?
- Did you watch in the company of others and, if so, did you influence one another's response?

Having answered the questions above, you will have made a start on some of the many and complex debates surrounding the media audience. As noted elsewhere in this book, it has often been said that we live in a 'media-saturated society'. It is certainly the case that we have access to an enormous amount of information delivered to us by the mass media. Just as media technology has become more complex and sophisticated, so have media audiences. A typical household in Britain contains a huge quantity of stored information not just in newspapers, magazines and books but also in DVDs, CDs and numerous files on the hard drives of personal computers and games machines. In addition, points of access to the media may include multiple televisions, radios and phones together with Internet access and the means of replaying electronically stored information (e.g. DVD, CD and MP3 players).

In most households it would be common to find many of these devices being used simultaneously, often by the same person. This makes for a very complicated picture of the media audience; and it does not end at the front door. Outside the home an array of mobile and in-car communication devices are available and we are rarely far away from the next billboard or poster. With all of this choice and diversity it would be strange if we were to play a wholly passive role in our relationships with the media. Far from it; we make selections about when, where and how we want to engage with the media. We expect a degree of control and participation. As an illustration, we could compare the soccer fan of thirty years ago with his or her modern equivalent. Of course, both could watch live matches, but the experience of football as a media event is very different. The fan of thirty years ago would be able to read match reports, listen to the occasional radio commentary and watch recorded highlights on television. Just some of the ways in which modern fans can use the media to pursue their interest include the ability to:

- receive text alerts from a favourite club
- read the club's own dedicated magazine
- play on-line games based on soccer skills or management

- watch live games on digital TV using the red button to select different perspectives
- email the club's own subscription TV channel with comments and suggestions
- post digital images on a fan website
- listen to commentary on DAB (digital) or Internet radio
- take part in Web-based discussion groups
- keep up with scores and the latest information via teletext
- phone the local radio station for post-match chat
- watch a DVD of last season's triumphs.

Of course it is still perfectly legitimate to talk of an audience outside the context of the mass media. Live performances of music and plays or sporting events take place in the presence of a live audience. These audiences react visibly and audibly to the spectacle before them. They are aware of one another's presence and it is relatively easy to count them. Frequently, the live audience contributes to the event by generating an 'atmosphere'. A stand-up comedian, for example, is very well aware of audience feedback by the presence or absence of laughter. An appreciative audience may stand up to register approval of a performance. Sometimes the outcome of a live event may be influenced or even determined by the audience, perhaps by demands for an encore or by booing a performer off the stage.

Case Study: The Changing Cinema Audience

In some ways, cinema still retains aspects of live entertainment. Older cinemas were built on the same lines as variety theatres or music halls, with social class divisions reflected by different seat prices in the stalls, the circle and the boxes. In the 1940s, it was still common for live entertainment to precede film features. A scene in the 1949 film *The Blue Lamp* shows precisely this kind of mixed programme at a London cinema. Until fairly recently, clapping, cheering, booing, jeering and general banter were commonplace at the cinema. Even today audience response of this kind is not altogether unknown, but cinema-goers in general have become quieter and more attentive.

The experience of film viewing in the modern multiplex cinema is very different to that in the Victorian music hall. Various explanations suggest themselves for this change in the pattern of behaviour of cinema audiences. These include the following.

- Short films, 'B' features, newsreels and the intermission (a break halfway through the film) have all disappeared. The experience of cinema-going is much less fragmented today than in, say, the 1940s and 1950s when audiences would still be expected to stand for the national anthem.
- Smaller audiences: modern cinemas are likely to boast anywhere between three and twelve screens so that crowds for each screening are quite small.
- The auditorium has a functional design, with larger and more comfortable seats.

continued

- Sophisticated 'wrap around' sound systems make it difficult to communicate with the person next to you let alone anyone else.
- Different expectations: cinema-going is still a social event, but the social aspect has become less significant now that there are so many alternative forms of entertainment, particularly home-based. Today, most members of the audience come to watch a specific film rather than for the social experience of visiting the cinema.

While cinema audiences are more likely to be hushed and reverential, this is far from being the case with big-screen sports entertainment. Sports fans often prefer watching televised matches in pubs and clubs simply because the group of viewers can generate an atmosphere which may have some resemblance to a live event. Sometimes, 'overspill' audiences for live events are entertained with huge outdoor screens, providing an alternative to the real thing.

The live audience is a useful starting point for an investigation of media audiences and is a means of understanding the many and various approaches to the mass audience. Media audiences are, however, very different from live audiences and we need to be wary of attributing to them the same qualities and properties. In no real sense is the media audience a unified and coherent body. Rather, it is atomised, made up of numerous independent individuals. While we may very well react visibly and audibly to a television programme or a magazine article, the creators of these messages will not be able to observe our reactions. Nor, indeed, will other viewers and readers of the same media message. It is certainly possible to estimate the size of a media audience, but such estimates are inevitably less reliable than the straightforward headcount of a live audience. Can a mass audience influence or determine the outcome of a media product? As we shall see later in this chapter, the topics of audience control and interactivity are at the centre of some lively debates in recent audience studies. For now, though, it is safe to say that any influence which the audience does have over the form and direction of a media text is relatively indirect and simple, though the same may not always be said of the audience's *interpretations* of a text.

This brings us to another problem in dealing with the mass audience, a problem inherent in its very nature: its size. Because the mass audience is, by definition, very large, particular techniques and devices are used to understand, describe and predict the behaviour of media audiences. Techniques such as opinion polls, surveys and audience ratings all deal in very broad categories of, for example, age, gender, social class and ethnicity. The results produced by these 'broad brush' approaches are valuable both to media industries and students of the media but they inevitably involve generalisations. Such generalisations are useful but they should not obscure the underlying reality that audiences, no matter how big, are always composed of individuals. The audience for, say, *Coronation Street*, is vast, yet the range and sophistication of individual responses to the programme are also impressive. Soaps such as *Coronation Street* provide the raw material for endless discussions and arguments between viewers (and, in some cases, non-viewers). These discussions begin to reveal the subtlety and diversity of audience reactions, with numerous shades of opinion represented.

As we move to a more detailed discussion and evaluation of audience theories and researches it is worth bearing in mind the following points.

- There are significant differences between media audiences and live audiences.
- Generalisations are legitimate and necessary in order to understand media audiences.
- In spite of such generalisations, audiences are not coherent entities, but collections of people who are individuals like us.

As Raymond Williams observed, 'There are in fact no masses; there are only ways of seeing people as masses' (Williams 1963: 289).

ACTIVITY . . .

1 List the differences between a live audience and a media audience.
2 Why do so many TV shows like to include a studio audience?

WHO IS INTERESTED IN THE AUDIENCE AND WHY?

It would be nice to think that every piece of research into the media audience is objective, balanced and reliable. It would be equally nice to think that commentators on the mass audience are impartial and fair. The real world, however, just isn't like this. Some research is careful, thorough and reliable while some is riddled with mistakes and inconsistencies. Many commentators and observers have vested interests or political agendas; others bring a less biased perspective to bear on the evidence. All of this has implications for us as students of the media. We need to approach research evidence and theories with an open mind, but we also need to maintain a certain level of healthy scepticism. Above all, we need to develop a critical approach by posing questions, e.g.:

- Who conducted this research?
- Who paid for this research?
- When did the research take place?
- Have the research findings been linked to proposed changes in the regulation and control of the media?

There are also questions to be posed about the methods used to collect and interpret data about audiences and we shall deal with these in the next section.

Broadly speaking, we can distinguish between three groups which all have an interest in the investigation of media audiences. These are:

- media institutions, e.g. television or newspaper publishing companies
- academics
- regulatory bodies including the state.

The first group, media institutions, is largely concerned with the relationship between audiences and profitability. Although it is certainly true that media organisations sell products such as newspapers, magazines, CDs and DVDs directly to the audience, a very significant proportion of their income is derived from advertisers. Advertisers are interested in media products principally because they are the means of building and maintaining audiences. From this perspective the audience is a commodity which media institutions create in order to sell to advertisers. Just like any other commodity, the media audience needs to be developed, brought up to date, refined and, above all, marketed to interested parties.

NOTEBOX

Demographic and psychographic variables

Segmentation is a process of categorising a group of people. It is a technique widely used in advertising and marketing. For the technique to be useful, the members of each sub-group or segment need to have some similarities in the ways in which they think or behave, and differences between themselves and members of other groups. Variables used to identify segments are:

Geographic:

- region (from neighbourhoods to continents)
- size and density of area
- climate.

Demographic:

- age
- ethnicity
- gender
- family size
- family life cycle (e.g. full-nest, empty-nest, double income no kids)
- generation (e.g. Baby boomers or Generation X)
- income
- education
- occupation
- education
- religion
- social class.

Although it is a crude and sometimes discredited method of categorising social class, the JICNARS (Joint Industry Committee for National Readership Surveys) scale is still widely used in media and advertising:

A   upper middle class, successful business or professional, or considerable private means

B	middle class, quite well off but not at the top of their business or profession
C1	'white collar', lower middle class, small tradespeople, administrative, supervisory, clerical jobs
C2	'blue collar', skilled working class
D	semiskilled or unskilled manual workers
E	casual workers or those dependent on social security schemes.

The chief problem with this scale is that it is based on the occupation of the head of the household. It does not reflect the enormous changes in the labour market or even patterns of pay in different jobs.

Psychographic:

These sub-groups or segments are based on the 'inner qualities' of a person, for example:

- personality
- lifestyle
- values
- activities
- interests
- opinions.

Psychographic variables often relate to the aspirations of consumers – the type of person they would like to be. An example is the following breakdown of aspirational types found in younger audiences:

- **trendies**: those who crave the attention of their peers
- **egoists**: those who seek pleasure
- **puritans**: those who wish to feel virtuous
- **innovators**: those who wish to make their mark
- **rebels**: those who wish to remake the world in their image
- **groupies**: those who just want to be accepted
- **drifters**: those who are not sure what they want
- **drop-outs**: those who shun commitments of any kind
- **traditionalists**: those who want things to stay as they are
- **utopians**: those who want the world to be a better place
- **cynics**: those who have to have something to complain about
- **cowboys**: those who want to earn easy money.

(Selby and Cowdery 1995: 25)

Demographic and psychographic information are often combined to create a profile of a typical audience member. This sort of profiling may create stereotypes of certain types of media user such as 'the *Guardian* reader', 'the *Sun* reader', 'the heavy metal fan' or '*Cosmo* woman'.

For further information on some of the more sophisticated methods of audience segmentation see Rayner *et al.* (2004: 104–10)

In order to sell their audiences to potential advertisers, media institutions need to describe them with great care. They do this by using demographic and psychographic variables (see the notebox on pp. 118–19). This can clearly be seen on the National Magazines website page for its magazine *Prima* (see below). The audited circulation and readership figures are given, together with the median age of *Prima* readers. Just as significantly, National Magazines offers a description of the magazine's 'core buyer'. This includes the age group (25–54) and social class (B, C1, C2) of the target audience. The 'core reader' is also described in terms of her lifestyle, attitudes and aspirations. All of this information is expressly directed at advertisers so that they can match the target audience for their products or services to the readership supplied by *Prima*. Tellingly, the *Prima* reader is described as a 'prolific, but discerning consumer'.

PRIMA

EDITOR: Maire Fahey

Total Circulation: 330,179 (ABC Jan–June 2004)

Adult Readership: 770,000 (NRS Jan–June 2004)

Women Readership: 730,000 (NRS Jan–June 2004)

Median Age: 45

1986 saw the UK launch of **Prima**, which has been the top selling domestic women's monthly ever since. Brimming with inspirational ideas, authoritative information, shared wisdom, as well as practical and trusted advice, the title now sports a fresh new look, is more contemporary and reflects the confident **Prima** woman.

Prima has always offered readers great value for money – delivering relevant features that reflect all aspects of our readers' busy lives. Containing the latest fashion and beauty trends, creative ideas for home and garden, health advice, life affirming features, consumer solutions, family life, cookery, and the exclusive **Prima** pattern and craft in every issue.

CORE BUYER – The **Prima** woman is predominantly BC1C2 25–54 years old, likely to be working, settled with a family and enjoying a full life. She is optimistic, down to earth, full of energy, creative, intelligent and confident. She loves her home, entertaining and looking after her family, and buys **Prima** for all the confidence and information it gives her, but she also buys it for herself! It provides her with a warm, supportive, positive experience.

She is a prolific, but discerning consumer, always seeking quality and value for money, whilst making the best choice available. She wants to feel that she is making the most of her life and herself. The combination of quality production values, stylish imagery, and stimulating editorial, means that **Prima** inspires trust, prompting women to follow its advice.

Women trust **Prima**.

(http://www.natmags.co.uk/students/demographic.asp)

Another of National Magazines' titles, *Country Living*, has a roughly similar number of readers although the median age is slightly higher. However, in the case of *Country Living* the brand promise, brand values and description of the core buyer show that this magazine supplies advertisers with a very different audience to that of *Prima*. These are 'upmarket homeowners' who are 'prepared to invest in products that combine quality, craftsmanship and lasting value'.

COUNTRY LIVING

EDITOR: Susy Smith

Total Circulation: 179,396 (ABC Jan–June 2004)

Adult Readership: 658,000 (NRS Jan–June 2004)

Women Readership: 474,000 (NRS Jan–June 2004)

Median Age: 50

Country Living was launched in May 1985 as the magazine concerned with all aspects of living in the country.

BRAND POSITIONING

Country Living is the **ONLY** complete lifestyle magazine with 'the country' as its enduring central theme. A uniquely evocative celebration of country style and all that is positive about the country way of life, **Country Living** reflects the interests of people living in the country whilst inspiring all those who dream of this ideal lifestyle.

BRAND PROPOSITION

The magazine for when your heart is in the country.

BRAND PROMISE

Country Living is renowned for its stunning, high quality photography and thoughtful, authoritative writing, combining traditional country style and values with contemporary relevance. Its inspiring coverage of country homes and gardens provides a wealth of ideas for readers to create their own country style wherever they might live. Its first-hand accounts of rural life, wildlife stories, campaigning issues and hard hitting opinion pieces keep readers informed, updated and entertained. It encourages readers to cook with fresh, quality produce; provides a showcase for traditional and contemporary arts and crafts; presents health, beauty and fashion in a refreshing, relevant way and suggests imaginative ideas for travel and leisure.

Above all **Country Living** provides access to an appealing rural world of beauty, tranquility and traditional values – an escape from the stresses and demands of modern life.

BRAND VALUES

- Escapism
- Visual excellence
- Seasonality
- Tradition
- Tranquility

- Inspiration
- Creativity
- Original Craftsmanship
- Quality

KEY EDITORIAL PILLARS

Rural affairs, country style decorating/furnishing, crafts & rural businesses, the country dream i.e. moving to the country & living the life, escapes i.e. country breaks, organic/country gardening, regional & home-grown food.

CORE BUYER

The core purchasers are upmarket homeowners 35+ who either aspire to the romantic dream of living in the country or are already living the life. United by a love of the countryside and a strong desire for a better quality of life, they are discerning but prepared to invest in products that combine quality, craftsman-ship and lasting value. They have a strong affinity with **Country Living** because it endorses the values they hold dear.

THE BRAND VALUES

- Escapism
- Creativity
- Tradition
- Visual excellence
- Seasonality

BRAND UNIVERSE

The **Country Living** brand universe includes all those who aspire to the romantic dream of living in the country, share a love of the countryside and have a strong desire for a better quality of life. They are discerning but prepared to invest in products that combine quality, craftsmanship and lasting value.

(http://www.natmags.co.uk/students/demographic.asp)

ACTIVITY...

Compare the cover of *Country Living* with that of *Prima*. Do the advertisements match the needs of the two sets of core buyers described in National Magazines' website?

Figure 5.1 *Cover of* Prima, *December 2004. The* Prima *woman loves her home, entertaining and looking after her family. Source: National Magazines.*

Figure 5.2 *Cover of* Country Living, *December 2004. Readers of* Country Living *either aspire to the romantic dream of living in the country or are already living there. Source: National Magazines.*

The relationship between the commercial media institutions and advertisers has a large part to play in determining the type of audience research which is carried out. In this case the collection of data about audiences is powerfully influenced by the requirement of advertisers. To take the example of a magazine, the potential purchaser of advertising space will want to know a great deal about the readership – not only how many people buy the magazine, but also how many read it. What sort of people are they? Where do they live? How much money do they have to spend and what sort of products and services do they spend it on? Answers to questions such as these determine how much money advertisers are prepared to pay for space in a magazine. However, the publisher of the magazine may not be seen as a totally reliable source in providing answers to these questions. Advertisers may ask themselves 'Can we trust the information that is being given to us about magazine readership unless it comes from a reliable and impartial source?' This is why many areas of the media including magazines and newspapers, radio and television have set up audience research bodies which are separate from both advertisers and content providers.

NOTEBOX

Institutional audience research: who does what

ABC: The Audit Bureau of Circulation is the publishing industry's regulatory body, providing circulation data for newspapers, magazines and websites. Its ratings are used by advertisers to set advertising rates. ABC Electronic is a wholly-owned subsidiary of ABC and, like it, is an industry-owned, non-profit-distributing organisation. It was launched in 1996 and claims to be the leading source of independently audited data for electronic media measurement in the UK. (See http://www.abc.org.uk.)

BARB: The Broadcasters' Audience Research Board is responsible for providing estimates of the number of people watching television. This includes which channels and programmes are being watched, at what time, and the type of people who are watching at any one time. BARB provides television audience data on a minute-by-minute basis for channels received within the UK. The data are available for reporting nationally and at ITV and BBC regional level and cover all analogue and digital platforms. (See http://www.barb.co.uk.) You can find out more information about BARB in Rayner *et al.* (2004: 99–100).

CAVIAR is the Cinema and Video Industry Audience Research run on behalf of CAA (Cinema Advertising Association). It conducts 3,000 face-to-face interviews annually with respondents aged 4+. The survey provides the industry with a wealth of information about cinema-going habits and film viewing in Britain. This includes cinema and specific film audience profiles; party size and composition; in-depth analysis of cinema-goers' last visit to the cinema; their experience in the cinema complex; and consumption of other media including pay-per-view films and digital TV. (See http://www.bmrb.co.uk.)

continued

AUDIENCE

JICREG: Launched in 1990, JICREG (Joint Industry Committee for Regional Press Research) has revolutionised the way in which regional and local press advertising is planned, bought and sold. It has become the main currency used by advertisers, agencies, regional press publishers and their sales houses. (See http://www.jicreg.co.uk/about/index.cfm.) For an example of a JICREG readership report, see Rayner *et al.* (2004: 101).

NRS (National Readership Surveys) Ltd is a non-profit-making but commercial organisation which sets out to provide estimates of the number and nature of people who read Britain's newspapers and consumer magazines. Currently the NRS publishes data covering some 250 newspapers, newspaper supplements and magazines. It provides an estimate of the number of readers of a publication and who those readers are in terms of sex, age, regionality and many other demographic and lifestyle characteristics. This is used by publishers of newspapers and magazines, advertisers and advertising agencies to plan, buy and sell advertising space in print media. (See http://www.nrs.co.uk.)

RAJAR (Radio Joint Audience Research Limited) was established in 1992 to operate a single audience measurement system for the radio industry – BBC, UK-licensed and other commercial stations. (See http://www.rajar.co.uk.)

Figure 5.3 Advertisement in the Evening Gazette, 15 October 2004. Publications like Colchester's Evening Gazette *use statistics provided by independent research organisations to sell advertising space. Source: Newsquest newspapers.*

NOTEBOX

The focus group

The focus group is a widely used method of market or audience research. Under the supervision of a trained facilitator, a group of 8–12 people are invited to talk about a product, service or idea. In traditional focus groups the members are carefully selected to reflect the target group. The discussion is free and un-structured, in the hope that new ideas and perspectives which the researchers had not thought of will emerge. A video record of the session is made so that researchers can examine every aspect of the group's response including body language, facial expressions and group dynamics as well as comments.

A recent variant is the on-line focus group. This is an attractive alternative as it can provide similar qualitative information rather more cheaply than the traditional focus group.

The fundamental reason why commercial media institutions conduct or commission audience research is because they need to deliver a clearly defined audience to advertisers. It has often been noted that media institutions do not, primarily, sell media products. Rather, they use media products to build an audience which can be sold to advertisers. There is also another reason, linked to this, why the commercial media conduct research among audiences and potential audiences. This is to guide the decision-making process about the launch or, perhaps, continued development of a media product. To use the example of magazines again, it would be rare for a publishing group to launch a new title based only on a hunch that it would be successful. In a situation such as this extensive work would be undertaken using focus groups and dummy issues of the magazine. Similarly, episodes of a new television series will be ruthlessly dispatched from prime-time viewing slots if audience ratings fail to match expectations. This reliance – some would say over-reliance – on focus groups, ratings and audience surveys has led to criticisms that sections of the media have become cautious, conservative and resistant to change. Where, critics ask, are the opportunities for exciting, challenging TV programmes, new magazines which break the mould or radio stations which lead rather than follow their listeners? The greater the commercial risks, the more likely it is that media producers will be tempted by the safety of tried and tested moneyspinners. In this way the music majors endlessly exploit their back catalogues of greatest hits by long-established stars, a successful television format such as reality TV will spawn numerous copycat versions of the same theme, and film producers will think nothing of radically changing a movie's ending to fit the requirements of the test audience.

Case study: Test Screenings

Film producers take a big gamble on a new movie so it is not surprising that they like to leave as little as possible to chance. This is why many (but not all) Hollywood films are tested on a sample audience before release. These 'sneak previews' are designed to gauge audience reactions so that last-minute changes can be made if the response is critical.

continued

Research companies are hired to recruit test audiences that are genuinely representative of the film's target audience. Members of the carefully chosen preview audience provide detailed feedback of their likes and dislikes through questionnaires or focus group discussions.

The results from test screenings may influence decisions about how, when and where the film is released. Some films may be put on limited release or release straight to 'sell-through' (DVD and video) rather than given full-scale theatre distribution. Additionally, the feedback may persuade the studio to revise its marketing strategy, cut scenes or characters, adjust the soundtrack or even change the ending.

Are test screenings a good thing? It depends on your point of view. Some argue that this kind of research makes films dull and mediocre because everyone is trying to please the same people in the same way in order to maximise the return on their investment. On the other hand, studios argue that these exercises help them to tailor their products to the preferences of the audience so that they can give us the films that we really want.

These different views sometimes result in friction between the creative team and the financial backers on a film project. Occasionally these are resolved by the later release of a 'director's cut' with the original elements restored.

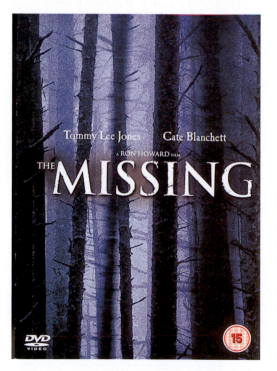

Figure 5.4 DVD *cover of* The Missing *(2003). DVDs give viewers the opportunity to see scenes, including different endings, which were omitted from the cinema release. The DVD version of* The Missing *includes a number of deleted scenes and alternative endings. Source: Columbia Pictures.*

PUBLIC SERVICE BROADCASTING AND THE AUDIENCE

Not all media institutions are commercial operations. The BBC, for example, derives the vast majority of its income not from advertisers but from the licence fee. Why, then should an organisation such as the BBC be every bit as concerned with the collection of audience data as any commercial operator? The first reason lies in the very nature of the licence fee. For years the funding of the BBC has been a political hot potato with many politicians advocating the complete abolition of the licence fee. Critics of the BBC argue that the corporation should become financially self-sufficient without having to rely on what is essentially a tax upon every owner of a TV set. They believe that market forces would have a beneficial effect on the BBC if the corporation was made to compete with other broadcasting organisations on a commercial basis. In response the BBC has lobbied robustly and effectively to convince the government of the day and the public at large that the licence fee represents 'good value for money'. Audience ratings have always been used to reinforce the BBC's position in this strongly contested debate.

It is also the case that programme-makers from news and current affairs to drama and light entertainment have always been strongly motivated by competition, to the extent that the relative viewing or listening figures are sometimes described as a 'ratings war'. This fierce competition, it is argued, helps the BBC to keep its programmes vibrant, dynamic and relevant to the audience. Cynical commentators have sometimes suggested that the BBC is capable of using audience figures for less laudable reasons. Some of the programming which helps the BBC to fulfil its public service remit, particularly arts and documentary programmes, have been moved to digital channels, especially BBC4. The very low viewing figures have been used to 'prove' that there is no need to meet minority tastes on mainstream channels.

The second broad area of concern with the media audience lies within the academic world. Here, different issues and questions come to the forefront. Academics have often been concerned with the effects that media messages have upon audiences and more recently with the various uses made of media messages by the audience. Some of these are explored in the section on audience theories (p. 131).

Research into media audiences is also carried out by or on behalf of government agencies or regulatory bodies. For example, in 2004 Ofcom published the results of a large-scale investigation of the television audience. This investigation was designed to find out just how well government policies on public service broadcasting were being implemented by major terrestrial providers in the run-up to the analogue switch-off planned for later in the decade.

THE SEGMENTED AUDIENCE VERSUS THE MASS AUDIENCE

The use of demographic and psychographic variables by the magazine industry helped to reverse a decline in sales between the 1960s and the 1980s. Publishers targeted their titles at smaller but much more carefully defined readerships, as we have seen in the case studies of *Prima* and *Country Living*. The number of magazine titles available has risen dramatically as publishers compete fiercely for more and more niche markets and targeted audiences.

In more recent years a similar process can be observed in the television industry where digital and satellite technology has seen a proliferation of the number of channels available to viewers. Some commentators have suggested that media consumption is in a long-term and inexorable process of change from mass audiences to segmented audiences. It is argued that narrowcasting is replacing broadcasting and those texts which can attract a substantial proportion of the population are diminishing in number. This may be the case, but media products with a truly mass appeal have nevertheless proved highly resilient. On television, the ratings are still dominated by programmes transmitted on BBC1 and ITV1. The film industry continues to rely on hugely expensive blockbusters which can only show a profit if they attract big audiences. Newspapers such as the *Sun* and the *News of the World* sell in huge numbers. In the UK 55 per cent of adults read a national morning newspaper and 80 per cent read a regional or local paper every week (*Social Trends* 33 at http://www.statistics.gov.uk). The recorded music industry is sometimes criticised for its concentration on those few performers who can be relied upon to produce big hits. Even in the obsessively niche-orientated magazine industry, Britain's best-selling 'paid for' title, *What's On TV*, has a readership of 4.2 million while the Christmas edition of the *Radio Times* sells 2.7 million.

It seems, then, that the process of segmentation may be developing without delivering a mortal blow to those media texts with genuine mass appeal. The truth is that we are all members of many audience groups, some of which are huge and some relatively small. Although it may be too soon to forecast the end of the mass audience, many have argued that the dispersal of audiences over increasing numbers and varieties of media products has led to a decline in quality. This argument asserts that 'more is worse'; that standards have been driven down by the huge choice available to consumers. David Hesmondhalgh has suggested that audience behaviour has changed in response to increased choice of media and media products available. Consumers demand 'bite-sized' products which can be integrated into complex patterns of media consumption.

> Ratings-hungry producers increasingly resort to shock tactics in order to keep the attention of audiences. This means much greater sexual explicitness which might help to challenge prudery and puritanism, and in some cases encourage people to experiment with different forms of sexual behaviour and identity. In many cases, however, it means an explosion of unsubversive titillation and unimaginative, unerotic pornography. The impulse to shock has also lead to much greater levels of violence in television as study after study has shown, though whether this makes people more violent has never been proved conclusively.
>
> (Hesmondhalgh 2002: 247)

More optimistically, Hesmondhalgh goes on to suggest that developments such as these may have contributed to a healthy scepticism among television audiences. In any event, debates about 'quality' are notoriously difficult to substantiate. Some quantitative evidence is available, for example the amount of money invested in media

Figure 5.5
Still from I'm
A Celebrity
Get Me Out
of Here.
Source: ITV

products such as television programmes or feature films, but few would accept that there is a straightforward relationship between quality and price. A related, but slightly different, argument is that audience segmentation is linked to a decline in the significance of media texts as contributors to public debates. In the 1960s and 1970s 'social conscience' television dramas such as *The Wednesday Play* and current affairs programmes such as *Panorama* wielded enormous influence. A famous example of this was the television play *Cathy Come Home* (BBC, 1966) which propelled the neglected issue of homelessness to the top of the public and political agenda. Today, programmes such as this are pushed to the margins of the schedules or onto minority channels. Their influence is slight as public debate is more likely to focus on the fate of contestants in *I'm a Celebrity Get Me Out of Here* or similar game and reality shows.

AUDIENCE THEORIES

Research in media audience is always based on some theory or other about the relationship between audiences, institutions and text. Sometimes researchers set out to prove the viability of a theoretical position but on other occasions theoretical positions are unstated but implicit in the design and execution of research projects. It is important for students of the media to be familiar with the nature and scope of audience theories so that we can understand the ways in which theory interacts with the collection and interpretation of data.

Audience theories have been around for almost as long as mass communications. Most theories, even now, focus on one question: How powerful are the media in influencing the ideas and behaviour of the audience? This is certainly an important and interesting question but it is one which takes a number of things for granted. Firstly, it assumes that the media are powerful in these ways and that the only issue worth pursuing is to discover just *how* powerful they are. Secondly, this question inclines to a view that the 'audience' may be seen as a single, undifferentiated unit. A third problem with this question is that it has tended, until quite recently, to draw attention away from numerous other issues and areas of concern about the relationship between audience, texts and institutions. For example, a preoccupation with the power of the media to control and influence our lives sets up a somewhat negative scenario in which any positive or beneficial aspects of the media are likely to attract scant attention.

Early media theories were influenced by the mobilisation of media technology in warfare and the use of the media for state propaganda, especially in the case of totalitarian dictatorships. Nazi Germany, in particular, saw the development of a sophisticated propaganda machine which relied heavily on film, radio, newspapers and mass-produced leaflets to circulate the doctrines of Nazi ideology. Hitler's propaganda minister, Josef Goebbels, recognised that the most effective form of propaganda always put entertainment first. In Goebbels's approach, propaganda should not confront the audience with new ideas, but gently build upon existing prejudices to gradually build up acceptance of the Nazi world view. In this way, German films of the time used historical costume dramas to promote the need for strong leaders, the right to 'living space' for the German people, racial superiority and, particularly, anti-semitism.

*Figure 5.6
Still from
Triumph of
the Will
(1935).
Source:
British Pathe
News.*

Against this background, it is hardly surprising that many commentators saw the mass media as a sinister and insidious force. This was certainly the position of the Frankfurt School, a group of Marxist intellectuals who developed a trenchant critique of mass communication. This group, originally attached to the University of Frankfurt, moved to the USA in 1933 when Hitler came to power. After the Second World War they turned their attention from Nazi propaganda to the role of the media in promoting the values of American capitalism. Two leading members, Theodor Adorno and Max Horkheimer, coined the term 'culture industry' to describe the forms and processes of a mass media which, they argued, exercised considerable power over the behaviour and beliefs of the audience. Theirs was a very pessimistic view of a population whose leisure time is manipulated by the 'culture industry'. In this view the passive audience soaks up the empty promises of mass entertainment, becoming willing victims who both produce and consume the products of consumer capitalism.

It would be a mistake, though, to assume that all advocates of 'effects' theory came from the same anti-capitalist traditions as the Frankfurt School. The rise of youth culture in the 1950s and 1960s was viewed with horror by many, especially in the United States. Rock and roll music, personified by Elvis Presley, represented a challenge to dominant conservative values because of its celebration of teen sexuality and its roots in black music. Youth-orientated films such as *Rebel Without a Cause* (1955) and *The Wild One* (1953) were accused of encouraging delinquency and driving a wedge between the younger and older generations. Ironically, UK commentators of the same period frequently attacked the mass media for undermining authentically 'British' (or 'English') culture by importing glitzy American products. Much of this scaremongering on both sides of the Atlantic came from the right of the political spectrum, but shared with the Marxists of the Frankfurt School a belief that media messages have a direct and obvious effect on the audience.

These views of the influence of the media are often referred to as 'effects' theories because they see such a straightforward link between the content of the media message and the attitudes or behaviour of audience members. A comprehensive critique of this approach can be found in David Gauntlett's 'Ten Things Wrong with the Effects Model' (in Rayner *et al.* 2004: 112–21). A rather more refined version of effects theory focuses on the long-term influence of exposure to media messages rather than the impact of a particular text such as a film or television programme. According to cultivation theory, the accumulated effect of many years of exposure to violent images and representations is a *desensitised* audience. Although many commentators subscribe to cultivation theory, the attempts to prove its validity have not been entirely successful, not least because it is almost impossible to measure an attribute such as sensitivity.

NOTEBOX

Media effects and drug metaphors

The idea that the effects of the mass media upon audiences is somehow analogous to the effects of 'recreational drugs' or 'drugs of dependency' has been around for a long time. The language with which media effects are described can be very revealing: for example, the 'hypodermic needle' model and the 'plug-in drug', as first radio and then television were known in the 1940s and 1950s. Today it is common to hear media users described as 'soap addicts' or 'video game junkies'; in other words, people who need a fix of their favourite media form.

continued

The media/drug metaphor works in a number of ways to suggest propositions and sets of associations such as the following.

- Like certain drugs (including alcohol) the media can offer an apparent escape from reality, an alternative to the dull routines of everyday life.
- Use of the media can induce a dangerous psychological dependency in members of the audience.
- While 'little and often' may be acceptable, overuse of the media, e.g. watching too much television, can be dangerous and akin to a drug overdose.
- The short-term pleasures of using the media mask the long-term dangers.
- Just as some drugs take away your self-control (being drunk, stoned or 'out of your head') so the media can influence you to behave in ways which are out of character. The implication here is that members of the audience are powerless to resist the effects of media messages.

In considering this metaphor – one which is still in frequent use – we need to be rather careful. It is a common rhetorical device to take something which has already been widely established as a 'bad thing', in this case drug abuse, and then to claim that a completely separate phenomenon shares all of the properties of that 'bad thing'. This way of pursuing an argument is often done by using metaphors and loaded questions (e.g. 'Do you want your child to become a mindless computer game addict?'). It is certainly wise to be suspicious of arguments such as this. Simply asserting that television is like a drug does not prove anything. On the other hand, we may want to admit the possibility that the mass media can be influential in many ways, possibly including some which are harmful, without necessarily accepting the implications of the drug analogy.

ACTIVE AUDIENCES

The next set of ideas to be considered is collectively known as active audience theory. Audiences may be seen as active in two ways. In one sense audiences actively create meanings from the material that is made available to them by media institutions. In the second sense, audience members actively select media products and decide how to use them alongside all our other daily activities.

The two-step flow model and the contexts of reception

A significant problem for the 'effects' approach was that the audience was viewed as an undifferentiated mass, with little recognition that individuals and groups within it may have different perceptions of different messages for all sorts of reasons. An early acknowledgement of this factor is found in the approach developed by Elihu Katz and Paul Lazarsfeld: the two-step flow model (later modified to the multi-step flow model). Katz and Lazarsfeld were interested in the role of the mass media in an election campaign, specifically the US presidential election of 1940. Their study led them to conclude that the media have a limited effect on people's opinions and voting behaviour, but that most people were influenced by opinion leaders who interpreted media messages for other people. The model they devised is based on a simple distinction between active audience members (opinion leaders) and the more passive members who are guided in their perceptions (see McQuail, D. and Windahl, S., 1981, pp. 49–51).

The two-step flow model was certainly flawed, but it does raise some interesting questions about the nature of media influence, questions which are certainly relevant today. Firstly, Katz and Lazarsfeld recognise that media messages are received in a social context, and that the social relationships of audience members may be at least as important as the content of the media message in determining a response. Also, Katz and Lazarsfeld saw that media messages, even persuasive messages, may result in no audience response at all. Conversely, a response may be elicited from members of the audience who have not seen, read or heard the message but have come under the influence of an opinion leader who has. The role of the active opinion leader is crucial here; this is the person who mediates the media message by either positive endorsement or negative rejection.

In 1940, of course, television had no role to play in political campaigning; Katz and Lazarsfeld focused principally on radio and newspapers. So how relevant is their model to an understanding of contemporary media audiences? It is certainly helpful to think of a social context of reception in which media messages are mediated by others. At a fairly simple level, we are all familiar with discussions about, say, a new film or a new CD in which our opinion forms or develops as a consequence of what others have to say. Sometimes as a result of this process, we may even form very strong views about films, TV programmes or pieces of music which we have not even seen or heard. On the other hand, it is quite possible to witness a media event but to have no reaction to it at all; until, that is, somebody else expresses a strong opinion on it. A friend may take very seriously a TV programme which made little initial impression on you and cause you to re-evaluate your response. The two-step flow model does, at least, seem to point the way towards a more productive and sophisticated view of the relationship between the text and the audience. We begin to see that meanings may be negotiated and subject to reappraisal rather than just packaged into the text by the institution and then soaked up by the passive audience.

There are, needless to say, plenty of criticisms to be made of two-step flow, but even these can prove helpful in developing more fruitful theories. The division of the audience into active and passive members does seem simplistic. Most of us would consider ourselves to be both the mediators of media messages (we sometimes influence other people's views) and the mediated (we are sometimes influenced by others). The transition between opinion leader and opinion follower could quite easily take place within the course of a single conversation. Also, an interesting twist on the leader/follower idea is that the self-referential (or even self-obsessed) nature of the contemporary media means that many of the mediating comments and conversations are witnessed on television and radio or in the pages of newspapers and magazines rather than among members of the audience. Every newspaper offers its readers previews, guides, reviews and evaluations of television programmes. New films or

MORE TOP TELLY MOVIES

TUESDAY

Hawaii
Channel 4, 1.45pm

First part of this epic adventure, charting the experiences of a couple who decide to head for Hawaii in an effort to convert the natives to Christianity. Julie Andrews (below) and Max von Sydow star. Concludes tomorrow. (PG, 1966) ★★★★

Cabin Pressure
Five, 3.40pm

Airborne disaster drama about a hi-tech new plane that more or less flies itself. But the triumphant first flight of the craft is thrown into jeopardy when an enraged mechanic sets out to take revenge for his dismissal from the project. With Craig Sheffer, John Pyper Ferguson and Rachel Hayward. (PG, 2001) ★★★

The Guru
Sky Movies 3, 9pm

Comedy, starring Jimi Mistry (left), as a wannabe dancer who heads for the bright lights of Hollywood. But his plans are scuppered when his only audition turns out to be for an adult film – and to add insult to injury, he doesn't get the part. But actress Heather Graham is on hand to offer comfort – and helps him become New York's best-loved sex guru. (15, 2002) ★★★

Equilibrium
Sky Movies 1, 10pm

Christian Bale stars as a cop in a world where the population is kept sedated to stop them experiencing emotion. His job is to wipe out the rebels who reject their medicine – but when he fails to take his own pills, he's drawn into an addictive new world. Sci-fi thriller, also starring Taye Diggs (above). (15, 2002) ★★★★★

An Almost Perfect Affair
BBC2, 12.20am

An ambitious first-time film-maker who channelled all his resources and energies into his latest flick is seizen him efforts officials. producer cloud has a silver leaog, and his efforts to retrieve it lead him into a passionate love affair with the wife of a well-known Italian producer. Can they keep their relationship a secret? Likeable romantic comedy, with Monica Vitti and Keith Carradine. (15, 1979) ★★★

WEDNESDAY

Kojak: Flowers for Matty
Five, 3.35pm

Lollipop-sucking detective Theo Kojak returns to track down a callous crook with an eye for fine art – and murder in his mind. Mystery, with Telly Savalas (below) and Andre Braugher. (U, 1990) ★★★★

Legends of the Fall
Sky Movies 8, 8pm

The lives of four men are thrown into disarray by Julia Ormond in this dreamy period drama. Dad Anthony Hopkins does a fine job of raising his sons alone, but a wedge is driven between them when one of the lads brings his fiancée back to the old homestead. It's not long before she's captured the hearts of his brothers with her good looks and charm – leading to tragedy. Brad Pitt, Aidan Quinn and Henry Thomas star as the troubled siblings. (15, 1994) ★★★★

Lethal Weapon 4
Five, 9pm

The final Lethal Weapon film reteams action men Mel Gibson and Danny Glover (right) once more this time after a Triad gang who are up to no good. The crooks are determined to get a vicious crimelord out from behind bars – can the daredevil duo put a stop to the plan? Thriller, co-starring Jet Li. (15, 1998) ★★★★

Mimic
FilmFour, 10pm

Mira Sorvino (below) ends up in New York's sewers, hunting oversized bugs that have developed a taste for human flesh and the ability to pose as other creatures – including humans. Thriller, with Jeremy Northam. (15, 1997) ★★★★

Jaws 2
BBC1, 11.40pm (Scotland, 11.25, Wales, 12.20am)

The good people of Amity think they can get their lives back on track following the horror of the first film, but it soon becomes clear that something big, bad and toothy is lurking in the water once more. Can leathery sheriff Roy Scheider make anyone heed his warnings this time – or will they insist on holding the teen yachting regatta regardless? Thriller sequel, with Lorraine Gary, Murray Hamilton and Joseph Mascolo. (PG, 1978) ★★★

THURSDAY

Lost
Channel 4, 1.35pm

Doting parents David Knight and Julia Arnell are forced to live through every mum and dad's worst nightmare when their 18-month-old son vanishes without a trace. Police are soon hot on the trail of those responsible – but will they bring them to justice? Unusual and effective thriller which explores not only the reactions of those directly affected by the disappearance, but also those of police and press. David Farrar and Anthony Oliver co-star. (PG, 1955) ★★★★

Touching the Void
Channel 4, 9pm

Premiere. This documentary, interspersed with dramatic reconstructions, makes for gripping viewing. It's based on interviews with mountaineers Joe Simpson and Simon Yates, who decided to take on the might of the Peruvian Andes. But a terrifying fall forces them to make a horrific choice, and leaves them each in a desperate, individual battle. (15, 2002) ★★★★

Mad Max 2
Five, 10.05pm

Sci-fi thriller, in which post-apocalyptic anti-hero Mel Gibson (left) becomes involved in an explosive struggle to resist a ruthless crook who's determined to secure a stranglehold on all the fuel produced by a ragtag gang of survivors. Cue non-stop stunts as battle commences. (18, 1981) ★★★★★

Igby Goes Down
Sky Movies 1, 10pm

Premiere. Kieran Culkin (below right) heads the cast of this black comedy, playing a young man determined to escape the influence of his frankly bonkers family by fleeing to Manhattan. Claire Danes also stars. (15, 2003) ★★★★★

THIS WEEK'S HIDDEN GEM

Memento
Channel 4, 11.05pm

Premiere. A man who's lost his short-term memory vows to beat the odds and track down his wife's murderer. Thriller, starring Guy Pearce (above left). (15, 2000)

FRIDAY

Banacek: Detour to Nowhere
Five, 3.35pm

Grizzled insurance investigator George Peppard is launched into action when he probes the hijacking of a truck, which was loaded with a fortune in gold – how could the vehicle apparently vanish without trace? It's not long before he finds the clues it seems everyone else has missed, but he's shocked to discover an old adversary is also on the case. Thrilling crime drama, also starring Christine Belford and Ed Nelson. (PG, 1972) ★★★

Punch-Drunk Love
Sky Movies 1, 8pm

Premiere. Oddball Adam Sandler (left) can't believe it when he finally finds a woman on his wavelength. But their happiness looks set to be short-lived, thanks to the intervention of a blackmailer, who's determined to do him out of house and home. Comedy, with Emily Watson. (15, 2003) ★★★★

Darkman
Five, 11pm

An explosion leaves scientist Liam Neeson (above) horribly disfigured – and desperate to visit punishment upon those responsible, no matter what the cost. Inventive comic-book horror, also starring Colin Friels. (18, 1990) ★★★

Bad Company
ITV, 12.30am

Double-dealing abounds in this thriller, as CIA agent Ellen Barkin gets embroiled in all manner of espionage, while teaching new recruit Laurence Fishburne how it's done. Frank Langella (below) also stars. (18, 1994) ★★★

Dearly Devoted
Five, 12.45am

Troubled teen Rose MacGowan is obviously not a girl to be messed with, so when her repeated amorous advances are rejected by her principled schoolteacher, she sets out to take a horrible, twisted revenge. It's not long before vicious rumours about the tutor are spreading like wildfire, ruining his career in the process – but things are about to take a decidedly sinister turn. Thriller with a definite air of tension, also starring Alex McArthur and Peg Shirley. (18, 1998) ★★★

32   TOP TELLY RATINGS: Don't miss! ★★★★★ Worth watching ★★★★ Good ★★★

Figure 5.7 *Your movie guide for the week ahead in* We Love Telly *magazine, free with Saturday's* Daily Mirror*. Stars, points and ratings help us to decide what to watch. Source:* Daily Mirror.

music CDs are given star ratings or points out of ten; television pundits steer us away from computer games to be 'avoided at all costs' or towards a new television series which is 'unmissable'. For these reasons, media messages rarely arrive cold or unexpected. New films are 'eagerly anticipated' and we are often well aware of the critical reception before we get a chance to form our own views. Most new media produced are trailed, advertised and mulled over by the critics and pundits long before they actually appear. For those of us who cannot wait to discover the latest development in the main television soap operas, weekly magazines are on hand with synopses of major plot developments in the forthcoming week. It seems that the active process of mediation begins before the media event has even take place, with the role of opinion leader largely incorporated into media messages themselves rather than being delegated to influential members of the audience. Whether or not the self-referentiality of the media influences the degree of audience passivity is open to debate. It could be argued that as viewers, readers and listeners, our attempts to persuade each other about the merits of this or that film or television programme are less consequential than the 'expert' commentaries offered within the media.

The cultivation of the opinion leader underlies many contemporary marketing campaigns. Often, though, the identity of such opinion leaders is dubious or even illusory. 'Viral' campaigns, particularly those which exploit the Internet, use the power of 'word of mouth' endorsements to promote products or services. For example, the 1999 film *Blair Witch Project* became a surprise hit after the production company created a sophisticated interactive website which contributed to an impressive Internet buzz even before the film's release. This technique has now been adopted for almost every major film release as well as for other commercial products. The Internet abounds with bloggers, amateur reviewers and first-hand commentators, and their views often seem more credible than the biased endorsements of paid-for advertising. Needless to say, the value of this credibility is not lost on the advertisers and marketers themselves, as the following excerpt from the promotional site of an Internet marketing company makes clear: 'One of the most credible sources of information is the word-of-mouth. Let us boast about you by making discreet postings to discussion groups, forums, bulletin boards, newsgroups, and chats' (http://www.webadvantage.net/default.htm).

Another point arising from the initial study from which Katz and Lazarsfeld developed the two-step flow model is the assertion that personal contact outweighs the influence of the media at least in the arena of political campaigns. Can this still be the case in today's era of highly sophisticated media campaigns (including viral campaigns) mounted by political parties, especially at election times? In a single month (March 2004) George W. Bush spent $41 million on TV adverts attacking his Democratic opponent John Kerry (*Houston Chronicle*, 22 April 2004).

ACTIVITY . . .

How do you decide which films to watch? How influential are opinion leaders and is word of mouth more reliable than the recommendations of experts?

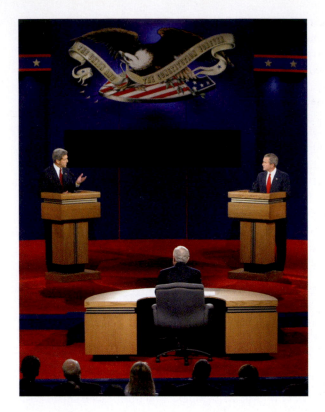

Figure 5.8 John Kerry and George Bush. Source: Reuters/Jim Bourg.

Uses, gratifications and the sovereign consumer

The two-step flow model saw the pendulum start to move away from the institution as the single most powerful element in the relationship between institution, text and audience. 'Uses and gratifications' moves even further in the direction of a powerful audience. The basic premise of this approach runs as follows. We all have various needs and desires, for example needs for entertainment, information and social interaction, which the products of the media help us to fulfil. Hence, we *use* the media to *gratify* our needs. As well-informed, discerning individuals we actively seek out those media products that we really want. In many ways this is an attractive principle. We would all prefer to see ourselves as thoughtful motivated consumers making careful selections from the products available in the media market place. It seems preferable to the image of the audience created in 'effects' theories: an undiscriminating mass that takes in media messages as blotting paper soaks up ink.

Uses and gratifications certainly does provide some positive and helpful insights into the actions and reactions of media audiences. We are reminded that the huge number of people watching, for example, *Coronation Street* will contain individuals who are motivated by all kinds of different impulses. These could include the following.

- A need for company: the characters become our friends. This may particularly be the case for those many viewers who have relatively little human contact in their lives. For such viewers, *Coronation Street* may provide a satisfying substitute for family and acquaintances.

■ The need to be a part of a group. If you work or socialise with people who are avid *Street* watchers, you need to keep watching in order to collect the raw material for the next day's conversation.

■ The need to identify with characters and scenarios. For many viewers TV drama facilitates the exploration of imaginary worlds. We ask ourselves: 'What would I do in his or her situation?'

■ Relaxation. Soap operas are relatively undemanding and can provide, for many, the sort of gentle stimulation in a familiar framework which helps to smooth the transitions from a day at work or college to a more leisurely evening.

■ The need for structure and order. Unless disrupted by a major news story or, more likely, a European football match, *Coronation Street* occupies regular and predictable slots in the schedule. This level of predictability offers a reassuring routine around which other activities such as cooking and eating can be organised.

USES AND GRATIFICATIONS

The list above suggests some possible motivations for choosing to watch a soap such as *Coronation Street*. Add some further possible uses or gratifications available to the soap opera viewer.

Select a newspaper, a magazine and a recent film. Repeat the exercise, identifying the uses and gratifications available in each case.

Uses and gratifications also links very conveniently with liberal-pluralist perspectives on media institutions (see Chapter 8). It confirms the idea of 'consumer sovereignty', the notion that we as users of the media exercise a powerful influence over the organisations that create media products. If we do not buy the magazines of a particular publisher, the company will go out of business. On the other hand, if we watch a particular television show in great numbers we will be rewarded by the commissioning of a second series. Because we as consumers wield such power in the media market place, media institutions do their best to cosset us; they conduct endless surveys to find out the exact details of our tastes and preferences, they fine-tune their products to meet the exacting standards of quality which we demand. Can the picture really be as rosy as this, with all-powerful consumers dictating to subservient institutions? As you probably suspect, there is another point of view which is critical of uses and gratifications and its underlying assumptions.

Uses and gratifications fits in with a broader view of social institutions called *functionalism*. Briefly, functionalism may be defined as a view which sees society rather as if it were an organism like the human body. Social institutions (the family, the education system, religious organisations and the mass media, for example) all work to keep the 'body' of society in balance by ensuring that the needs of the population are met.

If these institutions work properly we are all kept reasonably warm, dry, well fed and contented. Any members of the population whose needs are not met can become so frustrated that they represent a threat to society as a whole. This threat is then countered by institutions which protect the rest of society (e.g. the police, the courts, the prison system) or by institutions such as the mass media which can develop new ways of meeting these needs and restoring equilibrium.

One of the problems with functionalism is that it does little to explain the dynamic nature of society. If social institutions, including the mass media, are all working towards the maintenance of the status quo, how is it that societies change and develop so rapidly? Also, uses and gratifications (and functionalism generally) faces the thorny question of where human needs arise from in the first place. For example, if the 'needs' which are being gratified by television soap operas are innate, how did people manage for all those years before Granada television invented *Coronation Street*? If, on the other hand, we argue that needs are created by our environment – by the processes of socialisation and the actions of social institutions – then the rationale for the uses and gratifications theory faces a more serious challenge. The mass media are themselves an important part of our surroundings: part of the very social environment which is responsible for creating our needs. What sort of needs will the institutions of the mass media create? Fairly obviously, they have a vested interest in stimulating exactly the sort of needs which only they can meet: the 'must see' film and the 'must read' magazine. The idea of the powerful, rational, decision-making media consumer now seems rather less secure. The mass media, it seems, are largely responsible for creating the very needs which they then meet. The circularity of uses and gratifications seems to be pushing us back towards some of the principles of effects theory.

In further criticism of the uses and gratification, it could be asked just how many decisions about our personal media usage we really make. Does the following exchange sound familiar?

> PERSON A (*holding remote control*):   What do you want to watch?
> PERSON B (*slumping in armchair*):   I dunno. Anything. You choose.

This scenario does not illustrate well-informed consumers making rational decisions. Rather, the picture is of apathetic individuals simply allowing media messages to wash over them. Other constraints and provisos limiting our choice as media consumers include the following.

Expense

Only a minority of media products are free. Some, like subscription television services or broadband access to the Internet, can be quite expensive. While it is true to say that the real cost of consumer electronics has been dropping for many years, real expenditure has increased with the proliferation of communications technology: PCs, DVDs, games consoles, CD players, etc.

Unintended access

We are subjected to countless advertising images from junk mail to billboards, from radio advertisements to Internet pop-ups, few of which we actively choose in any real sense of the word.

Parental control

Parents may restrict their children's access to certain texts, e.g. *The Sopranos*, while imposing others which are felt to be beneficial, e.g. *Blue Peter*. Most of us can recall disputes about what may or may not be viewed, read or listened to.

NOTEBOX

Ethnographic research

Ethnographic research is a means of collecting qualitative information. Ethnography focuses on cultural forms and processes, often in everyday settings. Researchers use a variety of methods such as participant observation where they try to get as close as possible to the people they are studying. In the case of media audiences, ethnographic research has tended to focus on the contexts and conditions of media consumption.

The ideas underlying uses and gratifications were further developed by ethnographic researcher James Lull, but he moved away from the personal and psychological approach to focus more upon the ways in which the media, particularly television, are used in the domestic environment. Lull's team of observers spent many hours watching the behaviour of viewers in 200 American households. This is an example of ethnographic research; the researchers became almost a part of the furniture in the homes under observation. Lull was particularly interested in the ways television can be used to regulate relationships between members of a household. He found that on some occasions television brought people together for the ritual viewing and discussion of particular programmes. On other occasions individuals might use television as a means of creating their own space and avoiding contact with others. Lull described these types of use of television as *relational*. They contrast with *structural* uses such as having the television for company while doing household chores or using television to meet specific needs for entertainment or information.

ACTIVITY

Lull's study dealt only with television, but see if you can fit the use of these other media into his *structural* and *relational* categories:

- computer gaming
- surfing the Net
- listening to recorded music
- reading magazines.

continued

In which of the ways that Lull describes does your household use television?

How do you think the social uses of television may have changed in the light of the following developments?

- multiple television households
- time shift viewing
- prerecorded media (video and DVD)
- pay per view television in pubs, clubs, etc.

AUDIENCES AND HEGEMONY

The next set of approaches to the audience which we are going to consider draws heavily on Gramscian hegemony theory. This means stepping back for a moment from audience theory to answer two questions. Firstly, what is meant by hegemony? And secondly, who was Gramsci? The idea of hegemony can be used to describe a state of affairs where a powerful group in society (for Marxists this would be the ruling class) impose their ideas and values on everybody in a process of ideological domination. However, the concept of hegemony which was developed by the Italian Marxist theorist Antonio Gramsci (1891–1937) is rather more subtle than this. It is a concept which has been highly influential in media theory.

Gramsci certainly saw that dominant social classes play a very important part in forming the views, ideas and opinions that define a culture. He also saw the 'power' of a particular class in terms of its leadership qualities, its ability to persuade other groups in society to 'toe the line'. This leadership is only established through constant struggles in which the ideas, values and opinions of other groups in society as well as the ruling class have an important role to play. In this view, the ideology of the ruling class is powerful but it is not totally and invincibly dominant. In this sense, hegemony is a goal which cannot ever be fully achieved. The ruling class are not the victors of an all-out war, but they are the most powerful force in an ongoing struggle with their many opponents. In this struggle they use many techniques and strategies, including conceding the occasional defeat if it is in their long-term interests. Also, the ruling group may have to form short-term alliances with other groups or, perhaps, push some of its own members out of their powerful positions if they are an embarrassing liability. Gramsci often describes this struggle in the language of warfare: battles, strategic alliances, tactical defeats and so on. Another way of looking at it would be to see the process of ideological struggle as being like an athlete working out in the gym. By constantly engaging with its opponents in ideological disputes, the ruling class remains 'match fit'.

What does all of this mean for audience theories and the 'power of the media'? Firstly, it provides a framework which acknowledges that the production and reception of media messages can be negotiated. Many media messages are not in the interests of the dominant class and even those that are may be challenged by members of the audience. Secondly, this approach enables us to conceive of the mass media as a site where struggles over meaning take place rather than a straightforward agency of dominant ideology. Of course press barons and media moguls can and do use the media to pursue political campaigns in their own interests. But it is also the case that all kinds of oppositional and critical views find expression in newspaper columns and the broadcast media. Film-makers, writers and musicians who are very critical of capitalism and the ideological consensus are able to express themselves within the mainstream media, even though their voices may struggle to be heard above the din of the establishment. Sometimes these oppositional views and ideas propel themselves from the late-night television slots and the art house cinemas into the spotlight of public attention (think, for example, of Michael Moore's films *Bowling for Columbine* – 2002 – and *Fahrenheit 9/11* – 2004).

Voices raised in opposition to a dominant ideology have certainly made a difference. This can be graphically illustrated by comparing standards of acceptability in prime-time UK television over recent decades. Programmes such as the *Black and White Minstrel Show*, in which white performers 'blacked up', are no longer tolerated. In the 1970s, racist jokes were commonplace in early evening light 'entertainment' programmes and were defended by the media establishment on the grounds that objectors lacked a sense of humour and wanted to suppress free speech. In the same era television advertisers routinely assumed that women's roles were restricted to those of domestic slave or sex bomb. Contemporary prime-time soap operas have incorporated sympathetic roles for gay and lesbian characters which are in stark contrast to the crude and demeaning stereotypes of twenty years ago. Newsreaders, television journalists, continuity announcers and weather reporters are no longer compelled to speak in the Home Counties drawl of what used to be called BBC English. Their voices at least have begun to reflect the diversity of the population they broadcast to.

None of this is to say that racism, sexism or homophobic and class-based prejudices have been forever banished from the television screen. The examples above, though, indicate real and significant changes which have not 'just happened', but have been brought about by persistent and patient struggles over what counts as acceptable. Needless to say, such struggles are ongoing and today's ideas of common sense and acceptability are bound to seem dated in another twenty years. Change itself may be certain, but the direction of change and the outcome of these struggles between competing ideological forces are very far from certain.

Encoding, decoding

Stuart Hall drew upon Gramscian hegemony theory in developing the encoding/decoding model precisely because he wanted to focus on how dominant ideological messages can be resisted or, at least, reinterpreted by audience members. At the encoding stage the producers of texts create messages in the context of a shared system of signs, a code which they expect their readers, viewers or listeners to understand. Other contexts include the conventions of the genre and the constraints of professional practice. When we, as members of the audience, come into contact with the text we

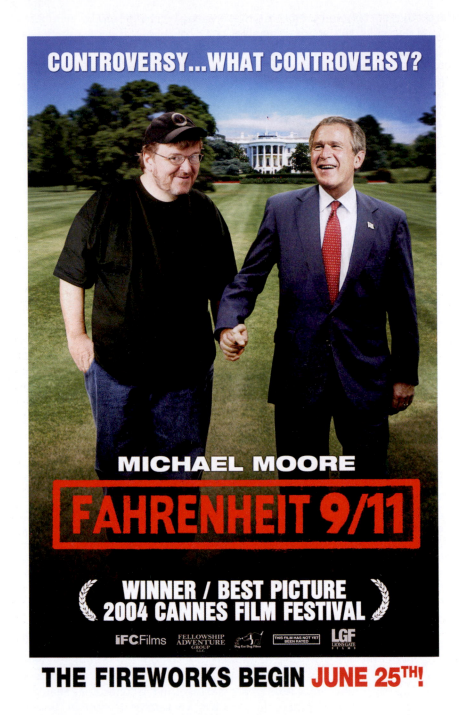

Figure 5.9 *Publicity poster for* Fahrenheit 9/11 *(2004).*
Source: www.michaelmoore.com.

Figure 5.10
Black and
white
minstrels.
Source:
Corbis.

certainly make use of our 'meaning-making' knowledge. We have a good idea of how the symbols, images and words make sense because we share a knowledge of their codes with other members of their culture. However, this decoding is an active process and does not depend solely on the content of the media message; it also depends on the particular way in which a particular member of the audience goes about deciphering the message.

As you know from your previous work on semiotics, signs operate at different levels. At the level of denotation there is not much room for ambiguity or mistakes (though they can occur). At the next levels of meaning – connotations, ideology or myth – the relationship between the signifier and the signified becomes less secure. For some people, an image of a person smoking a cigarette may carry connotations of relaxation or sophistication, while for others the connotations could be of ill-health or anti-social behaviour. Generally speaking, the context of the sign resolves the problem; if the smoker appears in a health awareness campaign we are steered away from the 'relaxed and sophisticated' connotations. Even so, we can only be *steered* in this direction; it is still possible to place a positive interpretation on the image. Notoriously, an anti-drug campaign of the 1980s, 'Heroin Screws You Up', presented the image of an emaciated heroin user as a warning of 'what could happen to you'. In direct contradiction to the message intended by the producers of the campaign, many of the target audience were attracted to the 'elegantly wasted' character. The images contained in the campaign helped to contribute to a style which came to be known as 'heroin chic' (see Figure 5.11).

Fundamentally, media messages are *polysemic*: they contain the possibility of numerous possible interpretations. However, readers are invariably steered in the direction of a

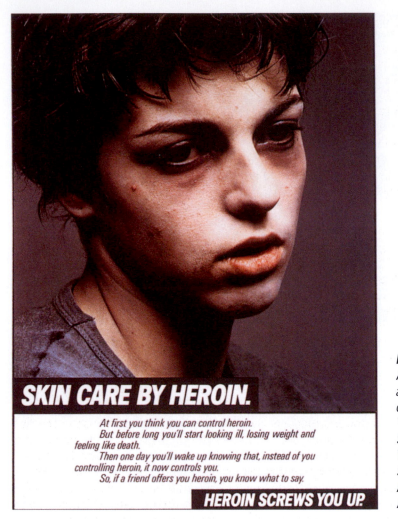

Figure 5.11
Anti-drug advertising campaign: 'Heroin Screws You Up'. Source: The Advertising Archive.

particular interpretation – what Hall calls the *preferred reading*. While it is likely that most readers will accept this preferred reading, Hall identifies two further possibilities:

■ *negotiated reading*: a qualified acceptance of the dominant reading in which some aspects are rejected
■ *oppositional reading*: total rejection of the dominant reading.

The tendency of an individual to elect one of these readings in relation to a particular text may well be influenced by his or her gender, age, ethnicity, class or some other social factor. The encoding/decoding approach is certainly about the power of the media over audiences but, as Justin Lewis puts it, it concerns 'the exercise of power within a set of shared cultural assumptions' (1991: 65). For a further discussion of encoding and decoding, together with an illustration of Stuart Hall's model, see Rayner *et al.* (2004: 96–8).

In some ways access to the preferred reading of certain media texts requires similar levels of cultural competence. This is the idea that people from different walks of life and from different social strata have different sets of skills when it comes to decoding messages. Members of an audience may reject the preferred readings of a text simply because it 'doesn't speak my language'. Similarly this can be linked to status and we are certainly aware of the different level of status attached to various media products. For example, magazines are often described as either *upmarket* or *downmarket*; popular music is bracketed as *alternative*, *chart* or *easy listening*; television programmes as *highbrow* or *lowbrow*. All of these categories reflect different levels of status attached to different media products. Most of us are well aware that others may make judgements about us based on their observations of the media products we watch, read or listen to. For this reason we are occasionally tempted to misrepresent our true patterns of media consumption in order to manipulate other people's perception of us.

The encoding/decoding model, then, is about contests over meaning. Meaning only comes into being as the message interacts with the receiver in a social/cultural environment. This *contest* over the meaning of signs can be seen particularly clearly in the case of controversial images, particularly of warfare. In these circumstances images can present a serious and powerful challenge to dominant orthodoxies if they offer interpretations which are not in line with accepted justifications for military action. In the 1960s the photograph of a little girl, terrified and naked, running away from a napalm attack became an icon for the anti-Vietnam war movement. More recently, images of Iraqi prisoners being mistreated in American-run jails in Baghdad have been a major embarrassment for the United States government. In cases such as these various interest groups rush to place their interpretations on the images in order to manipulate the process of meaning making. The idea that meaning making is an ideologically charged power struggle is vividly demonstrated. In the case of the Abu Ghraib prison photographs, some commentators referred to the 'unfortunate events' and 'alleged incidents' perpetrated by a tiny and 'unrepresentative minority'. Others interpreted the pictures as 'incontrovertible evidence of torture' and the 'tip of the iceberg'. As Stuart Hall put it (1981), media messages are 'structured in dominance': powerful groups in society rely on a shared interpretation of signs which is broadly supportive of their interests. However, this power to control the interpretation of messages is not absolute. Nobody can dictate to you, me or anybody else how we *must* perceive a message.

Occasionally media messages – especially highly charged images – threaten not only powerful vested interests but also the very consensus on which shared meaning making is based. Hence President Bush was at pains to stress that the Abu Ghraib incidents represented 'un-American behaviour'. The audiences' reading of the message in cases such as these may become a political battleground in a battle which is not only about interpreting events depicted in some photographs but about the core value system of a society.

Figure 5.12 BAFTA ceremony. Source: Ken McKay/Rex Features.

RECEPTION THEORY

For all its strengths, encoding/decoding theory has been criticised because it is somewhat abstract. It deals with ideas about the audience rather than real media audiences. In order to meet this criticism a number of studies set out to test the validity of the theory by measuring the response of real audiences to real media texts. One of the first of these was David Morley's study of the audience of *Nationwide* (1980), an early evening current affairs programme broadcast on BBC1 in the 1970s and 1980s. Morley assembled groups of viewers and played tapes of *Nationwide* to them. The participants in this experiment were divided into a number of categories including managers, students and trade unionists. Though Morley discovered some systematic differences in the responses of these groups to the programme, there were also significant differences within the groups. Some responses fell outside the three readings (preferred, negotiated, oppositional) altogether. The black students in Morley's study, for example, declined to find any meaning at all in *Nationwide*. Morley concluded that the relationship between viewers' socio-economic position and their reading of the texts was complex and multilayered. He also concluded that the context of viewing played a significant part in the ways in which audience members made sense of the text.

These two conclusions pointed the way towards a rather different agenda for audience research and audience theory. The emphasis was now placed upon the context of media receptions and the range of cultural resources used by the audience in perceiving media messages.

Morley's own research interests, as indicated by the title of his 1986 book *Family Television*, moved in the direction of empirical studies of media consumption in the home. Somewhat in common with Lull, Morley examined the ways in which people used television in connection with their personal relationships. Here, the conception of 'power' had less to do with a dominant ideology imposing itself on the masses through the medium of television and more to do with the micro politics of the household. As Morley discovered, domestic power relations are crucially influenced by gender. Men tend to see the household as a place for relaxation and leisure while women are more likely to conceive of the home as a place where tasks need to be done. These different conceptions affect the ways in which television is used. Men are more likely to concentrate single-mindedly on a programme whereas women are more likely to watch in a fragmented and distracted way, giving television only partial attention as other demands crowd in on their time. Morley also reported that men would frequently assert domestic authority by the simple tactic of holding the remote control. In Morley's study, gender differences were also apparent in the stated preferences for different programme types. Men claimed to prefer news, current affairs and documentaries while women expressed a preference for drama.

Other writers have speculated about the reasons why women prefer fictional programmes such as soap operas. Soaps have been described as a 'women's genre' because they present dilemmas about moral codes of personal conduct with a strong emphasis on emotional engagement. Soaps tend to defer narrative closure with multiple storylines operating in short, linear segments. It is argued that women have the particular cultural competences to decode these aspects of soap opera. Men, on the other hand, prefer narratives with a strong, conclusive and unambiguous climax as may be found in a sports broadcast or an action film.

TELEVISION SCHEDULES AND THE AUDIENCE

Since the publication of *Family Television* in 1986, patterns of media consumption and the sophistication of media technology in the average household have obviously changed greatly. To some extent, Morley's work was based on a version of domestic life in which a whole family would watch television together, choosing from the small range of channels available on the household's only television set – what Marshall McLuhan called 'the electronic hearth'. As we have already noted, contemporary households are likely to contain a diverse and sophisticated array of communication technology. However, this has put even more emphasis within audience studies on the relationship between our use of the media and the other components of everyday life. This is particularly the case for television schedulers for whom ideas of 'family viewing' and 'family entertainment' are still important considerations. Schedulers are the people who decide when particular programmes should go out. They operate in a highly competitive environment in which they play a key role in winning audiences for one channel rather than another. Schedulers are very well aware of the domestic routines which structure our lives and the times when we are most likely to eat, sleep, leave or return to the household. They aim to make the programme output of their channel or network an indispensable part of these routines in order to build the biggest possible audience. Just as long as we continue to prefer to watch 'live' television broadcasts as an event to be shared with others, then schedulers will continue to exercise a powerful influence over our viewing habits. However, their power may be on the wane as communication technology enables viewers to exercise increasing control over a 'personalised' entertainment schedule. According to David Bergg, ITV's director of programme strategy, 'It'll be dead, perhaps in five years, with the explosion of choice via broadband, video on demand. . . . The content of shows, their marketing and distribution will be more important' (Brown 2004).

BEYOND THE ACTIVE AUDIENCE

Can the pendulum swing any further in the direction of the audience? For some theorists the answer is undoubtedly 'Yes, it can'. These commentators have suggested that audiences are not just active in the ways in which they construct meanings, but positively subversive. In their view, the products of mainstream media culture can be appropriated by the audience to use as ammunition in ideological battles with the dominant value system. In the field of music this argument would point to home recording, illicit downloading, pirate radio, sampling and mixing as examples of resistance which use the technology and products of the mass media.

In support of this view, John Fiske has suggested that ordinary people frequently resist and evade the preferred readings of what he calls 'white patriarchal bourgeois capitalism'. Fiske acknowledges that there is a 'top down' force which attempts to impose a value system on media audiences, but he sees popular culture as a means of counteracting that power. This is not because ordinary people create their own cultural products but because they create their own meanings in a process which he calls 'semiotic democracy'. Whether or not you are convinced by this optimistic view of 'people power' depends to some extent on your view of the supporting evidence. Fiske cites the example of children making up their own rude words to a TV beer commercial and Madonna's use of religious iconography in her stage act. He takes a positive view of audience members using media products for fantasy or escapism. These strategies show that audiences are aware of their material situation: 'Dismissing escapism as "mere fantasy" avoids the vital question of *what* is escaped from, *why* escape is necessary, and *what* is escaped to' (Fiske 1987: 317).

In other words, Fiske is arguing that the mere fact of choosing to watch an escapist romantic comedy demonstrates the viewers awareness of personal problems which he or she needs to get away from, if only for the duration of a ninety-minute film.

These ideas and the quality of the evidence that supports them have attracted a certain amount of criticism in the world of audience theory. The idea of the 'resistant audience' has been dismissed as 'new revisionism' by theorists who maintain that the pendulum has swung too far away from the power and influence of the media institution. The Glasgow University Media Group has a long tradition of empirical audience research (research based on scientific methods) and is generally dismissive of the active and resistant audience approaches. The group agrees that people may respond differently to media messages but is highly critical of theoretical approaches which downplay the significance of media effects. According to Miller and Philo such theories have:

> tended to emphasise the ability of media audiences to interpret what they see and to bring their own experience and critical faculties to media texts. However, these have often been emphasised at the expense of questions of influence or effects, which have become objects of derision in some quarters.

> 'Active' audience theory inhibits the investigation of the role of the media in forming and changing people, societies, cultures and government.
> (Miller and Philo 1999: 24)

The work of the Glasgow Media Group has focused on audience reactions to events and issues such as the coverage of Northern Ireland and Palestine, images of mental illness and the reporting of the 1984 miners' strike. These studies start from the basis that there really is an objective reality which may or may not be reported in a fair and balanced way. One of their key findings is that the direct experience of audience members plays an important role in the interpretation of a media text. Commenting on the work of the group, Philo states:

> We normally found that if people had direct experience of an issue and that this conflicted with the media account, then they would reject the media message. An exception to this was where a great anxiety or fear had been generated by media coverage. When we studied TV and press reporting of mental illness, we found that it focused on violent incidents. People who worked in the area of mental health and who had professional experience tended to discount this media view and pointed out that only a tiny minority of people with mental health problems were potentially violent. Yet we found some cases where the fear generated by media accounts actually overwhelmed direct experience.
>
> (Philo 2004)

ACTIVITY . . .

THE RESISTANT AUDIENCE

How do people use the technology and content of the mass media to resist or subvert dominant ideology? Find examples from:

- video production
- blockbuster films
- TV advertising
- the Internet.

The same arguments about the audience's power, activity and capacity to resist have also appeared in recent theory and research in the area of Internet usage. On one side of the debate stand the optimists, who see the Internet user as savvy, well-informed and creative, and distinctions between production and reception blurred to the point of irrelevance. Optimists point to on-line and virtual communities in which members may interact not only with each other but also with the producers of mainstream texts such as films and television programmes. Websites encourage discussion and involvement rather than passive reception by users and the Web puts a phenomenal amount of information at the disposal of anyone with a PC and a modem. Politicians expect and get a great deal of comment and response via emails and feedback to their personal or government websites. This explosion of interactive communication has led some commentators to suggest that the Internet points the way towards a new democracy. Robin Cook MP stated that: 'The new technologies can strengthen our democracy by giving us greater opportunities than ever before for better transparency and a more responsive relationship between government and electors' (Coleman nd).

Ross and Nightingale see the Internet as a radical development for audiences and the study of audiences:

> The diverse character of contemporary audience net-work demonstrates the ways the information age is changing what it means to be an audience. Audiences are no longer passive receivers of media texts. They have outgrown the models proposed in 'active reception'. Audiences are learning how *to be* the media, how to net-*work*.
>
> (Ross and Nightingale 2003: 161)

It may be unfair to describe those on the other side of the debate about Internet audiences as pessimists, but they are certainly more dubious about the liberating and empowering aspects of this medium. Many of the more critical perspectives on the Internet point to the differential levels of access and use. Studies of Internet users have shown a very unequal distribution in terms of gender, age, ethnicity, region and social class. Another cause for concern has been the increasing levels of corporate domination of the Internet as big companies exploit the potential for making money from users. As we have already noted, the apparent independence and trustworthiness of the Web can also be exploited by 'viral' campaigns. There are also concerns that levels of control and surveillance are inhibiting the spirit of freedom, autonomy and creativity once associated with the net.

Jenkins suggests a path somewhere between the two sides of the debate outlined above. He argues that:

> It would be naïve to assume that powerful conglomerates will not protect their interest as they enter this new media market place, but at the same time, audiences are gaining greater power and autonomy as they enter into the new knowledge culture. The interactive audience is more than a marketing concept and less than 'semiotic democracy'.
>
> (Jenkins 2003: 280)

ACTIVITY . . .

INTERNET AUDIENCES

- Are you an optimist or a pessimist about the Internet?
- What arguments and evidence can be added to those described above to support you view?

SOME QUESTIONS ON MEDIA AUDIENCES FROM RECENT A LEVEL EXAMINATIONS (AQA MEDIA STUDIES MED4)

1   Assess the validity of passive and active theories of media audience. Illustrate your response with examples from your own media consumption.

2   Does the media construct viewpoints that the audience unwittingly accepts? Answer with reference to events and issues covered by the media.

3   The problem with media audience theories is that they ignore the role of pleasure. How far do you agree? Illustrate with examples from your own media consumption.

4   Why are television shows that feature 'real people' so popular? Illustrate your answer with examples.

5   Audience segmentation is essential to deliver audiences to advertisers. Discuss.

FURTHER READING

Barker, M. and Petley, J. (eds) (1997) *Ill Effects; The Media Violence Debate*, Routledge.

Brooker, W. and Jermyn, D. (eds) (2003) *The Audience Studies Reader*, Routledge.

Lull, J. (1990) *Inside Family Viewing; Ethnographic Research on Television's Audiences*, Routledge.

Moores, S. (1993) *Interpreting Audiences; The Ethnography of Media Consumption*, Sage.

Nightingale, V. and Ross, K. (2003) *Critical Readings: Media and Audiences*, Open University Press.

Philo, G. (ed) (1999) *Message Received*, Longman.

▼ 6 NEWS

In this chapter we consider:

- the changing nature of news reporting at the beginning of the twenty-first century
- the gathering and dissemination of news
- roles within the newsgathering process
- news agendas and values
- how news stories are constructed
- how news is presented
- a typical early evening television news bulletin.

Providing news has always been an important service offered by the media. From the first days of newspapers to the present-day twenty-four-hour digital rolling news channels the media have exploited technological innovation to disseminate news information to mass audiences. News is an important media commodity as it satisfies people's need for surveillance or their desire for information about the world in which they live. Indeed it can be argued that an important function of news is to help us make sense of a world which has become increasingly confusing, not least because of the amount of information that is available to us. News therefore can be seen as a commodity. As with any other commodity there is a market equation between supply and demand in which newspaper, radio, television and new media technology supply news to satisfy the demands of the audience. Also, like any other commodity produced for a mass market, news is produced through what can be recognised as an industrial process or production line. This process takes 'events' that occur in the world, and sometimes beyond, and turns these into familiar and digestible packages of information for us, the audience, to consume. It is this process that is the focus of much of what follows in this chapter.

The reliance of the news production industries on technology is a significant one. Firstly, it has until recently limited access to the production of news for a mass market to those people and organisations able to afford the expensive plant and equipment necessary for the process. In consequence news has been in the control of a relatively small number of wealthy and powerful individuals. Secondly, advances in technology have made the newsgathering process wider reaching, so that news can be obtained and relayed almost instantly from remote and often inhospitable corners of the world. Satellite and digital technologies mean that events from places we may never have heard of can be delivered to our living rooms within hours of their happening. Marshall McLuhan, the media commentator, famously described this electronic reduction of the size of the world as creating a 'global village' (McLuhan and Fiore 1967).

ACTIVITY . . .

How far do you think McLuhan's idea of a global village is reflected in television news bulletins? Consider for example what priority is given to events in remote parts of the world compared to those which are close to home.

News is available to audiences across a range of different media forms. News in the form of print media is primarily produced in newspapers, although there are a number of magazines that focus on current affairs coverage which is closely allied to news. The British press produce national newspapers in two basic formats, tabloid and broadsheet. These labels are also used to differentiate between newspapers which are serious and concerned with coverage of important national and international news and those which are more frivolous and at times scandalous in their coverage of more trivial stories. The distinction does not always hold water, not least because many of the serious broadsheets have recently changed the formats of their newspapers away from the traditional broadsheet to compact or even tabloid editions.

ACTIVITY . . .

It is sometimes argued that television news consumption is gendered in that it is largely males who are interested in news. Hence the role of the early evening news in attracting a male audience to hook them into the evening schedules. Do you think the idea of television news being primarily of interest to men is valid today?

Television news is available as regular bulletins on all the terrestrial channels and continues to play an important role in the scheduling of programmes, especially in the evening. In addition, the major networks all have dedicated rolling news channels operating round the clock, providing a constant supply of national and international news. Viewers need access to digital technology to receive these channels. Viewers can also keep up to date through the teletext news services providing twenty-four-hour news through both digital and analogue sets (see Figure 6.1).

Figure 6.1 *Teletext news index.*

Radio is another source of news. Most radio stations, national and local, provide regular news bulletins. In addition Radio 5 Live provides a service similar to the rolling news channels on digital television. Radio news is particularly useful to people who are on the move as they can access it via their car radio.

New media technology has also provided audiences with new sources of news. The Internet provides such a service both through websites such as the BBC News and Yahoo! as well as the websites of national and local newspapers, such as *Guardian Unlimited* (see Figure 6.2). More recently innovations in technology have enabled people to gain access to news information through their mobile phones, either via Internet access or subscription to news services providing specific news, such as sports or financial news, to their handset.

NOTEBOX

The relationship between the print edition and the on-line edition of national newspapers provides an interesting study. Many newspapers such as the *Sun* have become concerned that if the on-line edition replicates too closely the print edition, this is likely to reduce sales and ultimately threaten the production of the newspaper if sales of the print edition are insufficient to sustain it. This

continued

process is called cannibalisation and a survey by News International reported in the Media *Guardian* of 15 November 2004 suggested that 93,000 readers could potentially stop buying the paper. In consequence there is pressure to make the on-line edition less complete than the print edition, so that it acts more as a teaser to tempt readers to buy the newspaper itself. The *Guardian* offers Web users the opportunity to subscribe on a monthly basis to enable them to download the full print edition of the newspaper for use on-line. This latter option means that subscribers can read the *Guardian* anywhere in the world that has Internet access.

Consider some of the ways new media technology has influenced the way in which we consume news. Perhaps the two ways in which its influence has been greatest are the speed with which we now receive breaking news and the ability of the audience to select the type of news that they wish to access. News tickers on computer screens and public displays are now commonplace and bring us up-to-the-minute details of what is going on in the world. Similarly mobile phone technology has introduced us to the 'news alert' which means that we can subscribe to a service that sends text messages giving us the latest news direct to our mobile, wherever we happen to be.

Figure 6.2 *The Guardian Unlimited, www.guardian.co.uk. Source:* Guardian.

News alerts also represent the ability of the audience to make choices about the type of news that they receive. Alerts about a favourite sports team or rock band can be purchased via subscription to ensure that fans have the latest information. Similarly news groups bring together virtual communities of interest groups wishing to share information about any topic from postmodernism to bonsai. News groups also allow participation in the news process to the extent that the audience is potentially directly involved in posting news, thus reversing the familiar one-way process.

An extension of the news group is the weblog or blog. These sites are personal or sometimes political diaries in which people give out information about their daily lives and share their views with the world. Bloggers, as they are called, often take pride in keeping their sites up to date. They are also able to circumvent many of the restrictions or controls that governments are likely to impose on the mass media. So in war situations or times of repression, bloggers can become a key source of information about what is going on in a country. Blog sites are generally interactive, which means that debates about issues can also be generated in a similar way to newsgroups. Of course, surrounding blogs is the issue of credibility. Audiences will not always be able to verify the truth of what they see on such sites.

It is interesting to note how technological advance in one form can impact on another form. One impact of the Internet as a source of news and information is the way in which television screens are now used. It is common on a news bulletin to have information in the form of words and graphics running at the same time as the bulletin itself. The ticker tape and information boxes complement the information from the studio to provide the audience with almost instant updates of events taking place.

NOTEBOX

> The BBC now offers 10 O'Clock BBC News Extra as a variant of its late evening bulletin. This programme relies on digital technology to supply additional background information to complement the traditional 10 O'Clock News. This provides on-screen background information to the main story to give the greater detail normally found in a newspaper. In addition, the facility allows video material to be shown alongside the bulletin. When the death of Yasser Arafat was reported, viewers were able to access a video obituary outlining his life story through this facility.

One important aspect of news is that it must be up to date. Technology increases the speed with which news can be brought to us. Before the days of television, moving images of the news were available through such productions as Pathe News which was a round-up of the week's news shown at the cinema before the main feature. This need to be up to the minute with news is called contemporaneity. It implies that any news that breaks is featured in the next edition of the news media. With a daily newspaper this means the following day if the news breaks before the newspaper is printed, usually in the early hours of the morning. With a radio or television news service, breaking news can be announced almost as it happens. Traditionally there has always been intense competition within the news media to be first with the news.

Given this proliferation of available news sources, it is hardly surprising that there has been a decline in the consumption of news through the more traditional sources of newspapers and television.

National newspaper circulation

Dailies	October 2004	October 2003	% change	October 2004 (inc. bulks)	May – October 04	May – October 03	% change
Sun	3,277,968	3,458,269	-5.21	3,278,068	3,345,095	3,514,021	-4.81
Daily Mirror	1,770,407	1,943,382	-8.90	1,770,407	1,812,942	1,957,924	-7.40
Daily Star	878,393	908,037	-3.26	878,934	899,385	899,630	-0.03
Daily Record	474,848	503,668	-5.72	475,608	489,112	509,719	-4.04
Daily Mail	2,301,246	2,359,074	-2.45	2,415,032	2,319,330	2,342,745	-1.01
Daily Express	853,524	885,721	-3.64	915,324	882,966	918,099	-3.83
Daily Telegraph	861,072	890,274	-3.28	904,366	869,470	903,222	-3.74
Times	613,974	588,860	4.26	656,462	614,059	593,540	3.46
FT	408,917	412,781	-0.94	438,808	401,435	414,407	-3.13
Guardian	352,444	375,494	-6.14	378,426	351,240	373,402	-5.94
Independent	230,148	198,177	16.13	266,038	228,903	183,954	24.43
Sundays							
News Of The World	3,770,520	4,035,732	-6.57	3,770,620	3,784,089	3,901,150	-3.00
Sunday Mirror	1,637,847	1,628,441	0.58	1,637,847	1,589,068	1,624,326	-2.17
People	1,005,177	1,112,021	-9.61	1,005,177	1,015,764	1,106,797	-8.22
Sunday Mail	591,899	616,873	-4.05	592,309	587,427	621,419	-5.47
Daily Star Sunday	470,276	603,792	-22.11	470,276	497,486	521,004	-4.51
Mail on Sunday	2,346,717	2,322,372	1.05	2,437,748	2,279,851	2,263,986	0.70
Sunday Express	895,414	860,315	4.08	967,574	922,209	892,454	3.33
Sunday Times	1,346,312	1,374,589	-2.06	1,360,529	1,324,399	1,341,039	-1.24
Sunday Telegraph	658,673	692,683	-4.91	688,758	669,187	693,201	-3.46
Observer	424,623	446,831	-4.97	453,018	420,501	424,853	-1.02
Independent on Sunday	179,818	174,371	3.12	214,323	178,687	177,708	0.55
The Business	24,536	77,464	-68.33	214,962	24,779	71,815	-65.50

Source ABC All figures exclude bulks unless stated

% Change, year-on-year

Red-tops 6.0 Mid-markets 2.6 Quality papers 4.1

Newspaper performance by sector

% Change, Oct 2003-2004

News of the World -6.57 Sunday Mirror 0.6 People -9.6 Daily Star Sunday -22.1

Sunday red-tops' performance

Figure 6.3 National newspaper circulation. Source: Guardian.

As Figure 6.3 shows, there is a general trend for circulation figures for most national newspaper titles to fall, presumably as readers turn to other sources for news and information. As we have seen, new media sources of news also permit readers to set their own agenda, for example by choosing precisely the type of news they wish to consume, be it celebrity gossip, sport or international news. This move away from standardised texts to more differentiated texts, allowing the audience to choose the messages it wishes to receive from the many sources available, means that the audience for news, as with many other media products, is much more segmented and much less homogenous. For many media commentators this is a significant shift as it has an impact on the important relationship between the sender and receiver of messages in the form of news.

NOTEBOX

One impact on newspapers of such new sources of news as twenty-four-hour rolling news channels is that they are less inclined to compete for speed of delivery of news, but instead have refocused much of their content. In consequence national newspapers tend now to contain far more in terms of human interest stories, celebrity gossip and background features than they did previously. Such material is often referred to as infotainment.

ACTIVITY . . .

How do you get your news? Track your own news consumption over a period of a week or so and draw up a chart showing which sources you got news from. How far is your own news consumption individualised and how much of it is as part of a mass audience?

So where does news come from? Over a period of time the media, most especially Hollywood, have themselves created the myth of the raincoated hack pounding the streets in search of a story. If such an image was ever true, it has long disappeared. Today's journalist is part of a slick industrial process as much concerned with cost effectiveness as with investigative journalism. News is sometimes unexpected but most of the time it is carefully planned in advance, allowing the journalist ample opportunity to ensure that everything is in place to ensure that coverage is as smooth as possible.

At the centre of any news room, be it television, newspaper or radio, is the diary. The diary lists all the major events taking place on each day that are likely to be worthy of coverage. These will include court cases, for example major trials at the Old Bailey, parliamentary debates and royal visits. Coverage of such events by journalists can obviously be planned well in advance. Other sources of news are those which are managed by organisations, including the government, which want to get particular information across to the public. For example, the government may wish to tell the country about a new crime fighting or road safety initiative. There are a number of ways in which organisations can bring things to the attention of the media.

1   *Press releases*: a press release is a written statement circulated to the news media providing information in a readily digested form for journalists to use. Often a press release may simply be rewritten in the style of the newspaper that uses it, and thus become a news story. More likely a press release will alert reporters to a potential story by arousing their interest. For example, a publicity event might be staged which will provide an opportunity for a good press photograph or television news footage. A celebrity presenting a Lotto winner is a good example.

2   *Press briefings*: press briefings can be either formal or informal. They are devices much favoured by governments to pass information to the news media either on or off the record. Off the record means that the information is unofficial and the journalist is not expected to divulge where it came from. When phrases such as 'sources close to the Foreign Office' are used this is usually a sign of an unofficial,

off the record briefing. With governments, this is part of the 'lobby system' by which certain privileged journalists receive information about government thinking and plans. The system has been criticised for limiting information to a small clique of journalists trusted by the government. Press briefings are also used by other large organisations, such as companies, wishing to get information published in such a way that it is favourable to them. Richard Keeble (1994: 57) suggests there is a view that 'the lobby system is bound into a culture of secrecy pervading all branches of government and into which journalists are too often sucked.'

3   *News conferences*: these are a favourite device of the police in their crime fighting endeavours. News conferences are often called when a major crime is suspected, for example when it is feared that a child may have been abducted. News conferences are likely to be attended by journalists working across a range of media forms, but their emotional tone, often with distraught and weeping relatives, brings a strong sense of drama to television news bulletins.

4   *Public relations*: the need for a positive media profile is recognised not only by commercial organisations and public bodies, but also by individuals, usually celebrities, who need to keep themselves in the public eye. One of the best-known publicists is Max Clifford, who is famous both for representing the interests of celebrities and for selling stories from people intent on making money by destroying the reputations of celebrities. Public relations consultants not only send out press releases and other materials to try to obtain positive coverage, they also arrange parties and other entertainments to which the press are invited. These are particularly used, for example, when a new product is being launched.

5   *Publicity stunts*: given the visual nature of the news, organising news 'events' with a strong visual appeal is a surefire way to make headlines. The Fathers4Justice group is particularly adept at stealing headlines through outrageous publicity stunts which provide strong photo opportunities and news footage.

Clearly journalists are under a lot of pressure to report the messages that the influential people and organisations want them to.

NEWS ROOM ROLES

The news room is the centre of the newsgathering operation. This is the base from which journalists work and to which many will return to prepare their stories. The hub of the news room is the news desk, occupied by a news editor. The news editor's job is to decide what stories will be covered and to allocate the job of covering each story to a particular journalist. Usually an experienced journalist, the news editor will have a good sense of what is newsworthy so that he or she can decide not only what stories will be covered but also to what extent in terms of time allocated in a news broadcast or space in a newspaper. This latter function is called copy tasting and involves looking at incoming stories from staff reporters and freelance agencies to decide if they need greater coverage.

The news editor will be expected to work closely with the editor, who has ultimate responsibility for what is included in any particular edition, and the chief sub-editor whose job on a newspaper is to lead a team of 'subs' to ensure the accuracy of each story, allocate space for it and lay it out alongside any illustrations. These senior news room figures will usually get together with other senior figures such as the sports editor at a daily news conference. The objective of the conference is to decide on the news agenda for the day so that they have some idea of how the evening bulletin or the next day's edition is likely to look.

Lower down the hierarchy but essential to the newsgathering process is the reporter. On a local newspaper, journalists tend to be general reporters, sent out to cover anything from a golden wedding anniversary to a murder enquiry. At a national level, reporters usually have specialist interests and are graced with the name of correspondent. If you watch a BBC news bulletin, you will notice that political stories are usually covered by 'our political correspondent'. Other specialisms might include education, media, Europe or sports. As in newspapers, a reporter's by-line is likely to be followed by a description of his or her role, for example 'parliamentary correspondent' or 'consumer affairs correspondent'. By specialising in a particular field, a journalist will build up both expertise and contacts, people who will provide information in that area, and will thus be able to speak or write with authority on issues that are raised.

The news room is a professional working environment and, as in all professions, journalists have their own professional practices and codes of conduct. Much of this conduct is enshrined in the codes of practice laid down by bodies that oversee and regulate the news media. However, it is interesting to note that there are also professional issues which guide the selection and presentation of news. What becomes news is remarkably consistent across the news media. If you consider the lead stories in the press and on the radio and television, there is often considerable consensus as to what constitutes the most significant news event of the day. Journalists claim to have a 'nose for a story', suggesting that they have an instinctive ability to determine what is important in terms of the news agenda and what is not. Academic studies on the selection of news suggest that there are also other factors at play. A much quoted study by Galtung and Ruge in the 1960s offers a series of categories that have an influence on whether an event is newsworthy or not. Such factors as unexpectedness and reference to elite people, they claimed, play an important role in determining the prominence given to a news story. A more recent survey in which Tony Harcup (2001) revisits Galtung and Ruge's ideas by considering a thousand page lead stories in three national newspapers suggests an alternative list:

1   *the power elite*: stories concerning powerful individuals, organisations or institutions
2   *celebrity*: stories concerning people who are already famous
3   *entertainment*: stories concerning sex, show business, human interest, animals, an unfolding drama, or offering opportunities for humorous treatment, entertaining photographs or witty headlines
4   *surprise*: stories that have an element of surprise and/or contrast
5   *bad news*: stories with particularly negative overtones, such as conflict or tragedy
6   *good news*: stories with particularly positive overtones, such as rescues and cures
7   *magnitude*: stories that are perceived as sufficiently significant either in the numbers of people involved or in potential impact

8 *relevance*: stories about issues, groups and nations perceived to be relevant to the audience

9 *follow-ups*: stories about subjects already in the news

10 *newspaper agenda*: stories which set or fit the news organisation's own agenda.

ACTIVITY . . .

Using Harcup's list, investigate one or more editions of a national newspaper in order to determine whether this is an exhaustive list or whether there may be other factors that determine 'newsworthiness'.

One factor that you may have discovered to be important is that of convenience. Most newsgathering operations have their headquarters in London. This makes sense as the capital contains many important and newsworthy national institutions such as Parliament and government offices. It can, however, lead to a London bias in news reporting, with journalists reluctant to leave the capital unless forced to do so. In consequence important news stories that do not take place in the capital may be overlooked by the national news media. Of course, this principle can be extended further to argue that one key feature of news coverage is ethnocentricity. Events that take place close to home, or involve people from the United Kingdom, will receive more prominent coverage than events that take place in distant and remote parts of the world. In consequence the death of a single person in this country or even of a British person killed abroad will be deemed more newsworthy than a natural disaster, such as an earthquake or flood, which kills large numbers in a far-off developing country. Cultural distance is also significant in the coverage of stories: culturally, events in Australia are 'closer to home' than those in say an East European country like Bulgaria.

NOTEBOX . . .

Not all days are likely to provide an equal amount of news. When Parliament is sitting and business and financial institutions are open, there is likely to be a significant amount of news emanating from them. The weekend, however, is often a quiet time for this type of news and Monday's edition of most national newspapers often betrays this. It is also one reason why Sunday newspapers have a different feel to their daily cousins, with far more investigative and speculative stories. The summer months when many people are on holiday and government all but closes down is often called 'the silly season' in journalistic circles as this is a time for silly inconsequential stories used to fill space.

Of course, the idea that the news agenda is set by these news professionals has important implications. It can be argued that staff who work in the news media are recruited from quite a limited and elite background. Similarly there is pressure on those working in the news media to conform to the norms and professional working practices prevalent in the industry. Those who do not conform are likely to find their opportunities for career progression are strictly limited, if not non-existent. In consequence audiences receive quite a restricted view of the world as interpreted and presented through the news media, one which reflects the interests of the powerful at the expense of the powerless. This is further compounded by ownership patterns. Other than the BBC, which is a public corporation, all news media are commercial interests usually owned by powerful corporations or powerful men like the Barclay Brothers, owners of the *Daily Telegraph*.

ACTIVITY . . .

Consider some of the following possible news stories. What sort of prominence do you think is likely to be given to each? Give reasons for your views.

- FTSE rises
- Pound falls
- Petrol prices rise

- Bread prices rise
- London covered in fog
- Norfolk covered in snow

How far do you think the availability of photographs or videotape would influence this?

Another important consideration is the rise of 'spin', particularly from the government and other political parties, where there is cynical manipulation of news agendas to secure positive coverage of certain current events. In addition, there is also the issue of news stories that are simply ignored, often because they do not fit into the ideological position prevailing in the news room. Of course the setting of a news agenda by these professionals carries with it the danger that the audience's perceptions of the world become skewed by the way in which news is covered and the focus given to specific topics. The focus on crime, for example the abduction of children, can create an atmosphere which exaggerates such dangers out of all proportion and leads people to become overprotective. At an extreme this becomes a moral panic, a term coined by Cohen in *Folk Devils and Moral Panics* [1972] to describe the hysterical reaction that news coverage can create within society. Coverage of stories relating to asylum seekers and paedophiles has led to overreaction, creating tensions within our society. This is often because their behaviour is seen as deviant and therefore threatening to our society. The news media certainly seem to think that they have a key function in watching over social values and protecting our society from such deviant behaviour. A perennial example is to be found in media concern over the social issue of drug taking. Writing in 1973, Jock Young coined the term 'consensualist' to describe the model of society held by the mass media and implicit in their reporting of both deviant and normal behaviour. He argues that we live in a society where people have little direct experience of individuals with behaviour that contrasts with their own values and conventions. We rely therefore on the media to tell us about the 'social worlds'. In explaining the term 'consensualist', Young reveals the ideology behind media coverage of so-called deviant behaviour:

> Its constitution is simplicity itself: namely, that the vast majority of people in society share a common definition of reality – agree as to what activities are praiseworthy and what are condemnable. That this consensus is functional to an organic system which they envisage as society. That behaviour outside this reality is a product of irrationality or sickness, that it is in itself meaningless activity which leads nowhere and is, most importantly, behaviour which has direct and unpleasant consequences for the small minority who are impelled to act this way. The model carries with it a notion of merited rewards and just punishments. It argues for the equitable nature of the status quo and draws the parameters of happiness and experience. Specifically, it defines material rewards as the payment for hard work, sexual pleasure as the concomitant of supporting the nuclear family, and religious or mystical experience not as an alternative interpretation of reality but as an activity acceptable only in a disenchanted form which solemnises (their word) the family and bulwarks the status quo. The illicit drug taker is, I want to suggest, the deviant *par excellence*. For his culture disdains work and revels in hedonism, his sexual relations are reputedly licentious and promiscuous, and the psychedelics promise a re-enchantment of the world – a subversive take on reality. (Cohen and Young 1973: 327)

One criticism levelled at the news media is that they focus on the negative at the expense of more positive news stories that would show the benevolent side of people and society. Certainly events that are disruptive of the norm are more likely to find their way into the public eye than positive stories. Strikes, civil disobedience or even bad weather feature strongly in the news agenda, not least because they have a negative and disruptive impact on people's lives. The way they are presented also lends itself to a greater sense of drama, especially where direct conflict is involved, for example where protesters are confronting the forces of law and order and threatening disruption.

In many ways the debate around news values is at the core of a debate about the role of the media in our society. At the heart of this debate is the question of whether the media reflect issues, concerns and trends within our society or whether they in fact create them. Clearly there is no simple answer to this question. In his book *Sociology of Journalism* (1998), Brian McNair, points out that journalism is a disseminator of values as well as facts. Generally there will be some element of truth in stories covered by the news media but the focus of attention on a particular issue may easily snowball, so that relatively minor incidents which might normally be ignored will receive prominent coverage. For example, the story of David Beckham's foot injury prior to the World Cup finals in 2004 took on epic proportions as news media competed for the most up-to-date information on the star's metatarsal injury. What is clear is that the news media play an important ideological role in interpreting the world for us in such a way as to shape our social attitudes and beliefs.

Martin Bell, the former BBC war correspondent, provides an interesting insight into how the news media affect individual lives in this harrowing tale about a journalist in Sarajevo during the war in Bosnia:

This business I am in is not just physically dangerous, but morally dangerous too, and anyone contemplating a career in it could do worse than to ponder the following anecdote, which I hope is apocryphal, but believe is not. It is about a journalist who wished to write a profile of a sniper on a front line in Sarajevo. It doesn't matter on which side the sniper operated, for both sides have them and each side fears the others as much as it values its own. The sniper was peering out from between two bricks in his forward defences. 'What do you see?' asked the journalist. 'I see two people walking in the street. Which of them do you want me to shoot?'

At this point the journalist realised too late that he was in absolutely the wrong place at the wrong time, engaged on a story that was fatally flawed and that he should not even have considered. He urged the sniper to shoot neither of them, fabricated some excuse and turned to leave. As he did so, he heard two shots of rapid fire from a position very close to him. 'That was a pity,' said the sniper. 'You could have saved one of their lives' (Bell 1995: 173).

NOTEBOX

One impact of a system of news values that encourages response on an emotional level is that it potentially stifles debate into important social issues. For example, the use of drugs among young people or street crime are often reported in an emotional way. Hence much of the debate about how liberal or otherwise our society should be towards the use of drugs such as cannabis has been hindered by an emotional, if not at times hysterical, response to the topic.

Of course, we must realise that positions within the news media change. In the recent past there was a good deal of homophobic reporting in the press. Now we see a much more tolerant attitude put forward, and gay celebrities are a commonplace feature of news coverage.

A perspective on news agendas is offered by Edward Herman and Noam Chomsky in their book *Manufacturing Consent* (1994). They adopt the political economy approach to the analysis of the output of the news media. Their argument is that the need to make profits and maintain a stable business figures as an important dimension in how news media set their agendas. The influence of advertisers is clearly one important factor. If news media report stories that upset their advertisers, this important source of revenue is likely to be withdrawn. Similarly news media must take care not to upset their major sources of news, which in many cases is the government itself. If they do so, it is likely that they may be marginalised by these sources that have the power to shut out unfavourable news outlets. They will then be unable to compete in reporting important stories and as a consequence will lose readers and, therefore, profits. Herman and Chomsky are writing primarily about news reporting in the United States, but their argument can be applied equally in this country. The lobby system by which news reporters are briefed about government policy relies heavily on journalists maintaining the favour of their government sources. Negative reporting of government business can lead to lobby correspondents being frozen out from this major source of political stories. Of course, such a proposal runs counter to the widely held belief in Western democracies of the news media as guardians of our liberties. As Herman and Chomsky (1994: xi) point out:

> the democratic postulate is that the media are independent and committed to discovering and reporting the truth, and that they do not merely reflect the world as powerful groups wish it to be perceived. Leaders of the media claim that their news choices rest on unbiased professional and objective criteria, and they have support for this contention in the intellectual community. If, however, the powerful are able to fix the premises of discourse, to decide what the general populace is allowed to see, hear, and think about, and to 'manage' public opinion by regular propaganda campaigns, the standard view of how the system works is at serious odds with reality.

CONSTRUCTION OF A NEWS STORY

The concept of narrative is an important one in looking at how news stories are put together. Whatever the media form, news stories tend to share the same construction. The often used description 'story' is important here. Just as a fictional narrative unfolds to us information a little at a time, so too with the narrative construction of a news story.

Narrative is a means of revealing information in such a way as to both keep the audience interested and help their understanding of what is going on. In consequence it requires the narrator to pass over the information in a series of chunks that will build together to form a coherent narrative. Each news story is an example of a shorter narrative inside a larger narrative, i.e. a news bulletin or a newspaper. You may have noticed how similar in construction are the products that form part of each of these genres. Indeed it is also possible to identify important similarities across these media forms. Whatever newspaper you open, you will always have a good idea of where to find specific information. For example, sport often occupies the back of the paper while business news is somewhere around the middle. Television and radio news bulletins will also locate these items in the middle and towards the end. You may be aware from your work on both genre and narrative that some degree of predictability and familiarity is reassuring for an audience, so knowing where to find things produces a comfortable feel.

ACTIVITY...

Where news narratives tend to differ from fictional narratives is that while the latter work generally in terms of a linear or temporal narrative, news stories work in order of significance. This can be seen in the way in which agendas are set to prioritise stories into a hierarchical order, within a bulletin or on different pages of a newspaper. One criticism of television news presentation is that it succumbs to adopting fictional narrative codes by using storytelling devices to maintain the interest of audiences. Indeed, it has been suggested that television news has adopted some of the conventions of soap opera, with its interaction of familiar characters and serial storylines. Can you find evidence in recent news bulletins of this tendency? Is it more prevalent on one channel or another?

Individual stories are also built to establish narrative conventions. All media use some system of headlines as a means of interpellation to summon their audience. These headlines often work as an enigma, teasing the audience to want to find out more. Hence they become an important hook to capture the audience and persuade them to pay attention to what is to come. Similarly, all news media place a lot of importance on the opening of a news story. Print journalists call the first paragraph 'the intro'. Like the headline, the intro should grab the attention of the audience and convince them that they should read on.

Former editor of the *Sunday Times* Harold Evans (1972: 85) offers advice to young journalists on the dangers of writing long and wordy intros in *Newsman's English*:

> There is a typographical objection to long intros, too. They look shabby and uninviting to read. It should be possible to read the intro – and digest its meaning – in a quick scanning. If you have to read an intro with care it is a failure.

> A 40-word *maximum* would not be at all unreasonable: about 30 words is better. Editors of the spoken word in broadcasting especially should aim for the shorter intro. Long sentences with subsidiary clauses are a snare for announcers and a strain on the listener.

> A limit of 30–40 words is not hard to achieve. The skill is in achieving brevity without depriving an intro of precision. Anybody can write a 5-word intro: 'A man was killed yesterday.' That is not news. It is a vacuum. Filling it with just the right amount of detail is where the skill is needed. Too little specific content makes the intro vague; too much bewildering.

ACTIVITY . . .

Collect intros from a range of newspapers, national and local. How many of them do you think fulfil the criteria of achieving brevity, wit and precision? Try rewriting any that do not.

Paragraphs in general are important in a news story. They tend to be shorter than those in, say, an academic essay and each one is used to develop the narrative of the story a little further, rather like building blocks. You will often find that news stories have a structure in which the important information is given at the beginning and less significant additional material comes at the end. This is also the case with television news reports. One reason for this is that it allows material to be cut without destroying the sense of the whole item. It may be that pressure on space or time means that a story will have to be reduced or cut down. A sub-editor is then able to chop the story at a convenient point to fit in with the timing of the rest of edition or the bulletin.

ACTIVITY . . .

In order to make a complicated story more easily understood, journalists often resort to metaphor to help with the explanation. Conflicts, such as strikes or political arguments, are often reported through images of battle: 'all guns blazing' or 'battle lines are drawn'. Look at some examples of stories from news bulletins or newspapers and identify any metaphors that are employed. What do you think is the impact of this choice of language?

If you consider a number of news stories on a range of topics, you are likely to find that journalists often present them from a human interest angle. This means that people will be at the centre of the story. Clearly many stories are about people and their lives, but often political and economic stories, potentially quite dry and uninteresting, are couched in terms of how they affect people. For example, when the Chancellor makes a budget speech, it is often reported through how it will impact on the lives of 'typical' people, such as families or pensioners. This is one reason why quotes are an important aspect of news stories. Quotes give a story a human touch by emphasising the importance of the people in it. They also add authenticity, one of the reasons why press releases often contain at least one quote. They may vary from expert opinion, for example a hospital consultant talking about a flu epidemic, to that of the person in the street, often in the form of a 'vox pop' where a radio or television reporter interviews ordinary people to get their views on a news topic or issue.

NOTEBOX . . .

When a big story breaks, it is often in the interests of the news media to keep it going in some way. This is not least the case because they will have invested time and money in getting key personnel on site to cover the story and need to recover their investment by having a supply of 'follow-up' stories to keep it going. For example, after a great tragedy such as a bombing or a natural disaster, correspondents are required to file follow-up reports from the location giving details of how the event has influenced people's lives.

Look at a story as presented on television and in a newspaper. Analyse how it has been assembled. What similarities are there in the presentation of the story between the two media forms?

TELEVISION NEWS PRESENTATION

News bulletins are an important part of television output. The main terrestrial broadcasters construct their prime-time schedules around the early evening and the main evening news bulletins. Whenever a channel suggests changing the timing of a news bulletin, there is often a lot of angry debate in the country as to the desirability of doing so. Such an important role puts a lot of pressure on news to be entertaining as well as informative in order to prevent audiences turning over to other channels. This pressure has been increased by the arrival of rolling news channels such as Sky News and BBC News 24 which provide a round-the-clock news service that viewers can tune into at any time. This pressure is further compounded by newer channels such as Five and BBC3 introducing slick and fast-paced news bulletins aimed at the youth market – at people who are assumed to be uninterested in news and to have short attention spans.

At the end of this chapter we offer a detailed analysis of an ITV early evening news bulletin, but it would be useful here to look at some more general points about the nature of television news presentation and how it endeavours to capture and maintain the attention of the audience.

In Chapter 7, 'Comparative Textual Analysis', we consider paradigms and syntagms as analytical tools in exploring media texts. News bulletins lend themselves well to this types of analysis. Each story is chosen from a range of possible stories, most of which will have been rejected and excluded from the bulletin. The stories that are chosen then have to be fitted together in a sequence to create a bulletin which will tell a coherent narrative. Hence a series of paradigms are dovetailed into a syntagm. This syntagm is the running order in which the items are featured and will usually have the form of a hierarchy which relates to the seeming 'importance' of individual news items. The selection of a story may depend not only on its own news value but also on its relation to other stories in the sequence. Too many dark or heavy stories may have to be lightened with a less serious or even comic story. Too many stories on one issue, such as health or education, will rarely be included in the same bulletin, unless they can be closely related.

Firstly, the presenters themselves are a key part of the look of a news bulletin. Presenters are generally highly presentable, photogenic people. They tend to be good looking, well groomed and well presented. They speak with cultured and authoritative accents, which suggests they have been well educated. Indeed, it has been suggested that it is their appearance rather than their journalistic skills that qualifies them for the job. It is certainly noteworthy that many presenters become celebrities in their own right and some use their fame to develop careers outside news reading.

Presenters are required both to appeal to the audience and at the same time bring a level of authority to the news bulletin. Similarly the studio itself is carefully constructed to create a specific impression on the audience. News rooms are busy places and the news studio echoes this quality. Often the studio features the actual news room in the background, with journalists busy preparing stories for broadcast. This provides both a sense of urgency about the process, showing the newsgathering operation just next door to the studio, but also demonstrates that the process is in some way 'real', because it is happening now. News is being gathered as the bulletin goes on air. If a story breaks then we are bound to hear about it because the news room is just next door. Although the presentation may be studio based it is firmly rooted in the real world. This sense of the 'real world' is further reinforced by the way in which reports are seen on location. A piece to camera, where a reporter directly addresses the audience from the scene, again reinforces authenticity. News studios are usually quite clinical in appearance: stainless steel surfaces and suffused lighting with muted colours suggest a sterile place remote from the outside world, thus conveying the impression of objectivity and detachment – creating the idea that news from this studio is a product the audience can trust.

The way in which the news is presented to us has an important bearing on the possible readings that we can take from it. As we shall see later in the chapter, news on television is intended to be in some way objective and unbiased, not least by presenting the facts in a neutral and disinterested fashion. However, such factors as the facial expressions, demeanour and body language of the presenters work in subtle ways to limit the different interpretations that the bulletin is capable of. A raised eyebrow, the recent penchant for standing up to deliver certain items, all contribute to the way in which we, the viewers, are likely to interpret the events reported to us. Certainly the presentational style adopted by many newsreaders makes it fairly clear when our disapproval is sought, for example in the reporting of 'terror attacks'.

ACTIVITY...

In Chapter 5, 'Audience', you will have come across Stuart Hall's concept of the three positions that audiences might occupy: dominant, negotiated and oppositional. Watch a news bulletin and see if you can adopt oppositional reading of any of the items. How easy do you find it? What are the difficulties it creates?

Of course, it can be argued that it is impossible for news to be truly objective and unbiased. The very process of selecting, editing and presenting it is bound to carry some degree of interpretation on the part of the people who process the news. Rarely do facts speak for themselves. One of the mainsprings of narrative is conflict, and news stories are no exception. A 'good' news story will inevitably involve some degree of conflict, from all-out war to a dispute between neighbours or two football managers. It is, however, incumbent on the television news channels to represent both sides of the argument in such conflicts. This is one of the fundamental principles of public service broadcasting, enshrined for example in the BBC Charter. It is obviously important in political debates when both the government and the opposition viewpoints need to be represented. Objective and balanced reporting, however, should extend into other areas of news coverage. Industrial disputes, for example, should be covered in such a way as to represent the case put forward by the workers and that of their employers. Interestingly, studies by the Glasgow University Media Group back in the 1970s suggested that reporting of such events as strikes was rarely objective and always favoured the employers' side.

One problem with the issue of objectivity is that it assumes there are just two sides to an argument or that an issue can be reduced to a conflict between two parties. Often the complexities of a news item mean that there is a whole range of shades of opinion that must be taken into account if reporting is to be truly objective. Given the constraints of time in news bulletins this is clearly not possible. Certainly a complex issue like Western attitudes to Islamic fundamentalism cannot be adequately represented within the confines of a news story in a television news bulletin without some simplification and reduction of the factors involved.

As Mark Peace (1998) points out, an important aspect of news presentation that has a bearing on how an audience is likely to interpret a story is the positioning of the camera:

> The fact that the viewer is positioned behind the camera has a great deal of influence on the presentation of reality by broadcasters. It means that we assume the point of view of the camera, so if it is positioned looking, for example, from a factory towards a picket line, we can, at least literally, see only the perspective of the employers. This means that, photographically, the news will always favour a particular group, side, or perspective at any one point.

Perhaps the important issue that underpins the problem here is that of ideology. News texts are inevitably presented from an ideological viewpoint. They inevitably reflect the belief system that is part of our culture.

There is no such requirement for the press to be objective in its reporting. Indeed part of the popularity of the print medium is that it is partisan and is often quite unashamed in its reporting of specific issues. The *Daily Mail* and *Telegraph* align themselves with the Tory Party and adopt a line which is conservative, middle class, nationalistic and anti-European in both content and tone. Until 1997 it was usually quite clear which party each of the national newspapers had chosen to support. Indeed the *Sun* famously claimed that it had secured victory for John Major in the 1992 general election, with its post-election headline 'It's the Sun wot won it'. Following the realignment of the centre ground of British politics, the *Sun* supported Tony Blair in 1997 and 2001. Even the staunch opponent of left-wing politics, the *Daily Express*, supported the New Labour government.

Consider some stories that have been reported on the news recently. How far do you think the news teams have managed to provide an objective report of the events? How far do you think their reports are biased in favour of one particular viewpoint? Do you think it would be possible to be more objective within the confines of a news bulletin?

One important quality of news is that it is nearly always serious. It is also generally bad. Negative events are much more likely to make headlines than positive ones. The nature of news, then, is bound to influence the way in which it is presented to us. News is also an important part of the ritual of everyday life. Tuning into breakfast television, reading a newspaper on the way to work, listening to a news bulletin on the car radio, or switching on the early evening news as soon as we get home are all ways in which the ritual of daily news is reinforced.

It follows therefore that the presentational style of news is such that its gravity and role in our daily lives are accentuated. Let us consider the way in which television news is presented to us. At the end of the chapter we look in detail at one early evening bulletin, but at this stage it is useful to tease out some of the qualities that constitute a typical bulletin and give it this sense of gravity and importance.

■ *Music.* The opening music to a news bulletin has an important interpellative quality. It is instantly recognisable. It has a certain pomp about it which signals at the very beginning of the bulletin that an important programme is about to start so the audience should gather round and listen. (Listen to the opening music for bulletins on all the major channels and news channels. What do they have in common?)

- *Studio.* News studios differ from one programme to another but all share many distinctive qualities. In the clean, sterile, self-contained studio with subdued colours and clean surfaces, there is always evidence of modern communications technology, such as laptops and plasma screen monitors. Here is a place where important business is carried out in a neutral and dispassionate way. In some we see the newsgathering operation going on in the background to remind us of the resources being used to bring us our news bulletin. The BBC news studio was in fact for several years a virtual studio, basically a plain room with a computer-generated set to create the illusion of a fully equipped studio,

- *The presenter(s).* News presenters are always dressed quite formally to reflect the importance of their role. For male presenters this invariably means they are clean-shaven and wear a suit and tie. They often sit behind quite a large desk which has the effect of giving them a sense of authority. They always address the audience directly, reading from an autocue on the camera to ensure they hold us in their gaze. People who look you directly in the eye while speaking are generally held to be telling the truth. In fact, the presenters are about integrity and sincerity. We can trust them because they are authority figures speaking directly to us. The accusation has been made that presenters are chosen for their appearance rather than their journalistic skill. This phenomenon has been called Ken and Barbie news, suggesting that newsreaders are chosen for their doll-like attractiveness. Certainly it is interesting to look at the way in which magazine-style and regional news programmes often use a husband and wife team to introduce a degree of informality which distinguishes such programmes from the more serious national news bulletins.

Figure 6.4 *News desk. Source: Sam Barcroft/Rex Features.*

As Casey *et al.* (2002: 147) point out: 'The ambience of television news, then, is one of formality, sincerity and neutrality, bolstering the ideological claim that television news is essentially truthful.'

What other features of news presentation contribute to they way in which audiences are encouraged to receive it? You might like to consider what has been called the increasing informalisation of news presentation whereby presenters appear to be friendly and approachable people.

Interestingly, one impact of digital technology has been to increase the number of channels available to audiences and in consequence to heighten the competition between them in providing news. Given the pressure from news providers in other media forms, there is clearly extreme pressure on both new and existing channels to make their bulletins attractive and entertaining. Some of the newer channels such as BBC3 are also intended to reach the youth market which is traditionally resistant to the serious business of watching news bulletins. This has led to the introduction of strategies to 'liven' up news presentation. Perhaps a turning point was when Kirsty Young on Channel Five sat on her desk rather than behind it, thus introducing a level of informality not previously associated with news presentation. Similar strategies are now to be found in ITV news bulletins where presenters stand up and move about the studio in a carefully choreographed news presentation.

In addition there has been a move towards faster and slicker bulletins in which the news is delivered quickly and some would say superficially. Typical of this is the sixty-second news bulletin introduced on BBC3. The assumption is an audience of young people with busy lifestyles and perhaps short attention spans.

It is not only in its presentation that television news has battled hard to maintain its share of the audience. The content of television news has often been focused towards lighter, celebrity-based items seemingly at the expense of hard news coverage. This has led to the accusation that television news is becoming tabloid – that its agenda has shifted to the trivial and the scandalous at the expense of hard and significant news stories, reflecting the agenda set by the tabloid press rather than that of the more serious broadsheets. The real concern about this is that television news is seen as the prime means by which people get information about the world. If serious stories about political, social and economic issues are to be replaced by trivial diversionary stories, then ultimately the basis of a democratic society is threatened as people become ill-informed and apathetic about these issues.

The story in Figure 6.5 appeared on page 17 of the *News of the World* on 22 August 2004. The story is a page lead, the largest and most significant on the page. It is fairly typical of news stories that occupy the inside pages of a Sunday tabloid. It is quite a visual story, relying on three photographs of an immediately recognisable celebrity to draw the attention of the reader. These are paparazzi photographs, presumably taken by one

Figure 6.5 'Posh wants UK tot'. Source: News of the World, 22 August 2004.

of the many photographers who spend their working lives tracking the rich and famous to bring us details of their private and often mundane lives. Notice how the photographs are unposed snatches of real life taken with a long lens, meaning they are soft or out of focus. In part they offer us, the audience, reassurance that even celebrities have ordinary lives filled with shopping trips and child caring responsibilities, just like the rest of us.

The headline is a typical highly coded narrative enigma. It relies on the reader's ability to decode it. We need to know who 'Posh' is and what is implied by 'UK tot'. It relies heavily on the shared cultural experience of its readers to bring meaning to it.

NOTEBOX

The use of the word 'tot' is interesting. It is a slang term for child, but is used here not least to save space. Abbreviated forms of words are popular with sub-editors as they save precious space in headlines. In the subheading below, notice the use of the word 'vows' as a synonym for the longer word 'promise', although you may also notice that vow is a much more emotive word than promise. You may like to look at other headlines to find examples of short/emotive words being used.

The caption to the photographs uses an awful pun 'tum-thing to hide' and explains that Posh 'keeps us from seeing her stomach'. The word 'us' seems to refer to both the *News of the World* and the reader.

The story is an 'exclusive' which means that the newspaper is claiming that we will not be able to read it in any other news source first. Being exclusive is important in print journalism, especially in the highly competitive Sunday tabloid market, as it means a newspaper is able to publish news that competitors cannot. In some cases this can involve paying large sums of money to people for exclusive rights to their story, often on the condition that they do not speak to any other newspaper.

Notice the structure of the news story and its layout. The upper-case headline in large-point bold type at the top, an underlined subheading in a smaller point size, a by-line in upper case and a first paragraph or intro in bold, with two upper-case opening words. The remainder of the story is then set in 'body type'. The narrative flow of the story is reinforced through typographical devices as we move from the enigma of the headline through to the exposition in the story itself, from major to minor detail. This is sometimes called the inverted pyramid structure and is common across media forms. Not only does it give stories a narrative structure, it also allows sub-editors the opportunity to cut a story by omitting, say, the last three paragraphs or, in the case of a broadcast story, the last ten seconds, which is called an 'early out'.

The intro is basically a very simple statement consisting of a single idea expressed in one sentence. Such a simple and direct intro also has the quality of being freestanding; the intro could be the whole story in itself. The other paragraphs simply expand and develop this basic information. In fact throughout the story, a virtue is made of using simple paragraphs, each containing a limited amount of information but linked to the one that precedes it and the one that follows. In this way the narrative of a news story is built.

Perhaps one problem that the story raises is in its use of quotes. Quotes are used to give a story authenticity, but in this case the quotes are not attributed. We have no real evidence that the person saying these things about Victoria and David actually did say these things. The whole story is based on rumour, albeit one that did turn out to be true. The person quoted is variously referred to as: 'a friend', 'the source' and finally 'the pal'. Clearly if this person does exist, he or she would not want to face the wrath of the Beckhams for revealing the secrets of their marriage, unless the source is in fact the Beckhams themselves, who do occasionally enjoy the glare of media attention.

Throughout the story the newspaper is at pains to remind readers that it is the source of inside information. It celebrates that fact that it had previously revealed a supposed affair of David Beckham.

Ideologically the story is also interesting. The use of celebrities is a popular tabloid strategy. Marxists would argue that this is to create a diversion, keeping readers' minds away from real issues such as their own working conditions. It can be argued that our lives are so alienated from our society that we escape by aspiring to be like the rich and famous. Many would consider this a simplistic view, arguing that the reader's relationship with the text is much more complex than this. Certainly there is a sense that we all love to hate the Beckhams, seeing their wealth as trivial and absurd and certainly no guarantee of their personal happiness. Some would argue that we are still seeking to replace Princess Diana and that Posh is one figure whose lifestyle and love of publicity offer similar qualities to hers. Underpinning the story, however, is a strong sense of xenophobia. David Beckham may have gone to play football in Spain, but his wife does at least have the sense to ensure their child will be born in England and presumably, if talented enough, will be eligible to play football for his or her country.

CASE STUDY

ITV early evening news, Monday 21 September 2004

The ITV *News* is a key part of ITV's prime-time scheduling. On most evenings it immediately precedes the popular soaps *Emmerdale* and *Coronation Street*. Part of its function is to hook audiences into prime-time viewing and to act as a bridge between family programming and programmes aimed at children and teenagers.

This particular bulletin follows on from ITV's regional programming, with the presenter of the regional news bulletin introducing the programme and the presenters, Mark Austin and Mary Nightingale. While the regional presenter is making this announcement a sound bridge of music introducing the news plays in the background. This music has a powerful interpellative function of summoning the audience to gather for this important event. The music itself has an insistent rhythm, suggesting that a significant event is about to take place. The opening shot of the bulletin is a graphic showing a close-up of Big Ben. Mary then announces off-screen the main headline, 'Execution deadline passes', as we see on-screen an image of a blindfolded kidnap victim and then hear the sound of Big Ben striking. Big Ben is rich in symbolism. It is the clock on the Houses of Parliament and is associated therefore with parliamentary democracy. It is also especially accurate in its time keeping, suggesting the reliability of the news that is to come. It also symbolises London itself, being a key landmark, as well as the immediacy of the events being reported. Here is important information from the capital, the seat of power within the country. This impression of importance is supported by the way in which the animated graphic of Big Ben later dissolves into a globe shape which then fragments as the camera seemingly penetrates it and, in a seamless movement, becomes the remote studio camera that tracks towards Mark and Mary who are standing waiting for us, side by side, in the news studio. Both are soberly and formally dressed in dark suits; both have an air of seriousness and sobriety.

ACTIVITY . . .

There is a preponderance of the colours blue and gold in the title sequence. Why do you think these colours were chosen?

Mark and Mary are standing in front of a triptych of still images of the kidnap victim, Kenneth Bigley, with the Iraqi flag forming a background. Mary goes on to tell us that that the demands of the kidnappers have not been met: his fate is still unknown. Mark then announces the next headline, the death of football manager Brian Clough, and we see library footage of him rather incongruously leaving a horse-drawn carriage, then two former Nottingham Forest players at a press conference eulogising their manager. The next headline is about an investigation by the ITV news team into the 'care home crisis', a story about conditions in care homes for the elderly, which 'exposes the shocking way we treat the elderly'. Finally we have trailed an upcoming report of Prince Harry's work with AIDS patients in Lesotho, a teaser offering us a human-interest story to hold the audience through the heavier and more serious news contained in the bulletin.

Mary and Mark then walk towards the desk in the centre of the studio holding their scripts. Mary stops halfway and introduces the first report. She looks unblinkingly at the camera to indicate the seriousness of the item before turning to face a second camera which holds her in lock shot as she stand, legs apart in a commanding pose.

The studio from which the news is presented appears spacious and makes elaborate use of technology with images from around the world projected onto the rear wall. The appearance of the studio is clean and uncluttered, with suffused blue light and clean surfaces. It gives the impression of a control centre of a space-craft with its central circular desk and curved surfaces.

The headline story, the Iraq kidnap, is given a lot of prominence, running for nearly five minutes. It is angled from the viewpoint of the anguished relatives in Liverpool rather than attempting any analysis of the political situation that has brought it about. The only real political perspective is summed up by Tony Blair who in a speech talks of the conflict between democracy and terrorism. The report of the situation in Iraq is done entirely as a voiceover. There is no piece to camera from a reporter in Iraq. Indeed, the report seems to consist of library and agency footage with a commentary spoken by the international affairs correspondent, Bill Nealy. It is interesting to observe that the footage used of al-Qaeda suspect Abu Musab al-Zarqawi, the supposed mastermind behind the abduction, is poor-quality black and white – images which gives it a particularly sinister feel. Whether this was deliberately chosen or is the only footage available is open to conjecture. Certainly this man is demonised as having been responsible for the beheading of hostages on a previous occasion. The kidnappers' demands are presented as misguided, if not absurd. They are demanding the release of all women prisoners. 'In fact there are only two', we are told, with a graphic showing us their identities.

The report does end with a location report from outside the Liverpool home of Kenneth Bigley's 86-year-old mother. Unfortunately, a number of young boys are waving and pulling faces in the background, rather compromising this live report. Its language, 'appalling wait and ghastly silence', is emotive in order to give the human interest perspective.

The second item is about the death of former football manager Brian Clough, or Old Big 'Ead (a reference to his being awarded the OBE) as Mary introduces him. Obituaries of ageing famous people are pre-prepared by the media so that they can be pulled 'off the shelf' and inserted into newspapers and bulletins when appropriate. The obituary of Brian Clough consists largely of library footage detailing his colourful and controversial career during which he took an unfashionable club, Nottingham Forest, and made it the best in Europe. The item runs for four minutes and includes footage of Clough attacking fans who had invaded the pitch at one of Forest's games. Clough attracted a good deal of negative publicity during his career but he is represented here as a genius. The item is rounded off with a location reporter doing a piece to camera at the City Ground where fans are paying homage to the legend in the form of a vox pop comprising eulogies from fans of the club. The reporter describes Clough as 'a reporter's delight' because of his originality and outspokenness in post-match interviews.

NOTEBOX

A typical news report prepared for a television bulletin suggests some of the ways in which news is constructed and packaged for the benefit of audiences. Generally a reporter will be sent with a camera crew to film a report. An interview for the report usually has to be shot three times using different camera positions. These include a single take of the subject being interviewed, over-the-shoulder reactions shots of the interviewer, known as 'noddies', and two shots of both interviewer and interviewee and cutaways in the form of actuality. These different takes are then taken back to the news room where they are edited into a seamless narrative which appears on-screen as a natural-looking report of an event even though it has been highly constructed.

The next item is a crime story in which police are hunting a serial killer after formally linking two 'brutal' murders. The report consists primarily of library footage of earlier reports of the killing of two girls in south-west London, including images from the scene of one of the murders. It includes still photographs of the girls with a voiceover saying the murderer attacks 'blondes'. The police hold a press conference outside a police station at which a police officer explains that they believe that the man knows the local Twickenham and Richmond area. This is a typical crime story which shocks and frightens the audience into believing that there is a dangerous world outside their doors. It also represents the police as being active and efficient in seeking the culprit and thus making the world a safer place for the general public.

We then move back to the shot of the two presenters (holding their scripts) standing in the studio. They trail the item about Prince Harry which is coming up in the second half of the programme. This segment of the programme revolves around a virtual commercial break that does not actually exist but clearly the construction of the news bulletin requires a break at this point, dividing the programme into two halves. It presumably allows the audience to draw breath while at the same time creating the opportunity for another 'headline story' to open the second half of the bulletin. In this case the story is an 'investigation' into care homes for the elderly. The language used by Mark Austin to introduce the item is emotive. ITV News has 'uncovered a shocking care crisis' which is 'a shameful indictment of how our senior citizens are treated'. Notice also how news reporters frequently use the pronouns 'our' and 'we' to position the viewer in the report. The report reveals that ITV News has investigated 100 care homes and found 97 per cent to be falling short of the minimum standards of care.

This story is a good example of journalists in their watchdog role, protecting members of society who may not be able to fend for themselves. It opens with an emotive montage of images of elderly people using walking frames, shot from ground level as a voiceover explains a scandal that brings shame to the £10 billion care industry. The story focuses its human interest on the plight of 79-year-old Lily Leatham who suffered malnutrition and gangrenous sores within six months of going into a care home. The report is by Chris Choi. 'If this were children, there would be a national outcry', he asserts. The report is intended to shock and outrage the audience through a combination of focusing on the human aspects of the care home involved, Laurel Bank in Halifax, and the documentary evidence in the inspector's report on which the package is based, which is shown to us as a highlighted graphic to give the report professional authenticity. We also learn of the death of a man who was scalded in a hot bath in the care home through an interview with his son. The whole story is constructed from the viewpoint of specific people who have suffered because of the failings of care homes. It also features a former inspector who has broken ranks to talk to ITN about failing care homes. This report is the first in a series to be featured on ITV News about this issue. Having spent time and money on researching it, ITV News needs to get a return on its investment by using the report over several days of bulletins. Chris Choi ends his report in a 'well-run day care' centre where a clever dissolve ghosts him among a group of elderly people at a table, addressing the viewers from the chair on which he is sitting sideways, to give the impression that he is confiding information to us, the audience. He tells us that ITV News has checked on the inspectors and they tolerate failure time and time again.

The necessary balance to the report is given by an interview from the studio with David Behan, Chief Inspector for the Commission for Social Care, who appears to be in Bournemouth. He defends the position of the inspectors by explaining they are a new body which has just been set up. He promises action in the form of a review focusing on important issues. Mark Austin's interview style is tough and aggressive, interrupting David Behan to put to him evidence from the ITV report.

ITN is clearly proud of this investigative piece. It also invited the audience to email the news room if they have any stories that they feel need to be investigated. This posture of the news media championing the causes of ordinary people has been central to news production for many years. Tonight's item trails a report on the drugging of the elderly in homes, a technique known as the 'chemical cosh'.

The bulletin also includes two short reports, one on an Algerian released from Belmarsh Prison, the other about a looming strike at Heathrow Airport. Both stories are read by the newsreaders and occupy a small space in the bulletin compared to the other stories featured that evening. Clearly with the Iraq hostage story, the death of Brian Clough the care home investigation and the Lib Dem conference (coming up), there is little room for other stories. Both of the short reports might have formed quite a major item in a bulletin with less pressure from major news stories.

The Lib Dem conference is a good example of a diary job. News editors know that the conferences of the major political parties are held in the autumn of each year, usually in seaside venues. At least one terrestrial channel will have daytime coverage of most of the conference and all news media will have at least one political reporter at the conference. Most will have several and the television news media will have a crew on site for the duration of the conference. It is important to a political party that its conferences receive extensive coverage in the media. Generally, though, such coverage is carefully stage-managed. Political leaders are careful to avoid coverage from within their parties that seems critical of their policies. On the other hand, they will see the party conference as an opportunity to address an audience far beyond the party faithful in the conference hall. The conference is therefore a showcase whereby party organisers can make the public at large aware of their policies and raise the profile of the party leader. It is suggested that this is often achieved at the expense of stifling debate at the conference about issues of real concern to delegates. This stage-managing of conferences is a good example of political 'spin' designed to ensure that a positive view of the party is presented to the national audience.

The Liberal Democrat conference is being held at Bournemouth. The report of the conference is introduced by John Ray, 'Senior Political Corespondent' (*sic*), as the caption tells us. The report is a montage of images from inside the conference hall, actuality in the form of a photo opportunity of leader Charles Kennedy playing with some young children, a piece to camera by John Ray on the seafront and an interview with Lord Rennard, chief executive of the Liberal Democrats.

ACTIVITY . . .

The piece to camera by John Ray shows him walking towards the camera, asking how the Lib Dems' policy to increase taxes will go down in Tory-held seats, and making hand gestures to emphasise what he is saying. This style of reporters walking and talking is relatively new. What do you think is the impact of this style of presentation?

We are then taken back to the studio for a recap of the main headlines, followed by an insert from the regional newsreader who introduced the bulletin. There is a sense of closure at this point as though we have come full circle, back to the top of the bulletin which was introduced with news headlines. This is not, however, the end of the news bulletin; there is another report to come entitled 'Harry's legacy'. The story is about Prince Harry's work with AIDS victims in Lesotho. Something of a tradition has been established that the royal family often provide the heart-warming story at the end of the bulletin. It has been argued that this sort of story is aimed very much at getting female viewers back into the prime-time schedule. Clearly there is another ideological agenda at play here. Prince Harry and the royal family generally have an uneven coverage in the news media. For example, Harry's drinking in a local pub and smoking a joint made news headlines when he was sixteen. The images of him supporting AIDS victims is an opportunity for the press advisers to the royal family to show the prince in a more positive light as a caring human being, sacrificing his privileged position to help those less fortunate.

The ITV bulletin considered in this case study is fairly typical of early evening news bulletins. The agenda was dominated by one important and ongoing story. The remainder of the bulletin included a range of stories, some from the United Kingdom, others from overseas. There was a mixture of hard news stories, investigative journalism and lighter items. As you will have seen, the bulletin is presented as a narrative with the two presenters playing the role of narrators taking us through the events of the day. Ideologically it is interesting to consider the totality of the message that this news bulletin delivers to us. The world outside seems full of treachery in the form of kidnapping, murder, death and an uncaring attitude to the vulnerable within our society. The only hope of redemption is through the altruism of the aristocracy who kindly and unselfishly give their time for the salvation of the vulnerable and needy. You may wish to consider if this is a fair representation of the world in which you live.

EXAM QUESTIONS...

How have recent changes in technology had an impact on news coverage? Provide examples to support your answer. AQA June 2003

'Bias in news is inevitable.' Do you agree? Provide examples to illustrate your answer. AQA January 2003

Are news values treated the same way within the press and broadcast news? Give examples to support your answer. AQA January 2003

Who selects the news and why? Provide examples to illustrate your answer. AQA June 2002

FURTHER READING

Harcup, T. and O'Neill, D. (2001) 'What is News? Galtung and Ruge Revisited', in P. Rayner, P. Wall and S. Kruger (2004) *Media Studies: The Essential Resource*, Routledge.

http://www.aber.ac.uk/media/sections/news.html

Wilcock, J. (2001) *The Tabloid Press: A Teacher's Guide*, Auteur.

▼ 7 COMPARATIVE TEXTUAL ANALYSIS

In this chapter we consider the skills required for extending discussions about individual texts into explorations of groups of texts and from there into the wider contexts.

- We provide an extended semiotic toolkit.
- We explore the ways in which significant theoretical perspectives can be used to clarify the issues involved in textual analysis and comparison.
- We look in some detail at postmodernism as a perspective in action.
- We consider the importance to a text of its conditions of production.
- We look at the ways in which the contexts of consumption of media texts might affect their meanings and status.
- We offer a workable model of how to apply comparative critical analysis to the AQA MED6 unit.

PLACES TO TAKE OFF FROM: COMPARATIVE CRITICAL STRATEGIES

Textual analysis is fine but it has limitations. There is a danger of it becoming virtuosity for its own sake. You want to feel that you've ended up with more than simply a bag of tricks, that you've accumulated knowledge and understanding that might also be valuable. This is something to evaluate at the end of a course and is built in to all new specification A Level courses as the 'synoptic' unit. 'Synoptic' merely has the implication here of encouragement to 'pull it all together'. It is good and proper that we should pause at the end of a course and take stock. You should want to consider what your Media Studies course adds up to, what it has equipped you to do. 'What does it allow career-wise?' is certainly one dimension of this, but arguably a more important question is 'What does it enable me to do that I couldn't do already?' The course you have done may not get you that job you wanted as a TV presenter, but it should have given you some competences and sharpened your intellectual abilities.

In Media Studies that sharpening is likely to be in terms of critical skills which will allow you to better understand your surroundings, the world you live in. After all, it is the development of mass media communication that has literally made your village 'global', that has, in McLuhan's terms, 'extended your senses'. One thing we hope you have learned from reading this book is the importance of seeing media texts within such a wider context. Comparing two texts is a good way of gaining access to wider contexts. Considering their similarities and differences can help you do this. Remember that looking at groups of texts can also more readily reveal their ideological work. Also, texts from different eras or simply produced in different contexts can be useful in exploring the social impact of the media and how they reflect social values of the day.

This is exactly how the AQA Media Studies synoptic unit (MED6) works.

Texts

- **Text One** – part of title sequence for *Mission Impossible*, © Paramount Pictures (1966), Episode 9, first broadcast 1966
- **Text Two** – opening sequence for *Spooks*, first shown on BBC1, May 2002.

Task

Consider the two texts supplied. Account for the similarities and differences between them, using the key concepts and their wider contexts. Your answer should make use of your study of the media. You have **one hour** to complete this task.

Here is an invitation to 'showcase' your knowledge, to apply within a loose context of two related texts all that you value (and understand!) from your course. You are being asked to understand your course as a series of contexts and to see the final exam as the last of these.

Look back at Chapter 1, 'Wider Contexts'. The media reflect social and cultural values so an analysis of media texts must take these into account. In this context, an examination of how texts are produced and consumed is essential. Similarly we need to appreciate the ideological function of the text. This part of the book and of your course is where you confront this awareness and test your critical skills. In doing so, you will have to revisit many features of the course and, we hope, see their relevance in a new light. These circumstances really challenge you to prove yourself as a media student. What has the course provided that might help you with these texts?

Here is a little more semiotic theory that you may find useful. Semiotic theory suggests that communication comprises the creation and exchange of messages through the use of signs. Signs are in essence, then, the building blocks of communication and of meaning in communication. They range in size and substance from a technique to a gesture to a visual element in a photograph or even a word. Signs, effectively, have two parts: the thing which does the communicating, which Barthes labelled the 'signifier', and that which it communicates, the signified. The process of negotiation which goes on when texts meet readers is largely concerned with the different connections made by different readers between signifiers and what they might signify.

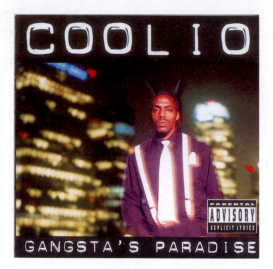

Figure 7.1 *Album cover of Coolio,* Gangsta's Paradise. *Source: Tommy Boy Records.*

You will remember that Saussure speculated on the different ways in which these connections can be made. He called his three tendencies 'icon', 'index' and 'symbol', which represent three kinds of relationship: 'resemblance', 'existence' and 'agreement'. They also represent three different ways in which audiences can be engaged. If we consider the CD cover in Figure 7.1, we can be encouraged by the text to take an interest in it in a number of ways:

■ by the highly motivated iconic images with which we are confronted
■ by the associations with a specific genre which are clearly evident
■ by the familiar symbols which represent the band and the title of the CD.

In this way we have interacted with the text and the ways in which it is communicating but we have not gone very far down the road to understanding how it works as a whole. Meaning-fixing devices like anchorage and relay will help to point the way, but the natural next step is to confront how the text has been compiled as a selection of signs. Barthes gave such a selection a useful name, 'syntagm', and it is the cornerstone of advanced semiotic analysis.

In a system of relay, Barthes explained, 'text . . . and image stand in a complementary relationship . . . and the unity of the message is realised at [the] level of the story, the anecdote, the diegesis' (1977: 41). (The **diegesis** of a narrative is its entire created world.) The easiest examples of relay can be found in any cartoon strip where meaning is created 'at (the) level of the story', in a fair and balanced relationship between text and images.

A syntagm is a chain of signs. Syntagms may be identified at the structural level where complex works may be broken down into their constituent parts: a novel into chapters or even books, a feature film into narrative segments perhaps. At the same time this analytical tool can be used to pursue potential significance in the smallest detail, to analyse sentence structure or choice of vocabulary in a single line or to deconstruct some small aspect of *mise-en-scène*. Syntagms set agendas or rather require us to do so. They are models of primary communication theory but more importantly they force a set of questions on us. They ask us to speculate on what texts consist of in order to clarify what there is to explore or examine or problematise. They then invite us to go further.

In any text, there are a number of interesting sign chains. Principal among them is the formal syntagm which asks us to consider the issue of focus or dominance in the text. In simple terms, we can always begin to 'understand' the text by trying to identify what is important in this particular sign chain. There may be four or five significant signs but usually only a couple of these can be described as 'dominant signifiers': these should become the initial focus of your analysis.

ACTIVITY . . .

Consider briefly the dominant signifiers on the Coolio CD cover in Figure 7.1. What are the most important elements that transmit the meanings?

Of course the identification of a sign chain implies that signs have been selected and it is often useful to consider what has been omitted. A useful first step is to go back to the significant sets from which particular signs are drawn: Barthes calls these paradigms. A paradigm is a set that releases one sign choice (at a time/place) at the expense of all the others, just as the selection of an England footballer deselects all others from the paradigm 'footballers eligible to play for England'. To change the selection is therefore potentially to change the wider meaning.

When analysing a text it can be helpful to consider the signs within a paradigm which do not occur in the actual syntagm. For example, a television newsreader may introduce a 6pm news bulletin by saying 'Good evening'. Other possibilities in this paradigm of greetings include 'Hi', 'Hello' and 'G'day' or no salutation at all. Thinking about these rejected alternatives helps to reveal the contribution which 'Good evening' makes to the text as a whole. You could say that the meaning of 'Good evening' is defined negatively; it is 'not-Hi', 'not-Hello' and so on. Paradigmatic analysis focuses on the creation of meaning by the deselection of signs in the paradigm. 'Good evening' does not have an intrinsic meaning, but the rejection of other signs in the paradigm locates its meaning within, for example, a spectrum of formality. The paradigm contains signs which are more formal and those which are less formal and our awareness of these allows us to understand the newsreader's level of formality and friendliness. Another example might be to look at the meaning/representation of the character James Bond in a series of films between 1962 and the present day. A significant paradigm in this case is that of 'casting', a set of five actors who have played the role. Each time a new selection is made it means a shift in meanings for the Bond syntagm.

What are the significant paradigms that have been activated by our CD cover (Figure 7.1)? Remember they can be more varied than merely paradigms of content: design features and camera angles also operate in a paradigmatic way.

What we are doing when identify paradigms is begin to see the text in one of its primary contexts: what is missed out or what might have been. We are beginning to expose the matrix or grid of relationships from which all texts are produced, the master set of permutations from which any specific combination has been constructed. From this point on the text is open in the sense that you have exposed its inner workings, even if this means you recognise it as being closed in that many of the possibilities that you have recognised have been denied. This puts you in a very strong position. You will have identified a number of leads and traced them to their sources. The text is now available to you as a collection of potential signifiers all of which might lead somewhere (in fact will lead somewhere if that's the way you want to go).

Having got really close, you take your next step backwards. Having engaged with the details of the text, it is often useful to spend a little time considering what other readers might make of its elements. Which perspectives that you have entertained on your course might offer an alternative view or simply a provocative or challenging one? Stuart Hall and his co-authors usefully remind us of three kinds of readings:

- dominant-hegemonic: the preferred reading: the version of the text the creator intends
- negotiated: the modified version of the preferred reading which we individually 'make'
- oppositional: alternative readings which run against the creator's intentions.

Oppositional readers often take up contrary ideological positions and offer a focus on the text that is theirs rather than the text's. These perspectives are often useful in providing insights which inform our own 'negotiated' readings of key texts. It might then be useful to remind yourself of some of these positions:

- **feminist:** where the specific focus is gender issues
- **Marxist:** where the specific focus is economic and social class issues
- **postmodernist:** where the focus is the contemporary context in which texts operate
- **poststructuralist:** where the focus is on the role played by audiences in the creation of meaning
- **postcolonialist:** where the specific focus is ethnicity.

Using perspectives

All the perspectives identified above offer positions which you can take up in relation to texts. They offer an important starting point and a sense of priorities. Remember you are trying to identify issues rather than allocate specific meanings, to see the texts as types rather than significant, discrete artefacts. More significantly, you are deconstructing the process rather than the product this time around; you are interested in the conditions and contexts in which these texts were produced and are understood. As a result, explanations of the process like those above are bound to be useful.

Feminists, for example, might see the 'Coolio' document presented earlier as a 'sad and brief chronicle of our times', as evidence of the most significant debate in contemporary society, that of gender. This is largely to do with an implication of this text, an attitude embodied in the male figure which makes assumptions about women and their particular functions, common in other texts from this generic set. Postcolonialists on the other hand would likely see in the very same 'attitude', an argument about black cultural identity which has a very different reading of this musical subculture. This might partly coincide with the Marxist insistence that the most important contexts of rap and hip hop are economic: it is an aesthetic and pragmatic response to powerlessness and poverty. Another way of looking at this is in terms of 'deeper' contexts. Consider a second text (Figure 7.2) as a contrast to or rather an extension of these arguments.

Figure 7.2 is at one level a historical document, and 'historical' always imposes an obvious depth. This need not be addressed with historical knowledge; you may not have the relevant knowledge or the time to go about finding it. What you always have, though, when faced with the historical, is something 'comparative', something which stands in a significant relationship to 'the way we are now'. The representation of gender is invariably a feature of this: of both male and female, and of their various 'relationships'.

ACTIVITY...

A feminist approach to texts should at least clarify some issues and suggest some priorities, both contemporary and historical.

1   What might these issues be for our first CD (Figure 7.1)?

continued

Our second text (Figure 7.2) was first offered in this format (as an LP record) in 1961.

2   What changes appear to have taken place in the packaging of music in the intervening period?
3   What do you think is the intended meaning of the second cover image? Who is the intended audience (then and now)? What stories are being told about men and, by implication, women?

Figure 7.2 *1960s LP cover: Cliff Richard,* 21 Today.
Source: Columbia Records.

Gender is, of course, only one of the approaches to such texts. Feminism has always been about more than representations of women. At the same time, feminism is not merely an appropriate tool for 'feminine' texts or ones with prominent female characters. Feminist readings are not just reserved for specific texts like *Thelma and Louise* (1992) but rather are available to all texts as one of a number of analytical approaches. In truth we are simply returning to our old friend, 'ideology'. Texts operate in contexts broadly defined by ideological needs, institutional practices and the conditions of reception. This is a way of saying that media texts are a product of the relationships between three important groups: producers, audiences and the society they come from. This being so, we should expect to find the marks of all three groups on the artefacts that are offered to us for analysis.

All texts of all kinds contain elements of the ideological blueprint of the society that made them or within which they were made. The ability to read these codes is a high-level critical skill, the ability to merely spot their traits is a matter of patience and practice. Theoretical perspectives like feminism or postcolonialism always give you a purposeful start since, if they do nothing else, they make you focus attention on the ways in which people are 'pictured'. This is always an interested as well as an interesting activity because it gets to the heart of meaning generation in our society.

The next text under consideration, Figure 7.3, is one that has a very specific historical context. It claims at least modestly to represent the events of 15 October 2004 for a national audience. It also has a very explicit and different function, described by its generic title as 'news', so Chapter 6 of this book might offer some useful leads. Before we even examine the text in detail, we have expectations about what we will get (in one way or another): an account of some things that happened around that date. The fact that there is an agenda emerging theoretically in advance of identifying the text is good news since it speaks of a common and significant context which will always inform our response to this kind of text. If we proceed in note form to explore this initial context we might expect a list like the one below.

- What is news? What is 'happening'?
- How does this differ from newspaper to newspaper?
- How are newspaper audiences different?
- What else do newspapers do (beyond supplying news)?

In other words, we are quickly on to another key concept: institution: issues of ownership, conventions and political bias. Some of these can be clarified by the arrival of the text (Figure 7.3).

ACTIVITY . . .

By looking at the newspaper front page (Figure 7.3), what information can you collect about its:

- news agenda
- audience/readership
- political bias?

Figure 7.3 *Front page of the* Sun, *15 October 2004.*
Source: Sun.

COMPARATIVE TEXTUAL ANALYSIS

Figure 7.3 shows the front page of a famous British tabloid newspaper: to some the most famous and to others the most infamous. Objectively relatively youthful (in newspaper terms), the *Sun* was perhaps the most successful newspaper of the second half of the twentieth century in terms both of the size of its readership and the extent of its influence. In a different context, a little research might have furnished the following, the authors' own version of the *Sun's* editorial column 'The *Sun* Says'.

The *Sun* Says

Cor what a scorcher

Forty years and counting for your soaraway SUN!

Some forty years ago, in 1964, out of the less than trumpeted demise of the *Daily Herald* rose a new light in the newspaper heavens: your own daily favourite, the SUN. Since 1969 it has been not only a handy size but also an extra pair of hands in the fight against cant and hypocrisy, thanks to our owner Rupert Murdoch.

Yes, occasionally we call a spade a spade and mister Chirac a worm, but 3.4 million of you can't be wrong. The highest-selling English language daily can say what it likes and all those frogs and Krauts in Brussels can take a running jump.

It used to be said that we didn't care who ran the country as long as she had nice boobs but we've grown up a bit since then. At forty we know what we like and the difference between an asylum seeker and an illegal immigrant: there is no difference (only joking)!

PS: for a very different 'history' of the *Sun* why not try Chippendale and Horrie (1993) or more scurrilously 'The History of the Scum' on http://www.kirkbytimes.co.uk?

What is required here is a much more contemporary response. What you need are 'leads' rather than historical facts, active readings of the way things are now. The list that follows offers a set of potentially meaningful contexts. These are arguments about the *Sun*, which are critical rather than descriptive.

- Some describe the *Sun's* approach as 'populist': it claims to speak to and for 'ordinary' people.
- The *Sun* is part of an international media group, News Corporation, which also has a controlling interest in Sky television (*Sun* and Sky are often 'seen' together).
- The *Sun* is largely right-wing on social issues: crime, gender, sexuality, ethnicity, irrespective of which party it supports (currently Tony Blair and New Labour).
- The *Sun* (established 1964) is an unlikely sister paper to *The Times* (established 1788). Other members of the News International stable of newspapers include the *Sunday Times* and the best-selling *News of the World*.

Clearly there is room for a feminist reading of the *Sun* and of this particular document, but there are other issues which are asking for a different kind of focus. One is to

SAYS

He's all talk

WHAT is the matter with David Davis?

The Shadow Home Secretary is either suffering from arrogance or ignorance.

The Tories rightly highlight asylum, immigration and border controls as issues which voters worry about.

They make a great song and dance about yesterday's debate in the Commons — so much so that hours before it takes place, Davis goes on the radio to stress it is "incredibly important".

But come the hour, Davis is nowhere to be seen.

When he strolls in late for the debate, he suffers the ignominy of not being allowed to get a word in.

It's not the first time he's let the party down.

Back in July, when the Government unveiled plans on law and order, Davis was in Washington and missed the chance to take on Home Secretary David Blunkett.

Leader Michael Howard rightly took him to task over that.

Davis makes himself out to be a tough guy. But he's all talk and no action.

There must be someone in the party who could do the job better than him.

Miracle boys

LOOK at the cheeky faces of the Hillier triplets on Page 29.

It's hard to believe the bouncing boys were 48 hours from death in the womb.

Doctors gave them only a ten per cent chance of survival.

But a remarkable laser operation after barely 20 weeks of pregnancy saved their lives.

Now we're delighted to report they have celebrated their second birthdays.

The boys are a wonderful reminder of the skill and dedication of doctors and nurses and a tribute to the remarkable advances made in medicine.

For once, the word miracle is spot-on.

Lighten up

THE trouble with so many of our major sports venues is that they're run by stuffy old men.

That's why Wentworth golf club booted out a former Page Three girl.

Well, we got our own back by sending a topless stunner to Wentworth.

And yesterday we did the same at Wimbledon and Lord's.

It certainly cheered things up on a rainy day.

And those stiff upper lips got considerably stiffer.

concentrate on the economic and social implications of the *Sun*'s specific context and operation and this might lead us in the direction of a Marxist perspective.

In many ways, the *Sun* is more than just a newspaper; it is a self-styled icon of 'Britishness'. As both a brand and a logo, the *Sun* has acquired a complex yet familiar set of associations which are well known to the paper's producers and readers and to the wider population. The *Sun* has become an institution, a cultural reference point for both its critics and its defenders. 'The *Sun* says' proclaims the editorial (Figure 7.4), an object lesson in the poetry of tabloid journalism: pithy, partial and uncomfortably precise: what the poet Carol Ann Duffy called 'the tits and bottom line of art'.

The *Sun* very clearly takes up a position on issues with only the merest pretence of objectivity. This is in itself not a problem: it is part of the particular dynamic of a 'free' press. It is, however, a place where a Marxist critique might choose to open avenues of enquiry. The fact that as students of the media you understand the polemical nature and traditions of the popular press is not to say that distinctions between news and comment are always apparent to the casual reader.

KEY TERM

POLEMIC The very idea of the 'polemic' (a piece written to provoke a response by taking an extreme position) is an element in an intellectual or subject-specific discourse or context: it was originally an academic exercise to demonstrate a person's skill in argument. The problem with understanding a 'polemical' popular press in this way is that the traditional function of the polemic is to open and keep open a debate about the issue concerned. The popular press is sometimes accused of closing down discussion rather than contributing to a well-informed debate.

Figure 7.4 'The Sun Says', 15 October 2004. Source: Sun.

Very often we do not distinguish clearly enough between facts (which are most often verifiable and reliable) and interpretation (which begins by being very selective with those facts and so creating its own agenda).

An interesting 'case study' in this respect was the nature of the negative side of the critical response to American film-maker Michael Moore's celebrated documentary *Fahrenheit 9/11*. An avowed polemicist, Moore set out to raise a series of uncomfortable questions about the events surrounding and following the attack on the Twin Towers of the World Trade Center. In doing so he presented a version of events that was at odds with that offered by the mainstream American news media, an 'independent' voice talking in the face of corporate news. Now Moore's documentaries are fairly well known, particularly his attack on American gun laws, *Bowling for Columbine*, but the '9-11' film provoked a specific kind of backlash. Rather than take issue with the version of events that Moore expounded, critics took issue with the character of Moore's film and questioned whether it even deserved the status 'documentary' and he the status 'journalist'. Revealingly they cited 'lack of balance' as its chief flaw as if the version by Fox News and CNN offered an objectivity that Moore's work lacks. A cynic (or at least a Marxist cynic) might argue that the only significant difference between these versions of traumatic events is that international news organisations have the resources to disguise their subjectivity with the 'liveries' of objectivity: schedules, personnel, sets and volume of coverage. The *Sun*, too, benefits from an institutional 'cloak' to some extent, largely because its admittedly radical stance falls within what Marxists would define as the dominant ideology (the prevailing values of society).

The *Sun* has always been a target for those on the political left who see it as a bastion of the political right, peddling views of the world which are self-perpetuating (it sells the very world in which it thrives). It is particularly involved in what Gramsci called naturalisation, turning opinions about the world into assumed common sense. In every issue inequalities of wealth are explained in terms of natural talent, hard work or even luck. All these either entice us to 'do better' or give up. Adopting a Marxist approach helps us to understand this and to set a new agenda. An interrogation of the *Sun* may begin by asking these questions.

- Who (precisely) is the audience?
- What is the *Sun* telling them?
- How is it telling them these things?
- Why is it telling them these things?

Althusser, you will remember, identified the media, along with education and the family, as a mechanism through which the dominant ideology is propagated: he labelled them ideological state apparatuses. Another Marxist critic Theodor Adorno suggested that the media are part of what he called 'the culture industry' whereby we are offered false needs and bogus values. You would not have to be very cynical to see this as a possible response to the *Sun*'s medley of celebrity scandal and big prize competitions. This, for Marxists, is a key 'voice' in the struggle between class interests, since its audience is largely working class and its attitudes those of the petite bourgeoisie (read by the 'have-nots', it has the attitudes of the 'partly haves'). This often allows the *Sun* to be radical and anti-establishment but not in a socialistic or even a liberal way. It is simply that the class struggle is being fought out through the channels of the mass media. As Voloshinov (1973) suggested, 'Sign becomes the arena of the class struggle'. Some Marxists then always find it relevant to ask the direct question: 'Which side are you on?' Answering the above questions is to some extent a drawing up of sides:

- largely white, largely working class, largely male (?)
- ENJOY YOURSELF: don't worry about the things you can't control (like politics); be honest (and outspoken), be straightforward (simple), be lucky, be happy
- by words and pictures: comic-book style, through energised, illustrated and effective narratives, in ways they understand and enjoy
- to enable them/help them to see their social position as natural and inevitable.

Already you can see how this brings a particular emphasis to the reading of a text. In fact it energises a new set of issues in a context where 'issues' are the essence. On top of this a Marxist perspective will also have things to say about the specific nature of the press as an institution. It will likely take issue with the whole viability of the 'free' press concept, preferring 'capitalist' to 'free', and suggest that the range of opinions offered to British readers is defined largely by the needs of the vested interests involved. In the case of the *Sun* these vested interests are international and high profile: those of Rupert Murdoch's News Corporation empire. Suddenly the range of opinions is shrinking further as the open promotion of this corporation's varied media interests (particularly Sky television but also Fox News) takes space that might once have been given to more traditional definitions of 'news'.

ACTIVITY . . .

Marx was especially interested in the relationship between theory and practice, with an emphasis on the latter. Look back at the *Sun* front page (Figure 7.3 on p. 194) and offer a bullet point analysis from a Marxist perspective. Identify the key issues as you see them.

This is an opportune moment to introduce a second text to extend the debate about newspapers and 'news'. The newspaper printed in Figure 7.5, like the *Sun*, offers a distinctive and definable perspective. In this case the angle is 'local'.

Figure 7.5 *Front page of the* Stourbridge News, *5 August 2004. Source:* Stourbridge News.

As we have seen, depth of content comes from breadth of context and this means plotting points of reference, which can then be joined up to provide a bigger picture. With this in mind:

1 What are the significant differences between the two newspaper texts (Figures 7.4 and 7.5)?
2 What relationship is established above between the text and its audience?

The *Sun* was forty years old in 2004. The most significant thing to happen to the local press since the 1960s is the emergence of the 'free' paper, delivered rather than sold. In a short period the whole relationship between some newspapers and their audiences was transformed and a tranche of local weeklies was removed. The paper featured in Figure 7.5, the *Stourbridge News*, was born in the first wave of free newspapers, swallowing in the process the *County Express*, a weekly broadsheet with a cover price. Despite the nominal 50p (where sold), VFD (verified free distribution) records the real (i.e. 'free') distribution as '51,513 copies every week': far more than the previous version, which local people paid for.

Take a minute now to contemplate Figures 7.4 and 7.5, as poles between which you might entertain a discussion on the nature of the press. The ground between is the work you've done and the experience you have as a student on a Media Studies course. It is first of all about having the confidence to allow the texts themselves to inform your narrative or argument. The details of the two texts will, of course, furnish further points of reference but this is a test of theory and practice. Much of the work is always about knowing what the persistent issues of Media Studies are. For Figures 7.4 and 7.5 an easy list would include:

- status/credibility of both texts
- functions of newspapers
- newsworthiness
- nature of audiences.

Questions about the form, style and content of the national and local press are found on most Media courses from GCSE onwards. Finding your level, therefore, is about realising the relative complexities of this area, recognising the issues and through these grasping the wider contexts. One of the widest contexts in this case is to pause to consider the functions of the mass media in general and the changing role of the press in relation to them. A list of functions might include:

- to inform
- to educate
- to advertise
- to persuade
- to socialise
- to control.

'To inform' comes perhaps a little too glibly for a medium that has since the Crystal Palace fire of 1936 (it occurred in the late evening, so radio got its first 'scoop') been struggling to compete with the immediacy of radio and television. 'To entertain' has become more of a norm, even for the broadsheets, whose cover CD ROM and numerous supplements would once have been signs of desperation. More interesting is 'to socialise' (though Marxists would perhaps see it as synonymous with 'to control') because long after newspapers have failed to offer us anything much that is significantly 'news', they will remain as vital elements in our social and cultural landscape. 'Socialisation', Basil Bernstein (1971) claimed, 'is a process for making people safe': implicit in titles like the *Guardian* and the *Daily Mirror* is the idea that they are places where values might be reflected and defended.

E. Katz, interestingly, argued that personal and social integration were goals of mass communication or, at least, needs gratified by our exposure to media texts. In other words, the media offer 'places' where we can form and forge our personal and social identities. This was partly the point that Fiske and Hartley (1990) were making in their formulation of 'bardic function' (they argued that TV had become the tribal storyteller of modern society) which perhaps overstated the extent to which the mass media had become the focus of our social learning. Neil Postman famously claimed that 'You have to watch TV to be American' and it is difficult to see how any smooth induction into contemporary British culture could avoid reference to television.

In the last thirty years or so such explanations of the media's role have been called into question. Postmodernists dismiss these grand explanations, these 'metanarratives' (super-stories). All the models of manipulation and control have equally been called into question, whether the focus be gender or class or genetic. The new orders of the day are uncertainty and flux: everything is changing so rapidly that no theory can hope to stand for long and no one's identity can be more than 'for now'. And 'now', of course, is the new focus.

POSTMODERNIST READINGS

Postmodernism is a productive perspective to adopt on the media partly because it has media representation and media technology at the heart of its insights. Modern media and technology, it argues, have created a reality that is in itself uncertain, where what is real is no longer a matter of straightforward fact. We live in a world of reproductions both materially and morally/spiritually. Baudrillard uses the biblical term 'simulacrum' to describe these 'copies', whether they be new trainers or new values. It is a world from which the old explanations have been removed and discredited. Pastiche and parody have become the dominant forms of expression and irony the dominant mode of address. Irony has even become a protection against those who think this explanation is beginning to sound a little like a metanarrative.

As the 'label' suggests, postmodernism arrived at the very moment that the last formal experiments of 'modernism' had run their course. The nineteenth century had produced a confident world order in which Europe (and especially Britain) had made empires and produced large-scale, confident art-forms: the novel, for example, had become a three-volume epic. In the early twentieth century modernism came along to reject all this, answering it with experiment and uncertainty. Arguably, postmodernism 'set in' when uncertainty had become a cliché and the unresolved ending had become once more a satisfying conclusion. All that was left was parody and cleverness and irony. Popular culture was at the centre of the movement: to its critics, it was too often style over substance with the medium as both message and metaphor: to postmodernism, that was the point. The 1960s was perhaps the key decade, a decade of contradictions: where popular music came of age and yet in which the most successful song was crooner Engelbert Humperdink's 'Release Me'. It was also the decade that produced the next text, Gerry Anderson's *Thunderbirds* (Figure 7.6).

Figure 7.6 *Still from the original* Thunderbirds. *Source: BBC.*

Anderson and his wife Sylvia dominated 1960s and 1970s television for children with their classic mixture of the old-fashioned and new-fangled: super-marionettes. A string of hit series stretched across more than a decade: *Captain Scarlett* (*and the Mysterons*), *Fireball XL5*, *Stingray*. However, it was *Thunderbirds* that made the greatest impression with its fantasy location (Tracy Island), its range of futuristic 'hardwear' and its

COMPARATIVE TEXTUAL ANALYSIS

genuinely creepy villain (The Hood). Even its rather 'wet' heroes, the Tracys, couldn't prevent it attaining cult status and the ultimate, if dubious, accolade of being turned into a mainstream blockbuster Hollywood film. Given that this has become in itself a significant film genre/sub-genre, the cult TV/cartoon tie-in recommends it itself as a place to explore issues in contemporary media. Imagine that your second exam text was simply an updated version of the first, a slice of *Thunderbirds* (2004), the movie (Figure 7.7).

As this book has persistently implied, your Media Studies course should have provided you with a set of useful critical tools and significant contexts. Media Studies hopes to turn you into a media commentator and a media theorist. Both require critical judgement and discrimination, together with the confidence or courage to express them. Discrimination is about choosing the right tool and trying to 'use' it on an appropriate issue. Again, while all the tools will tend to work on all the issues, clearly some combinations will bear more fruit than others.

The two *Thunderbirds* texts are a case in point and it's worth saying that in an exam context they would most likely have appeared as extracts/clips. They offer many potential lines of enquiry so the choice is genuinely yours. Much work might fruitfully focus on the historical dimension and start with a straightforward comparison of the texts in terms of, for example, the context of production and the conditions of

Figure 7.7 *Still from* Thunderbirds *(2004). Source: Universal Studios.*

consumption. The audiences for these two texts are very different, as are the social, economic and technological contexts. It is to be hoped, though, that with a grasp of some media perspectives your own analysis can be a little more ambitious.

In this case adopting positions that have previously been described as 'postmodernist' may prove useful. While it would be easy to talk about the 2004 film in terms of 'playfulness' and 'irony', it is not only in parody and pastiche that we find postmodern insights. The original series, too, gives much room for examining the ground rules, both for the specific text and for contemporary media.

ACTIVITY...

Choose one of the *Thunderbirds'* texts (Figures 7.6 and 7.7) and consider the usefulness of these postmodernist 'terms':

- hyperreality
- simulacrum
- bricolage.

The fondness that Hollywood has shown for often unlikely television shows provides an institutional context in itself and a series of questions. The issue here is not historical (or at least not in terms of what we need to know to watch the films) but rather cultural and critical. Ironically, one of the reasons why *Thunderbirds* (2004) flopped was because it didn't really understand what it was or what it was sending up. Unkind critics, who compared the film's live action unfavourably with that of the puppet original, were perhaps closer to the real issues than they imagined. What Gerry Anderson understood was the particular potential of puppets to deliver narrative entertainments in a surprising and yet charmingly traditional way. When translated into 'high tech' and 'live action', it is not surprising that 'surprise' and 'charm' are the first things to go. What remains then is at best an action film for children which has nothing to offer the adult in us. While *Starsky and Hutch* (2004) was capable of an ironic take, since the original was at heart a well-produced and performed crime series, *Thunderbirds* proved to be beyond parody. In fact *Thunderbirds* (2004) turned out to be far less sophisticated than the original.

Reduced to first principles, the 'postmodern condition' is just that: a state of affairs and not just a matter of style or manner of response. The condition for some is terminal and these critics would not be heartened by the evidence of *Thunderbirds* (2004). Lyotard himself has written scathingly on the proliferation of popular culture and its values. *Thunderbirds* (2004) appears to be trying too hard in a context where its predecessor was more obviously 'having it all'. While it seems unlikely that the term 'metanarrative' featured much in the development of *Thunderbirds* in the 1960s there are clearly messages here about the Western alliance (NATO) and its values. 'International Rescue' seems suspiciously like the role America still has in the world, the Tracys seem too like the Clintons/Kennedys/Bushes (even) to be ignored. By 2004, then, with revival imminent, there is in many ways a much more significant target in the water, a war in Iraq, but there is in fact not even the slightest desire to hit it. And when irony is employed merely for irony's sake, it is safe to assume we have gone too far.

Like the 'players' who appear within Shakespeare's *Hamlet*, the puppets strangely have a truth which comes largely from knowing what they are. It may be unwise to push these comparisons too far but it is certainly true to say at least that the puppetry is the source of the appeal on a number of levels. 'Seeing the strings' is in every sense one of the organising ideas, extending from the look of the piece through to its larger concerns with the kinds of stories it is telling and gently debunking. Alarmingly, they turn out to be the kinds of stories still being told with a straight face within the Hollywood mainstream.

ACTIVITY . . .

Look at the plot summaries of mainstream action movies and suggest the ways they might be adapted as stories about the Tracy family and their 'thunderbirds'.

Even the hardware seems less impressive, undermining the crass generalisation that technology adds to realism or at least spectacle. The toy-like miniature work of the original put aside realism in favour of narrative. All that CGI delivers is a kind of 'fantasy realism' where the original's suppositions about future transport are replaced by realisations which are as overblown as they are overwhelming. Even the oddly phallic look of the original models seems preferable to the 'Top Gun' feeling of the update. In fact the whole 'boys' toys' approach, complete with a sex kitten Lady Penelope relaxing unnecessarily in the bubble bath, seems more regressively sexist than the tokenistic but well-meaning quota-ing of the 1960s vintage. Lady Penelope was after all, despite the peroxide blonde hair and pink Rolls-Royce, a symbol of changing times: a significantly feminine aspect of the International Rescue team and as such actor rather than acted upon.

Perhaps a better model for the original *Thunderbirds* would have been something like the 2004 smash sequel *Shrek 2*. Here technology is married with narrative ideas and attitude to produce a challenging family film which is able to operate at more than one level for more than one audience. In the thinly veiled attacks on the corporate influence of Disney and the gentle exposure of the ideological nature of traditional stories, there is a genuine irony (an irony that has been worked through and is deserved). The story, across the two films, of Cameron Diaz's beautiful princess coming to terms with her trollish appearance, is proof enough of its mode of address. Modelling the CGI on Diaz herself focuses the gender debate in exactly the same proportion that putting a real Lady Penelope in the bath diminishes it.

THE CONDITIONS OF PRODUCTION

The argument on p. 205 ended up by disputing the simplistic view that advances in media technology improve the quality of media products. It argued implicitly that there are more abiding and prevailing aspects (character, narrative, theme) which will always exert themselves. If your analysis goes no further than 'primitive' and 'sophisticated', 'better' and 'worse', then nothing has been learnt about the contexts of production. Of course one of the differences between *Thunderbirds* and *Thunderbirds* 'remade' is technological and, by implication, economic but these limitations have both always existed and produced good work, even great work. In fact the German writer Goethe claimed that one sure sign of a genius was his/her ability to work within significant restraints ('the master', he said 'first shows himself when he is constricted'). Even in the context of Premiership football, economic power is no significant guarantee.

Obviously the conditions of media production have changed significantly since the early 1980s as case studies in all media fields might show: publishing, IT, radio, film, television. As students of media you should take an interest not so much in what has happened technically but rather in what has happened as a result of these changes. At the sharp end of this perspective is the book you are holding in your hand which, as the third in a series devoted to a developing area of the college curriculum, might never have been published save for the IT revolution which has allowed publishers to print smaller runs of books of all kinds. In the same way a casual look at any TV listings magazine will underline the very different ways in which television is being produced, ranging from national institutions like the BBC to small-scale cable stations like LIVE TV. A screenshot from something like LIVE TV's *Lie Detector* (in which pairs of friends or lovers had their 'stories' checked out by a lie detector test!) can raise an awful lot of issues, particularly if juxtaposed with the emblematic opening of BBC *News*.

ACTIVITY . . .

Choose a presenter-based show from a cable or satellite channel other than Sky 1 and compare the way it is presented with its equivalent on BBC1. It may be interesting to look, for example, at different kinds of news programmes. Look first at the *mise-en-scène*, the lighting, setting, costume, props and positioning. What are the significant differences between your chosen programmes?

They say that every picture tells a story but for your purposes it would be more accurate to emphasise the plurality of meaning, the polysemy: every picture actually tells a number of stories. Deciding which of these stories you want to pursue is one of the key stages of your comparative textual work. An excellent way of preparing for these challenges is to put yourself for a moment in the position of the person setting the paper. Try choosing pairs of texts across a range of media, which you think offer particular opportunities for analysis. Clearly texts are not chosen haphazardly; they are chosen to provide a certain amount of straightforward or even obvious critical work, historically or thematically perhaps. One paper for AQA's MED6 Unit, for example, juxtaposed Ridley Scott's *Gladiator* (2000) with Stanley Kubrick's *Spartacus* (1960), different versions of the distant past made across the recent past.

As one of these texts must provide a starting point of sorts for your work, it can be useful to identify a 'lead' text. This is a reasonable strategy, not only because it asks you to make an early critical judgement but because it is highly likely that one of these texts was the starting point for the task: you'll find this is most often the case if you devise your own pairs. In the case of the films about Romans mentioned earlier, it is likely that *Gladiator* is suggesting the agenda since it was a film widely talked about for its use of CGI technology. Issues of production are in this way immediately foregrounded and a whole host of questions is made active: about representation and realism as well as technology and economics. These may be very different questions to those that came out of BBC News and LIVE TV, though the conditions of production are again an important starting point: you would be quite likely to spend some time comparing the production values of a public-funded broadcaster like the BBC with the relative amateurism of *Lie Detector*.

THE CONTEXTS OF CONSUMPTION

All of this leaves only audience significantly unexplored. Though all the critical work to this point implies a relationship or relationships between text and readers, the identity of these readers still needs to be probed. As you know, media products are deliberately aimed at a researched demographic, the target audience, and yet most are also, in one way or another, hoping for that elusive ur-audience, the general public. Some betray themselves with taglines and trailers which speak of 'children of all ages' or 'all the family'; most advertise largely generic elements which are aimed to connect at a number of levels. Of course this is not to assume an uncomplicated relationship between texts and consumers: the more aspects you consider, the more interesting it becomes (and Chapter 5, 'Audience', should be a significant help in this case).

Print is arguably the most conservative and consistent medium: audiences settle down quickly and tend to change slowly. Moving image, because it conventionally exists in a number of different forms (and formats), is much more dynamic. Considering the target audience for a film like *Spartacus* or *Gladiator* prompts the question 'when?', or at least the response 'do you mean primary or secondary audience?' So as not to complicate the matter with the specific issue of 'history', let's take *Gladiator* as our example. Its audience penetration will necessarily have at least three distinct phases which represent to some extent the existences that the film enjoys post-production. These represent at least three very different contexts of consumption, albeit intimately connected ones.

Firstly, the film enjoyed exhibition in what Americans call 'movie theatres'. For a film like *Gladiator* many of these will likely have been multiscreen cinemas, showcasing the film across a number of screens. This will have defined *Gladiator* as a major film with all the requisite elements: a named director (auteur?), A-list stars, a significant understandable narrative, a recognisable central concept (genre, representation, theme). It would be possible to research the target demographic though it's equally interesting to speculate. Given the substantial business the film did, it seems likely that a broad audience base was established since stereotypically the film might be expected to appeal to:

- men: in terms of the nihilistic narrative and historical genre
- women: in terms of its advertised themes (love and family) and its charismatic male lead
- young people: in terms of its state-of-the-art CGI and eye-catching visual style.

This audience would have been strengthened across its relatively short lifespan by such matters as Oscar nominations and subsequent awards. This would also itself have been reinforced by the whole business of criticism and promotion (and often they're the same thing).

Of course the primary audience does in a number of ways constitute the secondary audience that will consume the film on video, DVD or even TV. At the same time, though, these 'sell-throughs' have a life of their own and considering each or any of them offers another context within which audience can be explored. Watching *Gladiator* on DVD in your Media or Film class is obviously very different to watching it in your local multiplex with a boy- or girlfriend or with your family one Christmas afternoon as a blockbuster seasonal movie. Terrestrial television is much less likely to be the place you first see a major Hollywood film these days. In some sense formats have become a kind of critical filter system through which we consciously and unconsciously process the latest cinematic fare and create a hierarchy of contexts for the 'presentation' of films. Such a hierarchy might look like this:

1   films you pay to see in the cinema as soon as they are released (pre-book even!)
2   films you pay to see in the cinema
3   films you rent/buy/pay-per-view as soon as they are available
4   films you rent/buy once they reduce in price/films you watch on your multichannel movie package
5   films you watch on terrestrial TV.

This 'pecking order' necessarily mediates the, for want of a better word, 'intensity' of the experience. Some films, of course, will function for us on a number of these levels and each of these 'viewings' will have its own specific context. Owning a film on DVD or video, either bought or home-recorded, does not preclude watching it on television but it does alter the emotional and psychological context. At best, with your 'greatest' films, you may find that this relationship is enhanced since you will believe you are seeing more.

PUTTING IT ALL TOGETHER

All that remains is to work through some examples to test your critical mettle and then examine what it is specifically that makes 'good' answers. What follows are a couple of sets of stimuli, or 'starting points' as we've called them, and then some extracts from examination answers at various levels of achievement. The notion of wider contexts is both a challenge and a useful prompt since it reminds you of the central (you might say 'narrow') context which exists in the paper and the 'examination' it represents. When mapping the broader issues, what we are crudely doing is indicating the 'other places' where the text–audience relationship is being conducted. Technically this represents the metacontext of the text: the context of contexts which so significantly relays meaning, which is only a complicated (or sophisticated) way of saying, as Margaret Atwood pointed out in *The Handmaid's Tale*, 'context is all'.

Hopefully this section has given you some clues but also, if you want it, a scheme or approach. Here is a thumbnail sketch of where we've been and thus where you might go.

- Establish a lead text/place to start.
- Clarify the key elements of the lead text's syntagm (sign chain) in terms of content, form and style.
- Identify the dominant signifiers: these become potentially the 'issues' of the text and the comparative work.
- Allow these issues to lead your comparisons with the second text and create critical contexts.
- Consider the way the texts are expected to be read (dominant-hegemonic).
- Consider key issues of representation via use of perspectives: feminism, Marxism, postmodernism.
- Explore key concept as context: 'ideology' (as a direct result of the perspectives above); also consider historical context as meaningful in this way.
- Address the institutional contexts of your texts.
- Explore finally the contexts of consumption as a way of putting the task to bed but leaving it awake: always leave something open and ongoing.

Practice, they say, makes perfect, so now it's your turn. What follows are two sets of paired texts, together with a few (hopefully) well-positioned prompts. For each pair the task is the same.

Task

Consider the two texts supplied. Account for the similarities and differences between them, using the key concepts and their wider contexts. Your answer should make use of your study of the media. You have one hour to complete this task.

The texts are shown in Figures 7.8 and 7.9.

From these might come the following prompts.

- In what ways does the first text (Figure 7.8) define film as a mass medium?
- List the ways in which it provides contexts which are: historical, economic, social, cultural, aesthetic.
- What is added to this debate by the second text (Figure 7.9)?
- In what ways does this film differ from those presented in the first text? Think genre, audience, institution, ideology, debates about culture.
- What might the broader differences be between popular and 'art' cinema in terms of media language, genre, narrative and representation?
- What clues are there in these texts to suggest the ideological position of Hollywood cinema?
- Consider broadly gender representation in contemporary cinema.

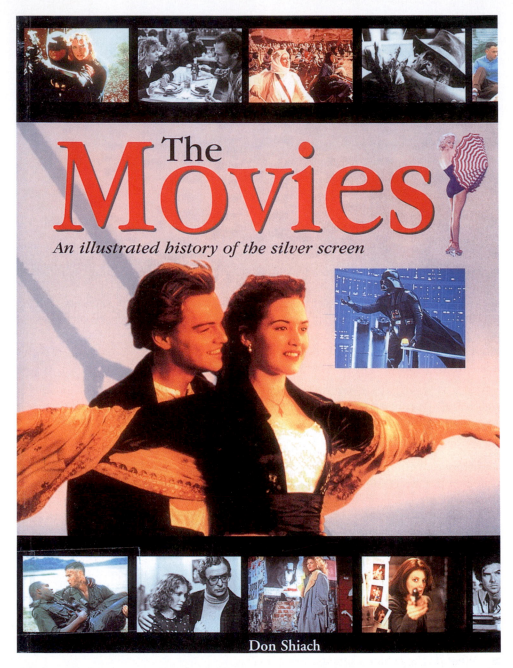

Figure 7.8 *Front cover of* The Movies: An Illustrated History of the Silver Screen (2000), by Don Shiach. Source: Hermes House.

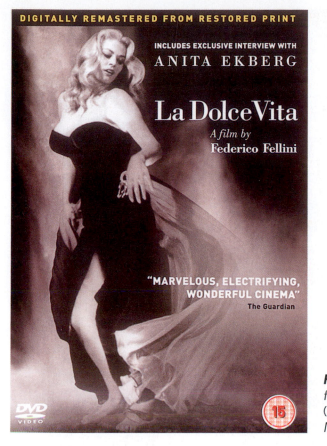

DIGITALLY REMASTERED FROM RESTORED PRINT

INCLUDES EXCLUSIVE INTERVIEW WITH
ANITA EKBERG

La DolceVita

A film by
Federico Fellini

"MARVELOUS, ELECTRIFYING,
WONDERFUL CINEMA"
The Guardian

Figure 7.9 *DVD cover for* La Dolce Vita *(1960). Source: Nouveaux Pictures.*

Remember the section title: 'Places to take off from'. These are not texts to waste your time trawling through, they are starting points from which you must break through to issues and contexts. This requires confidence which in turn comes from practice. Calling that Example A will allow this one to be 'B':

Here is a perfect chance to reflect upon the old and the new (and the old-fashioned and new-fangled, as both these magazines are currently in circulation). Again, a set of prompts might be the best place to get you started.

- Comment on the significant differences between these texts (Figures 7.10 and 7.11) at a production level: quality, context, the language of production.
- Examine the different ways in which they each address their audiences: who consumes, how are they addressed, how successful are they?
- What do they share as magazine covers?
- Comment on any issues of representation or ideology.
- In what ways has modern technology contributed to the meanings of both texts?

Figure 7.10 *Front cover of etc., issue 8, a magazine aimed at A Level students.*

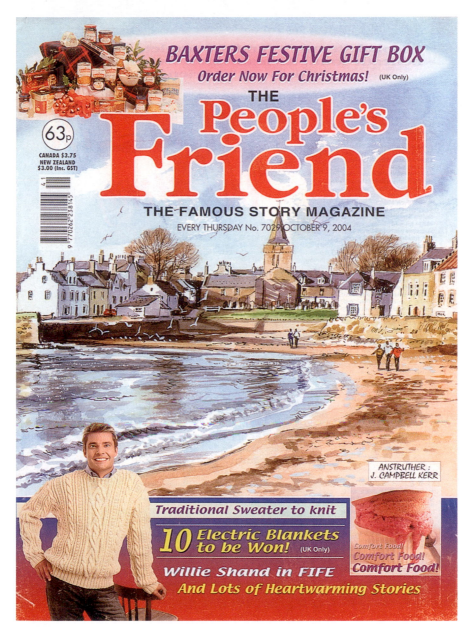

Figure 7.11 *Front cover of* The People's Friend, *Christmas special, 9 October 2004.*

Some final advice

To complete this chapter is to return to p. 186: 'Textual analysis is fine but it has limitations. There is a danger that it becomes virtuosity for its own sake.'

Remember that this is one of the places where your knowledge of wider contexts will be explored and tested. You must be prepared to engage with the texts only as a way of getting beyond them to a discussion of the forms, ideologies and issues of the media as a whole and in parts. It seems basic but any identified text will automatically furnish an important paradigm which can be addressed, whether it be newspapers, magazines or even television. The texts are intended to raise issues in the way all media texts do if we care to stop and think. They ask questions of our society and culture while at the same time downplaying their own role as messengers and meaning makers. It is our job as students of the media to ensure that these aspects are scrutinised and that all the implications are shared. Appropriately, that is also our job as citizens.

▼ 8 THEORETICAL PERSPECTIVES

In this chapter we shall discuss:

- the role of theory in media studies
- the popular culture debate
- semiotics
- poststructuralism
- postmodernism
- feminism
- queer theory
- Marxism
- liberal pluralism
- cultural imperialism and postcolonialism.

Throughout this book and, no doubt, throughout your Media Studies course, you have been discussing and applying theoretical perspectives. This is no place, then, to introduce theories. You have already used and explored them extensively. However, in a book about contexts, it is important to put theory into some kind of context as well as all those elements of the main object of our study, the mass media themselves. The discussions here are partly revision, partly critique and partly comparison of one theoretical position with another. Above all, though, this chapter attempts to explain and justify the use of theory as an indispensable way of opening our minds to all of the many and various meanings made available by the mass media.

If you are a Media student with a slightly jaundiced, perhaps even a cynical, view of theory, then you are not alone. Theory is not always the most popular part of a Media Studies course. For many, theory is seen as a tedious and abstract alternative to the 'nitty-gritty' of the subject, a boring and jargon-ridden sideshow to the main event. In this view theory is a strange concoction in which statements of the blindingly obvious are mixed with absurdly complex formulations which are almost impossible to understand.

You will not be surprised to learn that we disagree with this point of view. In fact, we'd like to argue that the 'theory is pointless' school of thought is itself a pretty good example of a theory. How so? Because it approaches a large and complex area – in this case Media Studies – and tries to make sense of it. It breaks Media Studies down into categories, theory and non-theory, and then it evaluates them. Theory, it concludes, is rubbish while non-theory is really quite excellent. Rather ironically, this is just what theories set out to do. They look at something which is complex and difficult to understand and try to make it comprehensible. They do this by, for example, breaking whatever it is down into its constituent parts and processes, categorising and labelling, offering causes and explanations, making connections between components and so on. Can you have a theory which claims that all theory is rubbish? Certainly you can, but we'd like to argue that it's not a very good theory. Apart from a certain logical incoherence, it's a theory that seems to duck out of asking difficult questions, that tells us just to accept things as they are. It's a theory which says that doing is always more important than understanding. We prefer theories that see doing and understanding as equal and complementary partners.

Rather annoyingly, theories often suggest that something which had always seemed perfectly simple and straightforward is actually complex. As we shall argue later, the mass media have a particular knack of making things seem so obvious and so natural that it would just be plain daft to criticise or ask for explanations. In these areas, especially, it is important to have theories which never take anything for granted, theories which ask *how* and *why* we see things as obvious or natural.

It is often said that modern life saturates us with information, that we are constantly surrounded by sources of stimulation which bombard our senses. The majority of this information takes the form of signs: pieces of information which *stand for* something other than themselves.

Sometimes, of course, we experience things very directly: the pain of twisting an ankle or the pleasure of resting after a hard day's work. But a great deal of information presents itself to us in the form of messages that we try to make sense of. All written and spoken language, for example, relies on learning and shared understanding. Visual images, whether they are photographs, paintings or television programmes, are two-dimensional. We have to learn how to recognise them and relate them to the world of our experience. Even the familiar objects of our daily lives can convey messages which have nothing to do with those objects' primary function. Chairs and tables, for example, may be plain or ornate, shabby or clean, made from natural or synthetic materials, co-ordinated or unco-ordinated, brightly coloured or dull, and so on. Invariably, we look for messages in these objects: messages about the objects' owners or the environment in which they are set; or, perhaps, messages about ourselves. We are always in search of meanings in everything we see, hear and touch (and even, come to that, what we smell and taste). We look for patterns to match up with our previous experience and understanding in order to make sense of the message. Secondly, we *expect* meanings to be indirect. For example, the clean-lined modern chair in a reception area *stands for* a dynamic, efficient organisation.

It is natural that you would like to be reassured about what you need to know about a subject, especially if you have to pass an exam at the end of the course. Media Studies does have a body of knowledge, but as we point out in Chapter 9, 'Passing Exams', it is much more about your ability to apply concepts to different texts, contexts, issues and debates. In consequence, defining a body of knowledge that you must know is neither possible nor desirable. It is, however, possible to suggest some ideas and theories that it would be useful for you to grasp, especially if you have to go into an exam room to demonstrate what you have learned about Media Studies. In this chapter we try to draw together some of the different theories and perspectives that have informed the development of Media and Cultural Studies into academic disciplines. Bear in mind that it is this theoretical base that distinguishes an informed and educated response from unsubstantiated opinions. Everybody has views and opinions about the mass media and we all enjoy a good argument about the strengths and weaknesses of films or pop singers, for example. The debates and discussions we have in Media Studies may be dealing with exactly the same topics but the context has changed to one in which we would expect more demanding criteria to be applied to the arguments. If it is useful, theory should supply these criteria, so that arguments based on sound theoretical foundations are more convincing and more insightful.

A word of caution is needed, though. Theory for its own sake is of dubious value. You need to be able to demonstrate that you have understood the theory and are able to apply it appropriately to the issues at hand. If you try to use terminology and ideas that you do not fully understand, your work will look at best contrived, at worst just silly. Assessment in Media Studies is based on your ability to relate theoretical perspectives to a range of texts and issues. The more confidently you are able to do this, the more convincing will be your work.

THE POPULAR CULTURE DEBATE

Media Studies is concerned primarily with what is known as popular culture. Popular culture consists of texts that have been created for consumption by mass audiences. Most television programmes are examples of popular culture, as are most newspapers, magazines and recorded music. Popular culture is sometimes referred to as low culture, a clearly pejorative term used to distinguish it from so-called high culture. Media Studies as an academic discipline is concerned primarily, but not exclusively, with popular culture texts. Of course, the distinction between high and low culture begs a lot of difficult questions, not least who decides which category best fits a particular text. Different theoretical perspectives take very different positions on the relationship between high culture and popular culture. For some Marxists, popular culture is a kind of drug which helps to distract the masses from an understanding of their own exploitation. For other theorists, popular culture offers an opportunity not only to understand but also to resist the structures of an unequal society. This debate is explored in more detail in Chapter 5, 'Audience'.

The popular culture debate also raises interesting questions about the *value* of cultural artefacts and media texts. We sometimes assume that texts have more value if they have 'stood the test of time'. This can be argued for centuries-old texts which are part of the literary and artistic canon such as Milton's *Paradise Lost* or da Vinci's *Mona Lisa*, but it is also an argument used to assert the 'classic' status of popular cultural texts such as Marvin Gaye's 'I Heard It Through the Grapevine' or the television sitcom *Fawlty*

Towers. One problem with the 'test of time' criterion is that it rules out contemporary texts by definition; it is impossible for a text to be simultaneously new and long-lasting. It also throws up some rather dubious examples. In terms of popular culture, *Carry On Nurse* and 'Chirpy Chirpy Cheep Cheep' are well-remembered and frequently revisited texts – but does this make them in any meaningful way 'better' than many less well-remembered films and songs?

Other contributors to the debate about the value of different texts have shifted the focus away from the texts themselves and towards the status of people who make influential value judgements. Looking at the 'canon' of great works of high culture, these critics ask why the work of women, non-white ethnic groups and non-Westerners is so under-represented. The conclusion often drawn is that the reason for the over-representation of 'dead, white European males' lies in the power structures of society rather than the quality of the work. Those in power assert the value of their favoured cultural products over all others. In this view, value has little to do with the text itself and everything to do with those who have the power to assign high or low status. In response to arguments such as this, the balance of power has begun to shift away from a traditional and exclusive 'canon' towards a version which is much more diverse and inclusive.

In contrast to the view that cultural value is simply a matter of elitism, others have argued that certain texts have an intrinsic worth which transcends the narrow self-interest of any group or individual, or even of any single culture. This kind of argument is often used to establish the innate superiority of high culture. The fact that a play or a painting, for example, is serious, difficult and inaccessible is seen as a virtue. Similar arguments are used in popular culture to differentiate between, say, alternative and chart music or 'highbrow' television and populist rubbish. The underlying idea is that the harder we have to work at retrieving meanings from the text, the greater our rewards will be. Low culture, on the other hand, is easy. It is superficial and therefore gives up its rewards very easily, but they are rewards which are shallow and insignificant compared to those available from high culture. Some versions of this argument have gone even further, to suggest that popular culture is positively harmful because it is emotionally and intellectually destructive.

Although this argument may have a bit more going for it than the 'test of time', it is difficult to escape from the rather snobbish connotations of 'difficult equals better'. As we saw in Chapter 4, 'Representation', simplicity can be an important quality of a text. A three-minute pop song may be based on predictable patterns and familiar structures, but it still has the capacity to be a really profound form of expression. Similarly, Chapter 3, 'Genre', showed how the constraints of formula and convention are not necessarily a barrier to creativity.

Postmodernists have yet another view on the issues raised in this debate. They have suggested that a feature of the contemporary 'postmodern condition' is the collapse of boundaries between high and low culture. This view is explored further later in this chapter.

These competing perspectives on popular culture are particularly significant for Media students because they touch on the thorny issue of relativism. The charge of relativism is often used by critics of Media Studies to attack the whole basis of the subject. Such critics argue that Media Studies has no objective basis; it is simply a collection of opinions, none of which has any more validity than any other because there is no agreed standard against which they can be assessed. In defence of Media Studies, we would argue that *all* knowledge and understanding is relative. There are no *absolute* truths or *absolute* standards, only useful agreements within a culture.

At this point it might be useful to try to explain what is meant by the word 'culture'. Dictionary definitions would lead us to believe that it is to do with socially transmitted behaviour patterns or the attitudes and behaviour of a particular class or group of people, as well as their intellectual activity in terms of art, for example, and the works they produce. Clearly, culture has something to do with the way in which a society decides what its values and beliefs are and the way in which these values and beliefs are transmitted through society. The media in particular and popular culture in general are central to this process of transmission. Much of the way in which we see the world is determined by our consumption of media texts. In terms of some media texts such as news bulletins and newspapers this is a fairly obvious link. In other texts, such as popular music, quiz shows or feature films, the relationship is more complex and more subtle. As you will see later in this chapter, it is even possible to argue that our very identities are shaped to a large degree by the media.

THE TOOLKIT OF THEORY

One of the key functions of media theory and more broadly cultural theory is to explore the relationship between the individual, the text and the transmission of culture and values within our society. Theory is little more than a toolkit that enables us to explore the ways in which media texts work in terms of both their production and their consumption. As a student, it is comforting to know just how much theory you need to have grasped in order to pass your exam. Unfortunately there is no simple answer to that question. So much will depend on precisely what you need to explore in terms of texts and contexts. In much the same way as if you are undertaking a repair job around the house or in the car, you will need a basic toolkit to get started. If you have other tools to hand, these may well be of use. The important thing is to use the right tool for the job and to use it correctly. So what do you need in your toolkit?

SEMIOTICS

The first item in any Media Studies toolkit has to be a grasp of semiotic theory. Semiotics deals with the production of meaning. A perfectly sensible view of meaning would say that as I am the writer of this sentence so I put the meaning into it and that you, the reader, are the receiver so you take the meaning out. However, semiotics does not see things in quite this way. Media texts are in essence a series of complex messages made up of signs. Semiotics is the science of understanding how signs work and how meaning emerges from the relationship between the sender and receiver.

Language and codes

The person most usually cited as the founder of semiotics is the Swiss linguist Ferdinand de Saussure (1857–1913). It may seem strange to put so much emphasis on language in a book about media, but the theoretical tools of Media Studies owe a great deal to the study of language (linguistics). This is evident in the use of expressions like 'the grammar of film', 'the language of television' or 'media literacy'. These sayings illustrate just how influential semiotic theory has been in establishing a key proposition: that all meaning systems such as film, television, photography, dress and appearance or ritual behaviour work in a very similar way to language. For this reason, all students of the mass media need to know a little, at least, about how language works.

Think about your own knowledge of the English language for a moment. If you can understand this sentence, you have a very good knowledge of an enormously sophisticated means of communication, whether or not you are a native speaker of English. You are able to express any number of ideas, opinions and emotions. You can explain, amuse, persuade and request information. You can describe complex processes and give simple directions. All of these can be achieved because you share with others a knowledge of language. Language is a code which works because a group of people (and in the case of the English language, it's a very big group) enjoy a shared understanding of its mechanisms. Understanding this code called the English language is not just a matter of knowing the meanings of a few hundred words. Of course it is important that English speakers broadly agree about the definitions of the words we use, but it is just as important that we are able to put words together into more complex chains of meaning such as sentences. Putting words together in this way depends on a grasp of the *rules* of language. Our knowledge of these rules enables us to express ourselves in the past, the present or the future. We are able to move from certainty ('I will come and see you tonight') to conditionality ('I may come and see you tonight'). We are so familiar with these rules that we are hardly even aware of them as we communicate using language. Often, the complexity of grammar is only appreciated as we try to learn another language. For our first language, though, we learn these rules and the meanings of words at a fairly young age, usually with little difficulty.

Simply put, then, language is a code which consists of signs (words) and a set of rules (grammar). Semiotics applies exactly the same model to all kinds of communication. Television, for example, includes signs such as type of shot, settings, graphics, camera movement, music and so on. It also draws upon a set of rules about how to assemble these signs into meaningful chains such as sequences, trailers or programmes. Just as we assimilate the code of language as we grow up, we also assimilate the code of television. Both of these codes change over time: the English language we use today is not quite the same as the English of fifty years ago, nor is today's television based on quite the same rules and signs as television of the 1950s.

In one sense, language is a part of television – one of the codes which operates within television. It is often helpful to break down a complex medium such as television into the various different codes which feature alongside language in a television text. These include the codes of narrative, codes of setting, and generic and editing codes, for example. The same can be said of other media as well. Advertising posters, films, magazines, radio shows and newspapers all draw on a variety of codes which are shared by producers and readers in order to communicate. Semiotics helps us to focus on signs and codes in different contexts in order to understand how meaning is generated.

STRUCTURALISM

Before returning to consider semiotics in more detail, this is a good point at which to consider the idea of structuralism. This approach also owes a good deal to Saussure and is closely linked to semiotic theory. We have already discussed how language (and other communication systems) relies on a shared understanding of 'rules' – even though language users may not be conscious of the use of these rules. As we are not usually aware that we are applying rules in our use of language, there would be little point in a linguist asking us what these rules are. Instead, linguists very carefully observe and record what people actually say, the surface structures of speech, in order to work out what the underlying rules are: the *deep structures* of language. Structuralists take the same approach to all other forms of communicative behaviour. By looking very closely at, say, a particular film genre, structuralists would claim to work out the deep structures being employed. Exactly as is the case with language, it would come as no surprise to find that neither the film-makers nor the film audiences were aware of these deep structures.

It seems perfectly sensible to argue that language is a cultural phenomenon; why else would kids in France grow up to speak French while kids in Chile grow up to speak Spanish? We might expect media codes to work in much the same way, so that a full knowledge and understanding of, say, Brazilian *telenovelas* (TV soaps) or Indian film would be confined to people who have grown up with or, at least, learned the rules of these codes. This view, cultural relativism, is not entirely shared by structuralists. The linguist Noam Chomsky argues that all children have an innate capacity to learn language. He calls this a Language Acquisition Device. It is as if all humans are hardwired like a new computer, ready to accept the software of the particular language to which they are exposed. This has led linguists to search for language 'universals': aspects of deep structure that are common to all languages. In anthropology, for example, Claude Lévi-Strauss searched for the principles common to all cultures and myths. In Media Studies, similar ideas have been used in approaches to narrative. Structuralists have investigated narrative using versions of the *binary oppositions* proposed by Lévi-Strauss to explore the possibility that all storytelling has deep structures. Examples of binary opposites include:

Culture	:	Nature
Man	:	Woman
Inside	:	Outside
Good	:	Evil

A structuralist analysis of a television drama would examine the ways in which tensions between these (and other) oppositions are introduced and resolved in the text. Also, the analysis would look for evidence of universal features of narrative development, such as those proposed by Vladimir Propp or Tzvetan Todorov. The idea is that the surface structure of drama has a deeper underlying resonance which helps to give us, the audience, reinforcement of our culture's 'rules' and expectations.

Structuralism has informed the approach to media analysis in both narrative and genre. Narratives offer us a limited range of character typologies, for example, hence we get stock characters in sitcoms and soaps. Genre offers us a similar idea that ranges more broadly, encompassing groups of texts and categorising them according to the characteristics they have in common. In searching for the underlying themes or characteristics which define a genre for both producers and audiences, we are looking for the deep structures or 'blueprints' underlying what actually appears on the screen.

Structuralism was highly influential in the 1960s and 1970s and became closely associated with some variants of Marxism such as those developed by Louis Althusser (see below, p. 235). More recently, though, the search for deep structures that are universal to all cultures has stimulated less interest than more relativist perspectives such as poststructuralism.

Signs and codes

What makes semiotics so important in Media Studies is the fact that it is primarily concerned with the receiver end of the meaning equation. Semiotics concerns itself with how audiences make meanings from messages. Perhaps the key term in semiotic analysis is reading. Reading has connotations of being active. To read something implies that you bring some interpretation or imagination to whatever it is you are considering in the same way as when you read a book. The idea of reading, therefore, privileges the audience, suggesting that what it brings to the text is as important, if not more important, than what the producer put into the text when it was created. Ultimately it can be argued that every single person's reading of a text is potentially different from everyone else's. Semiotics does, however, acknowledge that there are certain ways in which the meaning of texts can in some way be limited. Although our reading of any text is likely to be determined by our cultural background and our life experiences, texts can be created in such a way as to close down the number of potential readings that a text may be open to. Meaning can be anchored in a variety of different ways such that the meanings available in a text are finite and audiences are given a strong push into one area of interpretation. One way in which meanings can be limited is by how we derive pleasure from media texts. Many people enjoy Hollywood films. Even people who may not agree with the underlying philosophy of the film are often able to sit through a Hollywood movie and derive pleasure from it. Similarly, people who profess to dislike reality TV programmes on the grounds that they are demeaning, often find themselves hooked into watching episodes of the latest show. Devices such as narrative, genre expectation, recognition and identification are all likely to be at play in contributing to the pleasures available from texts like Hollywood films and reality TV programmes.

So the argument goes that sign systems share certain underlying structures and as human beings we learn to read these sign systems. In it is interesting to note that young children very often seem to be able to learn to read television before they can learn to read the written word. What we learn is to understand the codes by which television communicates to us. The problem is that these codes become so natural to us that we no longer recognise them as codes. Similarly, the conventions of most media products are basically the same. The structure of most newspapers and magazines has a good deal in common with that of other newspapers and magazines, even down to where we can expect to find specific items.

POSTSTRUCTURALISM

Poststructuralism takes up where structuralism leaves off. As we have noted, structuralists take the view that there are underlying structures or deep structures at work in all forms of communication and cultural behaviour. Poststructuralists are not at all interested in discovering these underlying principles because they do not accept the basic idea of deep structures. The search for meaning and coherence in texts is pointless, they argue, because meaning is just too slippery ever to pin down. As Rob Pope puts it:

> Whereas a structuralist approach would tend to treat a sign-system as a complete, finished, potentially knowable whole with a notional centre, a *post*structuralist approach would tend to treat a sign-system as an incomplete, unfinished and ultimately unknowable fragment with many potential centres or no centre at all.
>
> (Pope 1998: 124)

Structuralism seems to suggest that once we have discovered the underlying characteristics of a text, we can open it up to discover its meaning. Poststructuralists question the notion that this supposed meaning exists in the first place. The chief contribution to dealing with media texts made by the poststructuralists is their emphasis on the interpretation of texts rather than their production.

Poststructuralists have been responsible for extending the term 'text' to include anything that communicates in any way. We have already become used to the idea that a text can be any media product, but poststructuralists see culture in its entirety as a text which can be read. The analytical technique used by poststructuralists is called 'deconstruction', but the intention here is not to find out what the 'real' meaning is. Instead, the purpose of deconstruction is to explore the assumptions made by the text. These intentions may have very little to do with the intentions of the sender or author (hence the expression 'death of the author'). There may be so many interpretations that the 'meaning' of the text is unstable and temporary.

So what do we look for in a text when performing this kind of analysis? Ironically, deconstruction often involves a consideration of what is absent: the missing elements of the text. For example, the deconstruction of, say, magazine advertisements would involve a discussion of those types of people who are excluded from the images. Another technique of deconstruction is called *foregrounding*. This means moving the apparently trivial or insignificant elements of the text to the centre of the stage for our inspection. What is taken for granted in a text is often more evident in the background detail than in the carefully constructed foreground, so by inverting these we may learn more about the assumptions made by the text. These absences, gaps, silences and marginalia (background elements) help to reveal what the text is privileging. For example, West may be privileged over East, man over woman, science over nature, language over pictures. At its best, deconstruction can offer powerful insights into the workings of imperialist, colonialist or patriarchal discourses. At its worst, it can seem to privilege nonsense over sense.

Poststructuralists argue that without an audience a text has no meaning. Consider, for example, a film being projected in an auditorium at your local multiplex. If no one turns up to sit and watch the film, can that film be said to have any meaning? The poststructuralists' argument is that it is the audience that will bring unity to that text and hence give it meaning. Without an audience the text can have no meaning. Therefore, to suggest that there is a meaning in the text before it is seen by an audience is ridiculous. Of course the ultimate extension of the argument is that the text has the meaning that the audience chooses to give it. That places the audience in a powerful position and takes us a long way from the process model in which the producer determined the meaning of the text and the audiences were mere passive receivers of it. You may at this point wish to consider some of the ways in which this idea links closely to some of the theories of audience that you may already have looked at in Chapter 5, 'Audience'. Certainly one of the movements in audience theory was from the notion of passive and receptive audiences waiting to be injected with media messages which they would accept uncritically, to a model in which the audience is seen as both active and proactive in their use of the media. Pleasure becomes a key element in the dynamic relationship between producer, text and audience, with one aim of the audience being to maximise the pleasure that it can take from a media text, often regardless of the intention of the producer.

Many poststructuralist ideas are remote and difficult to grasp. Jacques Derrida, for example, argued that words are inadequate because they are so difficult to pin down in terms of their meaning: he would cross them out to indicate their frailty. It is, however, precisely this idea of the uncertainty of meaning that has made poststructuralism of such value to Media Studies. The argument goes that we are to a large extent defined by the language we use and by extension the media texts we consume. Hence not only the way in which we see the world but ultimately our very identities are determined by these cultural forces. Given that they are so unreliable and slippery in the meanings that they offer us, our very identities become uncertain themselves. It is as though the landmarks that we rely on to determine our own position, or identity, are so fickle that we are in danger of losing our own sense of who we are. Interestingly, this argument is perhaps much more scary than the hypodermic needle propaganda model, not least because there are no longer any certainties, any fixed meanings, even about ourselves.

POSTMODERNISM

One of the great attractions of postmodernism, in the eyes of many Media students, is that it roundly dismisses almost all the other theories on the grounds of irrelevance. According to postmodernists, any theory which makes claims about universal or underlying truths is just missing the point. And the point is that contemporary society and culture are so fragmented, so diverse, so full of differences, that no unified theory could possibly explain such a melting pot. This is what is meant by the 'rejection of metanarratives'.

Another of postmodernism's 'rejections' is the idea of cultural value: the notion that some cultural practices and products are simply and intrinsically *better* than others. This is certainly a convenient way of short-circuiting the popular culture debate described earlier.

Popular culture is no longer seen as the poor relation but simply as another means of expression. So rap music stands on a par with Shakespeare's sonnets. Bricolage, literally French for 'do it yourself', is privileged as a creative act: plundering the canon of 'great works' is playfully subversive. Above all, postmodernism abandons any notion of attempting to be new and different perhaps because the media universe is such a large space to fill that recycling the past is inevitable. We can see evidence of this kind of bricolage and recycling everywhere: pop songs which sample riffs and licks from the 'classics' of popular or serious music, the 'instant nostalgia' of television programmes like *Heartbeat*, advertising's appropriation of the icons of visual arts such as *The Scream* or *The Laughing Cavalier*. Of course, the meanings originally attached to these 'borrowings' from the past can be accepted, rejected or manipulated, often in the name of 'postmodern irony'. Lads' magazines, stand-up comedians, schlock films and homophobic rap artists have all dismissed the criticism that they are being offensive and tasteless on the grounds that they are expressing a form of 'postmodern chic'. Although it is difficult to pin down the precise meaning of postmodernism, there are at least three aspects which make it a particularly valuable conceptual tool for considering twenty-first-century media texts. The first is its interest in style over substance. Postmodernism concerns itself primarily with surfaces. As you will be aware, the media consist largely of 'shiny surfaces' that give the illusion of depth, like a film set. The form of a film or an 'alternative' CD may give us the impression that it is weighty and meaningful, but this impression may very well be limited to the form rather than the content; the text *looks* very significant, but that is as far as it goes. A postmodernist take on this would be to say 'So what? What you see is what you get.' In other words, we shouldn't even expect depth or meaningfulness. Just as there are no 'deep structures', there are no 'underlying meanings'; the signifier has detached itself from the signified. The cultural form which exemplifies this approach perfectly is the pop video. A dense array of suggestive signifiers may be compiled, drawing on all sorts of cultural reference points. But what does it all mean? If you are asking the question, you have already missed the point!

A second useful aspect of postmodernism is the way it conceptualises the relationship between the media and reality. One of the key figures in postmodern theory, Jean Baudrillard, has suggested three principles for understanding contemporary reality: simulation, implosion and hyperreality. For Baudrillard, we live in an era of media saturation in which we are bombarded with information and signs. So much of our experience is in the form of media texts rather than first-hand, direct experience that the signs become 'more real than real'. This is *simulation*: the part of our lives that is dominated by television, computer games, DVD, Internet chatrooms, magazines and all the other image suppliers. This is a very big part of many people's lives, maybe even the biggest and most important part. Consequently, Baudrillard argues, the distinction between reality and simulation breaks down altogether: we make no distinction between real experience and simulated experience. This is *implosion*. Hyperreality refers to the condition where the distinction between them has not only blurred, but the 'image' part has started to get the upper hand.

Here is an example which may help to explain the rather baffling concept of hyperreality. Let's imagine that I have never visited Paris. In spite of this I have a huge fund of impressions based on the simulations of Paris that I have seen in films and on television, usually to the accompaniment of accordion music. I have looked at magazines, travel brochures and my friends' holiday snaps. I have read about the entertainment, the food and the nightlife. The simulated Paris I know so well is a vibrant, exciting and stimulating city. One day, I decide to visit Paris for the first time. It is drizzling, my hotel room is cramped and dirty, nobody is particularly friendly and I get ripped off in a restaurant. Now I have a fund of rather negative 'real' experiences to add to my very positive simulated experiences. Which of these will win out to form my overall impression of Paris? If Baudrillard is right, they will all merge into one undifferentiated set of experiences, but the image-based simulations will be just that little bit more powerful than my direct experience. My Paris is hyperreal.

Finally, postmodernism is about playfulness. Taking ideas, styles and designs and playing with them is one of the hallmarks of postmodernism, particularly in such disciplines as architecture where postmodern buildings are recognisable for their witty designs. In the media this playfulness is evident, as we have discussed in Chapter 1 'Wider Contexts', in the way in which reality television extends the idea of playing with surveillance cameras.

It can sometimes be helpful to distinguish between optimistic and pessimistic postmodernism. The former embraces the enormous range of diversity in contemporary culture without finding a need to analyse and explain. It celebrates pleasure and playfulness and the debunking of traditional 'rules' about how we should behave or what we should like. Pessimistic postmodernism, on the other hand, is more likely to focus on the breakdown of meanings and the domination of simulation. Critics of postmodernism are scornful of the way in which postmodernists seem to sidestep issues of material inequality, poverty and deprivation.

FEMINISM

It is worth emphasising at this stage that most of the theoretical perspectives we are dealing with in this chapter do not see Media Studies as their main focus of attention. This is particularly the case with feminism. Feminists are not feminists because they want to analyse media texts but because they want to challenge the unfair and unequal distribution of power and wealth in patriarchal society. A patriarchy is a society based on male rule and male domination.

Feminism, then, is a political project which seeks to challenge power structures and change the roles and perceptions of women. In common with other perspectives such as Marxism and postcolonialism, a part of this political project is to understand how power works because without this understanding it is almost impossible to get things changed. This is why feminists have made such an important contribution to Media Studies. If the mass media play an important part in the reinforcement of patriarchal ideology, then it is essential to see how this process works, to criticise it and to find ways of using the media to propose alternatives to patriarchy.

Feminists are particularly interested in the contribution made by the media to society's dominant ideas about gender roles. You are probably familiar with the idea that gender and sex are dissimilar categories. Sex is a matter of biological differences to do with chromosomes, hormones and reproductive systems. Gender, in contrast, is about the cultural distinctions which we learn to make between masculinity and femininity. In other words, our sex (male or female) is determined at (or, really, before) birth, but we still have to learn how to think and behave as a girl or as a boy according to the expectations of our culture. As we shall see later, some theorists have cast serious doubts over this sex/gender distinction, but it is still an important point of departure for understanding the relationship between feminism and media studies.

It is widely acknowledged from many different theoretical positions that the mass media play a crucial role in socialisation, in teaching us how to behave and think in ways that our culture finds acceptable. A significant part of this socialisation process is to provide answers to the questions 'What does it mean to be a woman?' and 'What does it mean to be a man?' Of course, the answers to these questions are not always exactly the same, but we are all familiar with the kind of gender stereotypes so often reinforced by media representations. Rather crudely expressed, they look something like this:

Femininity	Masculinity
Caring	Tough
Nurturing	Providing
Emotional	Rational
Domestic, home-orientated	Public, work-orientated
Sensitive	Thick-skinned
Passive	Active
Gentle	Rough
Soft	Hard

You will probably look at these stereotypes and find them embarrassingly out of date, but the point is that they still describe very familiar versions of masculinity and femininity. Furthermore, it is easy to see how these qualities are associated with power. The list of stereotypically masculine attributes are also linked with influential roles, political leadership, higher status and well-paid jobs. The stereotypically feminine qualities are associated with lower status and more poorly paid work such as child care, nursing and teaching.

Everybody agrees that gender roles and representations have changed rapidly in recent years, largely because feminists have made a good deal of progress in eroding the stereotypes described above. But have they been replaced by different though equally disempowering stereotypes? In the view of some feminists, the key site of struggle has moved away from the attribution of low-value qualities towards the visual presentation of the body. In an influential book *The Beauty Myth*, Naomi Wolf wrote: 'Beauty is a currency like the gold standard. Like any economy, it is determined by politics and in the modern age in the West, it is the last, best belief system that keeps male domination intact' (Wolf 1991: 10).

Wolf argued that images of ultra-thin supermodels and the 'perfect bodies' glamorised by advertising, fashion and the media in general are indications of a patriarchal attack on women's bodies. Women's bodies and female sexuality have become commodities and the consequences of this are mental and physical illness, starvation diets and eating disorders.

The idea of the female body as an object was also explored by Laura Mulvey in an influential essay 'Visual Pleasure and Narrative Cinema' (1975). She conceived the term 'male gaze' to emphasise the extent to which so much of our media output (she was particularly interested in film) assumes that the spectator is male or constructs reality from a male point of view, from a set of largely masculine assumptions. Her idea was that the darkened cinema offered the perfect opportunity for the male viewer to drool over the erotic exhibition of women's bodies on the screen. Because female characters are invariably insignificant to the plot, female viewers also identify with the male character, enjoying the spectacle of women through his eyes. This idea, that the media encourage women to see themselves through the eyes of men, was also developed by Angela McRobbie in relation to girls' magazines. In a 1979 essay on *Jackie* magazine, McRobbie argued that the magazine worked alongside other socialising influences to reinforce an obsession with romance:

> The Jackie girl is alone in her quest for love; she refers back to her female peers for advice, comfort and reassurance only when she needs to do so or when she has nothing better to do. . . . To achieve self-respect, the girl has to escape the 'bitchy', 'catty' atmosphere of female company and find a boyfriend as quickly as possible. But in doing this she cannot slide into complacency. Her ruthlessly individualistic outlook must be retained in case she has to fight to keep him.
>
> (McRobbie 1991: 131)

Both Mulvey and McRobbie have found good reasons to modify their views in more recent years. To some extent, such changes of heart reflect the growing disillusionment with 'effects' theory which we discussed in Chapter 5, 'Audience'. Just as significantly, though, the landscape of gender representation in the media has changed enormously since the 1970s, not least because of the campaigns and critiques of feminist activists. As Gauntlett points out:

> Men and women are seen working side by side, as equals, in the hospitals, schools and police stations of television land. Movie producers are wary of having women as screaming victims, and have realised that kick-ass heroines do better business. Advertisers have by now realised that audiences will only laugh at images of the pretty housewife, and have reacted by showing women how to be sexy at work instead.
>
> (Gauntlett 2002: 57)

To acknowledge that these changes have taken place is not necessarily to say that the battle is over. Recent debates between second-wave feminists and postfeminists (see the Notebox below) have focused on the amount of progress that has been made. Some second-wave feminists have viewed the developments described opposite with a certain amount of cynicism and suspicion. They argue that many battles for economic and workplace equality have still to be fought and won, and that representations of strong, assertive women may be little more than marketing ploys. For example, powerful, independent female role models have become commonplace in car adverts as the automotive industry opens up a lucrative new market of female consumers.

Postfeminists, on the other hand, may well take a very different position on adverts such as these. What is wrong, they argue, with women expressing themselves in any number of different ways, whether through buying cars, clothes, make-up or anything else? If men can have fun with the products of consumer capitalism and popular culture, then why can't women do the same thing without being accused of being the dupes of patriarchy? If women *know* that femininity is a construct, then they can play with its signs, symbols and identities from a position of power. This is the territory of *semiotic guerrilla warfare* where the meanings of signifiers such as high heels, lipstick and designer clothes can be shifted from *powerless* to *powerful*.

NOTEBOX

The waves of feminism

First wave

From the mid-nineteenth to early twentieth century feminist activism was focused on the fight for social and political equality. The struggle for women's suffrage (the right to vote) was particularly hard fought.

Second wave

This was the liberation movement of the 1960s and 1970s (and beyond). It was characterised by struggles for equal pay, equal rights at work and better representation in public bodies like Parliament. Second-wave feminists established a very strong tradition of academic scholarship.

Third wave

The generation of feminists who grew up in the 1980s and 1990s have put less emphasis on battles for equality and more emphasis on the positive nature of ambiguity and difference. (Not all women are the same, it doesn't matter.) Third-wave feminists have links to postmodernism and postcolonialism and, in questioning the nature of gender difference, to queer theory.

continued

QUEER THEORY

In the introduction to feminist theory we looked at the contrast between sex (biological difference) and gender (culturally learned difference). This basic distinction is rejected by queer theory. Queer theory offers the view that all identities are social constructions; the ideas of 'male' and 'female' are just as much the product of representations as masculinity and femininity. Although often misconstrued, queer theory does not concern itself exclusively with homosexuality; it is about all forms of identity, especially those linked to sexuality.

Like feminism, queer theory is a political and cultural project, not just another way of analysing representations. In this case, the project is to subvert and undermine conventional attitudes to sexuality. Much of queer theory is heavily influenced by Judith Butler's book *Gender Trouble* (1990) and the title itself gives some indication of the theory's key objective: to break the link between the categories of 'sex' and 'gender' so that all forms of sexual identity can be accepted and celebrated. In order to do this, queer theory attacks the binary oppositions which underlie many traditional ideas about sexuality, for example man/woman, active/passive, gay/straight. Butler rejects the idea that any of us have an innate sexual identity. Instead, she focuses on *performance*, so that repeated performances and representations of heterosexuality will create the illusion that heterosexuality is not only 'normal' but right. On the other hand, performances and representations of alternatives such as drag queens, 'butch' lesbians, 'camp' gays and macho gays have the capacity to subvert and 'denaturalise' dominant heterosexual ideology.

Does queer theory have a role in understanding the mass media? It certainly offers us some interesting perspectives and lines of enquiry when we examine representations and identity. You could argue that 'gender trouble' is evident everywhere in the mainstream, let alone the alternative, media. Gay and lesbian characters appear in fictional narratives without self-evident tokenism. (A 'token' gay character would simply represent the liberal values of the programme-maker and little else.) Drag, camp comedy and references to transgressive sexuality (such as sado-masochism) are all commonplace on early evening television. Celebrities no longer feel that it is essential for them to project 'all man' or 'all woman' images of unambiguous heterosexuality.

But do these trends signify a move towards increasing tolerance of sexual diversity, as queer theory would suggest? Maybe so, but we should also consider other more cynical interpretations. Some have argued that representations such as these simply present titillating, transgressive alternatives to the 'norm' of heterosexuality. Images of alternatives to 'normal' heterosexuality are used because of their shock value, not because of any desire to promote or celebrate diversity. Ultimately, representations of alternative sexualities only draw lines in the sand which reinforce the dominance of conventional heterosexuality. Proponents of this side of the argument might point to the ease with which drag and camp have been successfully and unthreateningly incorporated into mainstream entertainment. Does anyone really believe that the pantomime dame or the camp character in a television sitcom does anything to subvert gender categories?

Like most theories, queer theory does not provide all the answers but it opens up new ideas and, inevitably, new conflicts and debates.

MARXISM

It may seem strange that the ideas of an economist and philosopher who died in 1883 should have any relevance to an understanding of today's mass media. After all, the mass media in any form other than printing did not even exist at the time when Karl Marx was writing. Furthermore, many have argued that Marxism has become totally irrelevant since 1989. Why 1989? Because this was the year that the Berlin Wall came down, signalling the decline and fall of Communism in Eastern Europe. The film *Goodbye Lenin!* (director Wolfgang Becker, 2003) provides a fascinating insight into events just before and after the destruction of the Berlin Wall. Immediately before this period almost half the world's population lived in countries whose political system was described as Communism, a political philosophy indelibly associated with Marx. Marx, of course, was the author of one of the most influential books ever written, *The Communist Manifesto* (1848). In it he wrote: 'Workers of all lands unite, you have nothing to lose but your chains.'

Many workers and political activists were inspired by the vision of Communism and they struggled for decades to overthrow established ruling classes. Their greatest success was the Russian Revolution of 1917 which established the era of Communism in Russia. Subsequently China, Eastern Europe, Cuba and many other national liberation movements embraced Communism as a principle for social and political organisation. Within just seventy years of the Russian Revolution, though, Communist regimes began to falter. Marx had always regarded capitalism as a fundamentally unfair and corrupt way to organise society but it seemed that by 1989 capitalism had triumphed over its Communist adversaries. Even China has begun to move towards some of the key principles of capitalism: competition, profit making and free enterprise. Where capitalism finds itself challenged in the modern world, the threat is more likely to come in the form of political movements which Marx abhorred: nationalism and religious fundamentalism.

In view of this, why should we even bother with Marxism as a theoretical perspective? The main reason lies in the explanatory power of Marx's ideas. Although Marx himself argued that the 'purpose of philosophy is not to understand the world but to change it', his work has probably been most influential as a means of interpreting the world. We cannot do justice to the depth and breadth of Marxism as a perspective here, but a basic familiarity with this approach is essential to the understanding of media theory. As we shall see, 'Marxism' does not just refer to the ideas of Karl Marx himself, but to a huge body of work generated by numerous academics, scholars and revolutionaries who have adapted Marx's ideas. Unsurprisingly, there are many disputes and differences of opinion among those who describe themselves as Marxists.

In Marx's view all social and cultural institutions such as the family, the education system and the legal system as well as the mass media are shaped by the economic basis of society. This means that an understanding of the economic sphere is essential to any understanding of the role played by the mass media in society. For our purposes, this means that we need to know something of the ways in which capitalism works. In capitalist economies, one group of people (the ruling class or bourgeoisie) own the capital (money) to invest in factories, offices, machinery, new technology and land; in other words, in almost all those things necessary to produce wealth. The one thing that this group of people does not own is sufficient labour to create profitable products and services. Labour is owned by the second and much larger group in society, the working classes (or proletariat) who sell this labour in order to survive. Labour may be manual or intellectual, so that in Marxist terms the tractor driver, the neurosurgeon and the most highly paid footballer are all members of the working class. However much (or little) workers are paid for their labour, there must always be a 'profit margin' so that the true value of the workers' labour is not returned to them. This is why Marxists see a conflict in the material interests of the two classes; the capitalist class wants to pay as little as possible for labour, while it is in the interests of the working class to have the full value of their labour. This is the crux of the Marxist analysis of the mass media. Capitalism, in this view, has little to offer the working class as it fails to rewards their efforts adequately and often ensures that the satisfaction or pride gained from paid employment is minimal. Social institutions like the mass media play a key role in ensuring that the working class remain happy with their situation despite the inherent unfairness of the system. Marx described the situation in which members of subordinate class cannot see that they are being duped as 'false consciousness'.

We have already explored some of the complexities of the concept of ideology. In Marxist terms, though, ideology can be defined fairly simply. It consists of the lies, deceptions and misinformation peddled to the working classes in order to maintain the state of 'false consciousness' which prevents workers from seeing their true or material interests. If we apply this approach in a crude but straightforward way to the mass media it would suggest that:

- the institutions of the mass media are owned by the ruling class
- institutions of the mass media are used to indoctrinate the masses into a belief that capitalism and its values are 'good for all'
- workers in media industries are exploited by the owners just as in any other industry.

In other words, the function of the mass media is not just to make money for the owners but also to serve the ideological interests of the ruling class. Ideology masks the conflict between classes and promotes the view that the inequalities and inefficiencies of capitalism are 'natural' or 'common sense'.

One thing that Marx argued as an outcome of ideology was the alienation of 'wage-slaves' (the proletariat/working class) from the means of production (control of the production of wealth). In modern industrial societies, Marx claimed, there is often a disconnection between the maker and what is made. Nowhere perhaps is this more significantly true than in media industries where the identification of privileged individuals (writers, directors, stars) plays down the roles of thousands of others. A Marxist perspective might emphasise the ways in which this reinforces the ideological practice whereby key values of capitalism, like individualism and hierarchy, are headlined to the detriment of oppositional elements like collectivism. How many films can you think of in which a group of people (a trade union, perhaps) act heroically to overcome problems and triumph over evil? For every one of these you can probably think of dozens in which the hero is a lone individual who defies the odds to win through.

Put at its crudest, this theory says that great films, for example, are the results of genius directors and not of the co-operation of colleagues working in a significant team: competition rather than collaboration. Of course everyone knows that there is a long list at the end of films and television programmes (or close to the contents pages of glossy magazines) but this does little to redress the imbalance even if we stay in the cinema long enough to read it.

KEY TERM

THE AUTEUR THEORY Conceived by a group of French intellectuals and film critics in the 1950s, the auteur theory suggests that films (or at least some of them) are 'authored', most conventionally by the director who usually exercises artistic control. This extremely influential theory launched an era of hot-shot directors which has lasted on and off for over fifty years. This has made the serious consideration of films as art more straightforward since it identifies an artist. But at what cost? Many film-makers are outspoken critics of this approach since it undermines the creative contributions of a host of tradesmen and technicians. Some directors such as Quentin Tarantino and Steven Spielberg receive star billing in the promotion of their films while others are more anonymous.

One of the attractions of a Marxist approach is its underlying simplicity: the function of the mass media is to disseminate ruling-class ideology. However, as we saw in Chapter 5, 'Audience', the simplicity of this analysis is also its weakness; it just doesn't seem capable of capturing the subtleties and complexities of the relationships between media institutions, texts and audiences. The notion of false consciousness is particularly problematic as it carries the assumption that the mass of the population are just too stupid to realise that they are being duped. The associated idea of a passive, powerless and reactive audience has been rejected by most theorists, and latter-day Marxist commentators have tended to utilise elements of structuralism in order to develop more sophisticated analytical tools. Three theorists have been particularly influential in this way: Voloshinov, Gramsci and Althusser.

For the Russian linguist Voloshinov, there are no meanings outside culture. We only interpret words, images, clothes, behaviour in the context of our own culture; there are no 'natural' meanings. It is the work of ideology to try and 'fix' these meanings, but in order to do so other possible interpretations must be negated. This directly contradicts the idea that one sort of consciousness can be 'false' while another can be 'true' because all meanings are the product of ideological struggles. This directs us towards a rather different interpretation of the role of the media from the 'classic' Marxist account outlined earlier. The economic sphere is still important, but it is no longer the 'bottom line', because our understanding of the world can be influenced by many other factors including the mass media. The mass media are where ideological struggles over the meanings of signs are fought out. Crucially, this is why the meanings of signs and of media texts change over time. The use of racist and sexist stereotypes in television light entertainment of the 1950s, 1960s and 1970s did not strike viewers of the time in the same way as they strike us when we look at them today. This is because long, hard struggles over the meanings of these texts have forced a change in what is regarded as 'normal' or 'acceptable'. Voloshinov helps us to understand that 'normality' and 'acceptability' are themselves constructs, the temporary outcomes of ideological battles.

The Italian writer, Antonio Gramsci, provides a useful slant on Marxist teaching to bring into focus the way in which the culture industries, including the media, can be used as a means of social control to ensure that the ruling classes maintain their hold on power within a society. Gramsci uses the word hegemony to describe this process. The concept of hegemony implies that the media are one means by which people are persuaded to behave in a way that is favourable to the interests of the elite groups which hold power within society. Rather than relying on force, for example the army and the police, dominant groups exert control by persuading the proletariat that the way that society is organised and power is distributed is in fact in their interests. Thus they secure the consent of subordinate groups by creating a consensus. In many cases this consent may well not be to the advantage of the subordinate groups and it is possible they are actually being persuaded to act against their own interests.

This may not seem very much different from the view of ideology advanced by 'classical' Marxism, but as the discussion in Chapter 5, 'Audience', shows, Gramsci's concept of hegemony is particularly helpful in understanding how a ruling elite goes about the business of exercising social control. Invariably, the ruling bloc is made up of a series of alliances: disparate groups with different agendas which have to be welded together in order to present a shared understanding of the world. In Gramsci's conception, the dominant class is not like a huge, impregnable machine which efficiently snuffs out all opposition. Instead, the hegemonic bloc is a collection of groups and individuals in loose alliance; some of its members are in the ascendancy and some are in decline. Sometimes subordinate groups are drawn into the alliance while former members are evicted. These changes in the ruling group are in response to the ideological attacks by subordinate groups. Hegemony is certainly a goal, but it is one that can never be fully achieved. Ruling groups are engaged in a constant struggle for ideological domination. As in a military war, there are advances and retreats, battles won and battles lost, alliances made and then broken but unlike a military war there is no possibility of an end point, no conclusive victory or defeat.

Once again, this offers us a helpful insight into the relationship between the media and the ruling class. Like Voloshinov, we see the media as a location where ideological battles take place rather than a means of brainwashing the masses. We need not be surprised to see ideological disputes within the ruling bloc taking place in the pages of newspapers or on the screens of television. Think about how the mass media have handled three very different but highly contentious issues in British politics in recent years: intervention in Iraq, swapping the pound for the euro and the banning of fox hunting. It would be difficult to sustain an argument that the media have smoothly slipped into gear to propagate ruling-class ideology in each of these cases. Newspapers have taken different positions; politicians and pundits have poured out vitriol on the radio and television. There is no clear consensus but there is evidence of the kind of ideological struggle in which competing forces seek to formulate new versions of 'common sense'. Hegemony theory directs our attention to the use of signs, connotations, myths and meaning making as weapons in these battles to win consent.

Like every theoretical position, Gramscian hegemony theory has its detractors as well as its advocates. Critics have argued that there is no coherent 'dominant culture' of any description and that we need look no further than economic imbalances to understand power differences in society.

Louis Althusser is another Marxist theorist who moves away from the idea that the economy is the 'bottom line' in all explanations of society and culture. The mass media play a key role in the ideological system whereby individuals are 'constituted as subjects'. The 'subjects' here are all of us; Althusser suggests that every aspect of our individuality is brought into being by ideology. In this sense, ideology is not just a type of information transmitted to us in various ways, it is everything we do and say. We live and breathe ideology. In Althusser's view, the idea that we are free agents capable of independent decision making is an illusion. Far from this, he argues, we are the 'effects' of ideological structures, brought into being by patterns of discourse or interpellations. Put another way, we are as we are because of the ways in which we are addressed. There is no 'real me' separate and distinct from the person created by ideology.

Like Gramsci, Althusser acknowledges that ideology is not necessarily uniform but addresses us in different ways depending on, among other things, our class position, age, gender and ethnicity. The consequence of this is that the individual or 'subject' is not unified but fragmented. It is as if the ideological struggles referred to by Gramsci and Voloshinov are being fought out in our heads without our conscious knowledge. In some senses, Althusser seems to be returning to the conception of 'the masses' as passive victims of 'false consciousness'. A problem with this approach is that (unlike Gramsci) Althusser does not recognise the possibility of alternative ideological positions associated with subordinate groups. If ideology is as powerful and pervasive, as good at disguising its own existence as Althusser suggests, how would we ever know that it was there?

In concluding this section, we should reiterate that we have only scratched the surface of a set of ideas that is as vast and diverse as it is influential. Perhaps it is worth recalling that Karl Marx cited as his favourite motto 'De omnibus dubitandum' ('Everything should be doubted').

LIBERAL PLURALISM

Marxists, of course, are intensely critical of capitalism. They argue that capitalism contains within itself the 'seeds of its own destruction' and that the internal contradictions of competition and the need to constantly create new markets will eventually see capitalism consigned to the dustbin of history, along with feudalism. As we have already noted, though, capitalism has proved to be highly resilient and shows few signs of being on its last legs. On the contrary, the global position of capitalism is strengthening rather than weakening.

Liberal pluralism could be described as the dominant perspective associated with contemporary capitalism. It is *liberal* in the sense that individual choice and freedom are seen as a crucial human right, and *pluralist* in the sense that democratic societies allow a range of political views and opinions and a range of political parties between which the population chooses in free elections.

How, then, would liberal pluralists defend the role of the mass media in contemporary society against the charges of Marxist critics? Some of their key points would be as follows.

- With only a few essential checks and balances, the media are completely free to express themselves in any way they see fit.
- The free media (especially the free press) serve an important democratic function by monitoring the activities of politicians and powerful institutions. Corruption cannot thrive under this scrutiny and even the most powerful can be brought down, as President Nixon discovered when the *Washington Post* exposed the Watergate scandal.
- A democratic society needs an educated, well-informed electorate and the mass media help to ensure that people have a good understanding of the issues when they vote.
- The logic of the market place controls quality and value in the mass media just as it does in any other industry. If we are not satisfied with any media product we 'vote with our wallets' and spend our money elsewhere. Media companies are constantly on the lookout for gaps in the market; as soon as a new area of demand is identified a new product will be launched to meet that demand.
- The state (government) has the power to intervene in order to address any problems which might arise from the operation of the free market. It can do this in two important ways. Firstly, the state can act to prevent very powerful companies from wiping out the opposition by simply acquiring or merging with all the operators in a particular field. For example, the British government could stop a single owner

from buying up all the daily newspaper publishers or all the commercial radio stations. Secondly, the state can invest in public-sector corporations such as the BBC. The public sector, in theory, can set priorities and make decisions which are not based purely on the need to generate profits.

From these points, you can see that liberal pluralists see the mass media as having a generally positive and beneficial role in contemporary society. This does not mean that the media are beyond criticism in this perspective. On the contrary, liberal pluralists would expect the mass media, in common with all other social institutions, to be the subject of healthy debate and criticism.

ACTIVITY . . .

How do you think Marxists would respond to the liberal pluralist defence of the media's role in democratic, capitalist societies?

CULTURAL IMPERIALISM AND POSTCOLONIALISM

In studying the media you should be careful to avoid losing sight of the process by which media products are created. A perspective in Media Studies that puts a lot of emphasis on the conditions under which products are created is called the political economy model. This model sees media output as being shaped significantly by the economics of production. A major exponent of this approach, Noam Chomsky, explores the idea in his book, *Manufacturing Consent* (1988). He is particularly concerned with American news media and their coverage of news stories. He argues that decision making in such issues as news agendas is determined by the need for the institutions which report the news to remain profitable. In the newspaper industry, for example, the main source of revenue is advertising and newspaper sales. If news items appear in the paper which upset advertisers they are likely to take their business elsewhere and threaten profitability.

This idea as it relates to news media is explored more fully in Chapter 6, 'News', but it is an important perspective through which to consider a range of media industries and their output. It links closely to the idea of globalisation as increasingly the major media players are multinational companies with interests across the globe. This has important implications for the way in which institutions such as Western television and film companies can have an impact on the cultures of developing countries. As was seen in our discussion of the Marxist approach, an important function of the media is in winning the support of people to the interests of the dominant classes. The media also constitute a potential tool for control by dominant Western cultures over those of developing countries. The Western way of life and its economic and political systems can be imposed on other societies as its lifestyles are sold through media products such as films and television. This is known as cultural imperialism, a term which clearly echoes the empire building of Western countries across the world by the might of their armies. Obviously the most dominant culture exporting media products is the USA, the most powerful country in the world. Hollywood cinema is a good example of cultural imperialism. Indeed, even developed European countries express concern at the way in which American films are able to swamp and dominate home-grown products. Countries like France, for example, go to great lengths to ensure that their own national film production industry remains strong in the face of US imports.

It is against this backdrop that we consider our final theoretical perspective: post-colonialism. As its name suggests, postcolonialism is a perspective that looks at media and cultural studies, among other things, in terms of the aftermath of colonialism. Most European countries, including the United Kingdom, have a history of military impe-rialism. They would conquer less developed countries across the globe and impose their rule upon them, usually to ensure a supply of cheap materials from that country to help support the development of European economies. Former British colonies include India, South Africa, Australia, Jamaica and the United States. At one point in history Great Britain ruled half the world. These colonies eventually became inde-pendent and set up their own governments. However, it can be argued that much of the culture of the imperial countries, for example their language, still lingers on in the former colonies as a reminder of colonial rule. Furthermore, the process of decolonisation has not prevented the Western powers from tightening their economic grip on the rest of the world. The wealth of the economically developed countries increasingly depends upon the cheap labour and cheap raw materials supplied by the Third World.

Postcolonialism as a field of study gained prominence in the latter half of the last century. The Palestinian-American scholar Edward Said's critique of Western representations of the Eastern culture in his book *Orientalism* (1978) is a key text for postcolonialism as a theoretical perspective. In essence, the postcolonial argument is precisely that non-Western cultures are represented through Western eyes largely because of the impact of cultural imperialism through the power of Western media. It can be argued, for example, that whenever Islam is represented it is shown through a Western per-spective that usually fails to understand the nature and complexity of Islamic belief and culture but instead reduces it to a few stereotypical characteristics. In this way the sense of oppression is just as great as if colonies still existed.

It is not just the case that Western cultures are imposed on other cultures. In just the same way that imperial powers extracted profits from the colonies, cultural products were also appropriated. This happened quite literally in the case of the artefacts that were stolen to be put in the museums of European capitals but it also occurred at a more profound level in the formation of cultural stereotypes. Western culture has often defined itself in relation to the 'other' of non-Western cultures. The latter are seen as, variously, exotic, exciting, dangerous, romantic, mysterious and threatening. Complex, sophisticated cultures are reduced to a few simple components whose sole function is to serve the interests of the dominant metropolitan culture. For example, advertisers offer consumers 'a taste of the East' or 'the mysteries of the Orient' and film producers scour the globe for locations to serve as a tastefully exotic background to the latest action adventure film.

Postcolonialism as a theoretical perspective has a particular relevance following the events of 11 September 2001 and the subsequent invasions of Afghanistan and Iraq by American and British forces. The latter are clearly an example of military imperialism in which the Western powers are intent on imposing 'democracy' on Islamic countries in the belief that it is in their best interests.

Postcolonialism certainly helps to direct us towards a number of questions when we come to study the mass media. Some of these questions are about the products, practices and representations we encounter in the media and some of them are questions about ourselves. For example:

- Are ethnic stereotypes challenged or reinforced?
- Do the contemporary media represent the ethnic diversity of society?
- Who speaks for whom in the media? Are members of other cultures given the opportunity to represent themselves or are their ideas and opinions 'filtered' by a cultural intermediary?
- Who do I identify as 'belonging' in my culture? Do I belong?

FURTHER READING

Woods, T. (1999) *Beginning Postmodernism*, Manchester University Press.

Young, R.J.C. (2003) *Postcolonialism; A Very Short Introduction*, Oxford University Press.

In this chapter we will consider ways to maximise your performance in Media Studies exams. The approach will be both theoretical and practical.

WHY DO WE HAVE EXAMS?

At the end of your Media Studies course, it is likely that you will be expected to take exams. Few people actually enjoy taking exams. The thought of sitting in a room for an hour and a half and tackling a series of questions you have not seen before is quite off-putting. Certainly, for most students it is a much more demanding form of assessment than submitting a piece of coursework. The reason why we have exams is to check what you have learned on your course, and more specifically in Media exams to test how well you are able to apply what you have learned.

Media Studies exams differ somewhat from those exams that ask you to memorise information and then regurgitate it under exam conditions. Media Studies exams are usually much more about testing your ability to apply what you have learned. As you will be aware, Media Studies is very much a discipline which is driven by concepts. An exam is, therefore, likely to test your ability to make use of these concepts than it is to find out if you know the date the first local radio station went on air.

Probably the best and most positive way to approach a Media Studies exam is to see it as an opportunity to showcase what you have learned. If you enter the exam room expecting that the exam exists simply to catch you out, then you are unlikely to do well. Media Studies examiners take some pride in setting exams that they consider to be student friendly and enabling. This means that they enable you to show off what you know rather than try to trip you up and discover what you don't know.

Of course that does not mean that this is an heaven-sent opportunity to blag your way to an A grade. What you write in the exam should be firmly rooted in:

1   your grasp of Media Studies concepts and theories as tools for analysing and contexualising texts

2   the ability to apply these concepts and theories to a range of texts that you have researched for yourself

3   a willingness to think about and respond to the specific demands of the question which you are seeking to answer.

If you demonstrate all these things, then you will produce a high-quality response that will earn you a good grade.

You need vision as much as you need revision if you are to succeed in exams. Many people would argue that exams are not the fairest test of what you know about a subject. In fact some would argue that the only thing they really test is whether you are any good at passing exams. What we mean by vision is that you must learn to remove some of the mystery from exams and from preparing for them. As the candidate, you should be the centre of the process, knowing what you need to do rather than worrying about what you might not know. This is essential to good preparation for your exam. Revision is seen as a virtuous activity, largely because, like other virtuous activities such as taking medicine or going to church, it is seen as unpleasant. It also implies a number of unhelpful things about knowledge and understanding. It suggests that courses of study can be reduced to a series of knowable units and that at the end of the course it is necessary to spend time relearning these. Learning on Media Studies courses is much more of an organic process than this.

It may be true to say that after a year of Media lessons you may want some time to look back at what you've done but that is not the same as suggesting that the course is something that is to be memorised for a test. At best your relationship with the material will be already memorable, dynamic and, most importantly, ongoing, with the exam as a timely opportunity to demonstrate your confidence.

One way to make sure you feel able to demonstrate your confidence is by collecting information about the exam you are taking in order to maximise your advantages. This allows you to take the initiative and make informed decisions. Talking and working through past papers is an excellent way to explore how a module of work looks when it is transformed into a unit of assessment. This 'research' should be a natural part of your preparation: in practice, it is never too early to have a look at the kind of exam paper you will ultimately face.

In Media Studies it will be very likely that the exam paper will be largely intelligible to you. In fact, it is highly likely, if you are in your second or third year as a Media student, that you will at least feel able to have a go at most of the questions in advance of the module, with some likelihood of at least limited success. You should not feel undermined or alarmed by this; it is often a feature of these kinds of 'critical' subjects (Literature and Film are similar) where depth of analysis and understanding are the crucial issues. Take the paper reproduced below: it is unlikely that students from any discipline would have problems with the general issues. By comparison, non-physicists would probably find an A2 Physics paper entirely inaccessible, but that is a statement about difference and not necessarily about demands. Given this paper, specialism must be defined in other ways.

Section A The Production and Manufacture of News

1   **Either** (a) Have recent advances in technology had an impact on news coverage? Provide examples to support your answer.

   Or   (b) How are news values affected during 'times of crisis'? Discuss with examples.

Section B Representations

2   **Either** (a) Do stereotypes change over time? Answer with reference to specific examples.

   Or   (b) How far is it possible for the media to produce fair and accurate representations? Discuss with reference to **either** social groups or places.

Section C Genre

3   **Either** (a) Account for the popularity of **one** genre of your choice. Illustrate your answer with examples.

   Or   (b) 'Parody aims to mock in a critical way.' (*Fredric Jameson*) How has parody been used in contemporary genre?

The fact that these questions seem accessible and that you feel you could readily have a stab at them must be a strength, not a weakness. What they do is to set a bottom line from which you can work. Clearly what is required of you is to demonstrate the benefits of the Media course you are on by answering these comprehensible questions with more understanding, assurance and technique than you would have done without doing the course. It is the job of this chapter to provide you with the techniques, and the job of your course to provide the understanding: assurance will hopefully come as a result (and if not, with a result!).

Knowing what you are up against will puncture the mystique of the exam as something unknown and therefore unknowable. The fact is that although exams are unseen, their formats are not: they are available in advance. Recognising this shifts the balance of power from the exam to the candidate and you can concentrate on a short period of preparation rather than a prolonged period of revision. If the course has engaged and interested you, the exam should be both a natural end point and a straightforward demonstration of your abilities. As a rule of thumb, three days are more than adequate for this final job of synthesising materials for use in periods of around forty-five minutes.

Similarly it is useful to consciously restrict your physical preparation, your syntheses, to an appropriate size or scale. A single A4 side per theme or section translates well into what you might reasonably be able to use in forty-five minutes. It is also useful, at least psychologically and symbolically, to be able to lay out your preparation for a single exam (two hours maximum these days) on a flat surface in front of you: what you can frame with your arms should be a notional maximum.

COMMON SENSE PREVAILS . . .

All the advice offered in this section makes one assumption: that exams are stressful events that need to be negotiated. This understanding is behind all the suggested techniques that follow since in each case what we are addressing is the fact that undue anxiety will not help your performance. Most teachers and examiners would not wish candidates to have access to answer books or pens in the first ten minutes of any exam. Since this is impossible, try the following 'programme', which should at the very least calm you down. There are two simple ways to miss out on your share of more marks (if you ever need to!):

- poor time management
- lack of focus on questions.

Unnecessarily forfeiting 20 per cent of the marks by missing part of a question through poor timing puts awful pressure on your performance in the rest of the paper. Most examiners will tell you that they regularly see exam scripts in which for a number of reasons half of the questions are in effect unattempted. The mathematics of this tell their own story;

NOTEBOX

> In a regular A Level exam where an A grade might be 70 or 80 per cent of the marks and an E grade 40 per cent, losing even 20 per cent of possible marks by missing part of the paper has a strong impact on your prospects. It effectively means that you are increasing the percentage of marks required for each grade so that E suddenly requires half of the marks available and A is set perhaps as high as 90 per cent.

Here are some suggestions that will help to keep you on track. Use them as a checklist.

- **Read the rubric**: your research should have given you sound knowledge of these matters but a simple check of 'how many questions from how many sections?' will prevent the worst disasters such as doing all eight essays instead of choosing two (although you may have spent the day before laughing at the story about the idiot who did all eight!).
- **Read ALL the questions**: a pen or pencil is useful to underline or circle key words. This can serve the additional purpose of testing whether attractive questions are

really as attractive as they appear. Perhaps in the course of thinking them over you may uncover an attractive question in an unattractive 'cover'. Remember key words are of two distinct varieties: key subject words (which you tend to identify), but equally importantly key questioning words, which tell you what it is you have to do (explain, consider, evaluate).

So, for example, an annotated version of the exam question on p. 242 might look like this:

Section C Genre

3 Either (a) <u>Account</u> (give reasons) for the <u>popularity</u> of **one** genre of your choice. <u>Illustrate</u> (back up) your answer with <u>examples</u> (own choice texts).

Or (b) '<u>Parody</u> (what is it?) aims to <u>mock</u> (make fun of) in a <u>critical</u> (making serious points) way.' (*Fredric Jameson*) <u>How</u> (in what particular ways?) has parody been used in <u>contemporary genre</u> (today's text varieties)?

■ **Make *informed* choices**: this also is partly a function of sound research and preparation. Your preparation may have favoured one topic, say News, over another, say Representation. The exam will offer questions on both and the Representation question will doubtless be intelligible and accessible but that doesn't mean it suddenly becomes an option. As we have seen, exams test detailed knowledge and depth of understanding so it is rarely wise to pass up something you have prepared for something 'spur of the moment'. 'Informed' also relates to the bullet point above: time spent sizing questions up is never wasted since it allows you to choose between the substance of questions rather than the impact. In the exam question given above, this candidate has identified an uncertainty in their own knowledge of alternative (b) in the key word 'parody', which recommends (a) as a choice.

■ **Focus on answering the question**: in one episode of the classic BBC sitcom *Fawlty Towers*, Basil suggests that his wife Sibyl's specialist subject is 'the bleedin' obvious' and you may feel the same about this obvious bullet point. However, as we have suggested, irrelevance is a popular weakness. There are two key causes and the first you should have avoided by the right kind of preparation: it is the over-preparation of generic answers which most often renders the question set irrelevant. Don't go in to the exam determined to write a pre-prepared answer regardless of the question you are asked. The other issue is efficient planning. Planning takes many forms and is very much a matter of taste but it is also a necessity. Where answers underachieve, the most significant failing is irrelevance, not ignorance (and certainly not stupidity). In timed conditions there is a tendency for answers to grow away from questions. Paragraphing is the key since it

encourages you to see answers for what they really are: an introduction, a conclusion and three (or more) points developed in paragraph lengths. This also allows you to renew your angle on the question a paragraph at a time.

- **Timing**: many words have been wasted over the years discussing 'timing' when it simply boils down to two simple steps.

  1 Work out how much time you have per question.
  2 Stick to this.

  The rest is common sense including making sure you allow time for reading the questions and checking things through. Forty-five minutes, for example, is not how long you have to write but how long you have to deal with the question (read, plan, write, check).

- **Checking through**: we all make silly mistakes so a read through is essential. Misplaced words can play havoc with the kind of arguments you are trying to advance and being convincing is half the battle.

CONCEPTS AND CONTEXTS: THE MEDIA STUDIES FOCUS

What is left is to consider how all this general advice comes together in the particular context of your Media Studies exams. What is the 'flavour' of these particular exams? What are you expected to do? For this you have to reconsider the nature of Media Studies as a subject, since the examinations you will take are designed to 'examine' this very thing. The key is the ability to see the wood from the trees.

Let's return to our first observations about Media Studies exams: the fact that, even to a non-specialist, these questions appear comprehensible and accessible. Given that the course concerns the ways in which individuals, institutions and society communicate, it is not in the least surprising that the content of the course is in the public domain. Implicitly, this confirms that content as special learnt material is not the focus here. Media Studies privileges the higher-order skills of analysis and evaluation over simple subject knowledge. The key words are 'concepts' and 'contexts' rather than content: content is much more about providing evidence to support your arguments rather than the simple accumulation of facts.

In this way a Media Studies exam is more invitation than ordeal. It offers a context in which you are encouraged to develop arguments and support them on your own terms. This is a common thread across all Media specifications: the stated target of all advanced work in Media is 'critical autonomy'. In other words, your Media course is hoping to enable you to find your own voice: to have your own 'takes' on the material presented and to use those cornerstones of the subject, the key concepts, as foundations for your own critical framework. Step one in this appropriately ambitious project is having the encouragement and confidence to select your own evidence, to choose your own texts or at least your own readings of these texts. Any attempts by your teachers, however well meant, to impose readings at this level must be mediated by this knowledge. If everyone writes the same analysis of the same texts then 'critical autonomy' will be nigh on impossible to achieve/prove and the highest marks will be lost. All of the evidence available supports and encourages your right to choose.

Not only are the philosophical and educational arguments overwhelming but even a cynical and pragmatic approach tends to suggest it is in all senses 'valuable'.

The marking scheme is a useful resource. It is a series of instructions to the people who are going to mark your papers. It changes little from session to session, which again reinforces the priority of concepts over specific content. A Level marking schemes are arranged in bands which reflect levels of achievement, rather than grades. They are collections of positive statements which your work must match to 'score': there may be five or six of these, running from 'excellent' to 'unable to meet A Level standard'. In each band there will also be five or six 'kinds' of statement reflecting the range of performance required; for example, one might measure the degree of 'critical autonomy' or knowledge and application of key concepts.

To find the exercise most useful it is best to look beyond the highest band, which is designed to describe exceptional performances and is always reserved for high A grade work. Better to look at the next band down, where 'good' work is rewarded. The example in the box below is typical and shows various ways in which a piece of work can be rewarded rather than a set of demands that all must be met.

General assessment criteria

21–25 *marks*

Good knowledge and application of the key concepts to texts, issues, ideas, debates and their wider contexts.

Good evaluation of texts and ideas using the key concepts.

Proficient knowledge and application of relevant major ideas, theories, debates and information. Good evaluation of relevant major ideas, theories, debate and information on the basis of the available evidence.

Good, detailed personal evaluation of texts or issues where relevant.

Good knowledge and application of relevant historical, political, social and economic contexts. Good appreciation of the contextual demands and implications of the questions asked.

Good evidence of critical autonomy and independent thinking, particularly in relating texts to a range of wider contexts.

Good understanding of major principles and an ability to apply them.

Good exemplification of arguments/principles from a range of sources.

Well written, and clearly organised and presented.

The interesting words in the General assessment criteria are those that provide clues to what is required and what is valued. In this section of the marking scheme we can start with those words and phrases that are qualified by the chief band descriptor 'Good'. This is a fairly small but vital set since they tell you exactly what you must do ('well'). It is to show these:

- knowledge
- application
- evaluation
- appreciation
- evidence of critical autonomy
- exemplification
- understanding.

These are then backed up with an awful lot of emphasis on thinking for yourself and using the experience of the course you have done to support your views. These requirments may be gathered in two groups:

1 the 'stuff' (what?): concepts, texts, issues, ideas, debates, contexts, arguments
2 the 'style' (how?): relevant, personal, contextual, critical, independent thinking, range.

All these are indications of what is to be rewarded here: your own response to a set of key ideas which raise a number of issues and debates which you will evidence with material from your own texts and contexts. 'When you are doing these things', the marking scheme assures, 'you will be getting marks'.

UNSEEN TEXT EXAMS

'Doing these things' is also a good prompt for dealing with unseen exams in which texts are unleashed either when or just before you write about them. As has been stressed repeatedly in this section, these texts are opportunities to show what you can do and what you know and should be approached as such. Preparation, as usual, is key and the fact that in Media Studies you may be faced with texts from different media is an exciting and interesting part of the challenge.

What you will need to do either in the provided viewing time for moving image texts or in the equivalent time for print texts is learn to annotate 'with attitude' and anticipation. Annotation in this context is very much the first part of planning. Of course the texts must be carefully considered, but only in terms of what you can do with them and what they can do for you. This is the attitude John Fowles (1969) has suggested novelists have to their characters; 'I could really use you'. In the case of comparative

textual analysis there is at least the opportunity to set your own agenda with the notes you make. These should be more concerned with the nature of the task than the integrity of the individual texts.

This process begins with the headings/questions you use to organise your responses to the materials at first sight or through multiple viewings. Think about using a style of note making that suits the nature of the task. This means that simply writing about the texts 'in order' is unlikely to be the best fit. This 'linear' style also has the tendency to make your writing a laborious 'walk through' of your notes. As the question is encouraging you to go beyond the text and to consider wider contexts, theoretical perspectives, issues and debates, a more discursive style is needed which looks for contexts rather than a single narrative. A simple grid has much to recommend it as it is practical and also symbolic of the need to establish relationships between contexts. The heading for each 'box' is flexible to some extent but equally there are some strong clues as to what will be valuable. The example (Figure 9.1) mixes space for general comments and specific prompts.

At least with all the prompts on one page you should be in a decent position to see the connections and themes of your texts. You can then make your own choices about which way to go in the confident knowledge that this is what you are encouraged to do. If you collect information in this way you have your evidence available to you in one place without it imposing a structure on your answer. With the issues clarified you can then set your mind to writing these up using media terminology appropriately and constructing your response so it is logical and accessible to the examiner.

Never lose sight of the game and never lose heart: the only real consolation of exams, apart from the ultimate reward of a result, is that they provide a significant and necessary end point for courses or modules. An exam is something like a game, a performance and a contest, though the other contestants have no direct bearing on your success. The important thing is that you 'play' in a way that will allow the examiner to allocate most marks to your performance. The performance that you require is, of course, the one where you prove you are a Media Studies student by displaying the understanding and attitude of mind that this role entails. This means having knowledge and insights but it also means using the specialised terminology of the subject.

You will need to 'showcase' your knowledge within an efficient structure. There is little room for structural sophistication in forty-five minutes so 'transparency' is usually the best model. The essay structure is a shop window: it should not impede sight of your 'wares'. A flexible version of the five-paragraph essay mentioned earlier invariably reaches the spot.

Figure 9.1 (opposite) Planning grid for textual comparisons.

TEXT A: General	TEXT B: General
SIMILARITIES	DIFFERENCES
KEY CONCEPTS	THEORY
ISSUES/DEBATES	WIDER CONTEXTS

A PRACTICAL APPROACH TO ESSAY PAPERS

In an essay of five paragraphs each will normally function as follows:

1 **introduction**: address key words, set agenda
2 first main point and evidence
3 second main point and evidence
4 third main point and evidence
5 **conclusion**: air other points, leave the reader something to think about.

No essay can be attempted without three main points (at least). If you can't find three, choose again. Beyond this it's just about having the confidence to revel in the freedom and respect a Media Studies course affords you. This is a subject which, above all others, empowers its candidates, not least by putting them and their experiences at the centre of the course. The matrix that is the modern media not only provides you with a context but also with an abundance of potential examples. Media Studies offers you some key concepts with which to wrest or persuade meanings from massive multinational and international channels of communication in a context so contemporary that it includes the morning of the exam.

▼ 10 CRIME FICTION

In this chapter we show how an evolving genre, crime fiction, has interacted with broader patterns of historical change: social, cultural, political and economic. The material here supplements the genre case study (pp. 64–71) to demonstrate how the analysis of media texts is always enriched by a consideration of context.

HISTORICAL BACKGROUND

Call the cops! Waking the Dead, Rose and Maloney, CSI, The Shield – if there were as many police on the streets as there are on the screen criminals wouldn't dare leave home.

(Shelly Vision, *Daily Mirror*, 1 October 2004)

It is difficult not to sympathise with this newspaper columnist as the cop show has come to play such an important part in the television schedules. In this section we look at the historical development of the crime series and explore the reasons for its phenomenal success as a TV genre.

Crime fiction, of course, has a much longer history as a genre than television has as a medium. Sherlock Holmes, for example, was well established in the public's imagination in the early part of the twentieth century. The genre was well established in novels, magazines, theatre, film and radio long before the advent of television. It is important to acknowledge the influence of these other media on television crime fiction, particularly in the early days of the 1950s and 1960s. It was certainly the case that audiences for the first television crime series already had a powerful set of expectations based on their knowledge and understanding of the crime genre in other media.

In contrast to some other fictional genres such as science fiction or horror, crime is also represented powerfully in non-fiction formats. This means that the expectations and perceptions of the crime series audience are inevitably influenced by what they

have read in newspapers or heard on broadcast news about criminals and their victims, the police and the legal profession. Both fictional and non-fictional genres contribute to our perceptions of crime-related issues.

'Evening all' – early cop shows

The need to offer reassurance has been one of the factors influencing the development of the genre. In the 1950s fledgling television producers looked to other forms of media for programme ideas. The public service remit of the BBC meant that the work of public servants (e.g. nurses, doctors or the police) was suitable material for early drama. The earliest cop show, *Dixon of Dock Green* (1955–76), was inspired by the 'social problem' film of 1940s and 1950s British cinema to such an extent that the main character, George Dixon, was resurrected from the dead, having been murdered in the 1949 Ealing Studios film *The Blue Lamp*. Dixon reflected a world of policing where the bobby on the beat was a figure who commanded respect, criminals were, on the whole, 'decent', and would-be juvenile delinquents were saved from a life of crime by a clip around the ear and a threat to tell their mothers. Dock Green itself was a mythologised working-class area of London. The values of the community and those of the police were shown to be closely linked and mutually supportive. As PC Dixon, actor Jack Warner cut a reassuringly avuncular figure, always ready to provide a clear-cut moral framework for the audience. At the end of each episode Dixon delivered a monologue straight to camera, drawing conclusions and lessons from the tale we had just seen. Most of these lectures were variants on the theme of 'It just goes to show, crime doesn't pay'.

This representation of the world of crime and policing was, however, a long way from the reality of 1960s London. Organised crime was becoming increasingly difficult for the Metropolitan Police to contain and East End gang lords like the Krays and the Richardsons were household names. The postwar optimism that crime would wither away as 'things got back to normal' turned out to be naïve in the extreme. Crime rates rose steadily in the late 1950s and early 1960s and, for the first time, law and order became a significant political issue. Television responded to the claims that Dixon was no longer relevant and *Z-Cars* (1962–78) offered a new, gritty and more realistic reflection of the police. *Z-Cars* also benefited from new developments in technology and television techniques. In the early days of *Dixon of Dock Green* all scenes were filmed in studio-based sets and the need for live broadcast meant that the overall visual style was extremely static. *Z-Cars* was able to benefit from new technology which allowed exterior scenes to be recorded and fed into live broadcasts, creating a sense of realism with real establishing shots and some location filming.

Z-Cars was set in a fictional northern new town and at the level of content tried hard to raise the difficult social questions of the day. Issues like immigration and racism were addressed, but the private lives of the police officers themselves also came under scrutiny. Storylines based around domestic violence and alcoholism caused by the pressures of the job were included and initially the programme drew criticism from the police authorities who were worried that public confidence in the force would be undermined. If Dixon owed much to the postwar 'social problem' films, the film references of *Z-Cars* were the social realism films such as *A Taste of Honey* (1961) and *This Sporting Life* (1963). *Z-Cars* followed these films by putting an uncompromisingly authentic northern working-class culture onto the small screen.

The senior officer in *Z-Cars* was also a stark contrast to the characters of Dock Green. Detective Inspector Barlow, played by Stratford Johns, was forceful, blunt and certainly capable of bullying both suspects and his own juniors. However, the crimes dealt with by Newtown police were invariably small scale and community based. Criminality was seen in a social context. The 'real enemies' were not so much evil wrongdoers as the conditions of deprivation and poverty which caused crime and despair. In *Z-Cars*, the police officers themselves were almost as likely as the criminals to be the victims of alienating urban life. Their attitude towards juvenile delinquents, petty criminals and assorted miscreants was usually a tough but sympathetic humanity. This liberal view of crime was an influential component of the British genre.

From realism to naturalism and back again

British television cop shows of the 1970s were noticeably influenced by domestic political concerns and by the growing popularity of American television and film crime fiction. In 1970 the Labour Party lost the general election and was replaced by a Conservative government led by Prime Minister Ted Heath. Law and order issues played an important part in the election campaign and the new government arrived with a mandate to get to grips with serious crime. The period was characterised by social and industrial unrest and successive moral panics about crime waves. A more aggressive and confrontational approach to law and order displaced the emphasis on crime as a social problem. Then (as now) many politicians wanted to encourage the perception that they were 'tough on crime' and they avoided any association with policies that could be seen as liberal or permissive. The predominant attitude towards criminality and any perceived threat to social order could be summed up by the phrase 'Crack down and crack down hard'.

Z-Cars, still going strong in the early 1970s, began to shift its emphasis towards organised crime, particularly in its two spin-off series, *Softly, Softly* (1966–76) and *Barlow at Large* (1971). The idea that the police were in the front line in a war against crime began to take hold in this period, steadily marginalising perceptions based on the 'bobby on the beat' or the citizen in uniform. In new series such as *The Sweeney* (1974–8) and *The Professionals* (1977–83) the main characters were men of action who acted decisively and impulsively to foil and capture villains. In this respect the influence of American films and television programmes played a significant part. As the western genre declined in popularity, the cowboy was replaced by the modern crime fighter as the pre-eminent icon of the American screen. However, many of the key characteristics of the western hero were retained. The cops in films such as *Dirty Harry* (1971) and *The French Connection* (1971) and television series such as *Kojak* (1973–8) and *Starsky and Hutch* (1975–9) were rugged, individualistic maverick types who had scant respect for rules and regulations. Problems were generally solved by deeds rather than words. As was so often the case in westerns, these fictional heroes subscribed to and enforced a code of 'natural justice' which was sometimes in direct contradiction to the law.

The Sweeney (based on cockney rhyming slang, Sweeney Todd = Flying Squad) explored similar territory. The all-action style of the series was enhanced by high production values, fast-paced editing, frequent car chases and fight scenes. Lead character DI Jack Regan (played by John Thaw) was certainly prepared to 'fit up' villains, bribe informers, plant evidence and use violence as a form of persuasion. In addition, Regan led a turbulent and unstable private life, signalled by heavy drinking and casual affairs. As police officers, though, Regan and sidekick DS George Carter (Dennis Waterman) inhabited a well-defined moral universe. Although prepared to bend the rules, they were indefatigable and incorruptible in their single-minded pursuit of the villain. The audience was clearly positioned to sympathise with this approach to policing in which the ends justified the means.

This theme of ends justifying means was taken up much more critically by two highly acclaimed series of 1978. The four-parter *Law and Order* caused a storm of controversy with its frank exploration of corruption and abuse of power in the police, prison and legal services. The prison service was sufficiently outraged to ban the BBC from filming in prisons for a year. The impact of *Law and Order* was heightened by its use of a flat, understated drama-documentary style. For the audience, it felt as if we were spying unseen on the activities of the police, lawyers and prison officers, discovering most of them to be corrupt, incompetent, or both.

Out pushed the boundaries of the genre in a slightly different way. The main protagonist was Frank Ross (Tom Bell), a convicted bank robber just out of prison after an eight-year stretch. Ross sets out to discover the identity of the informer who put him behind bars and in the process begins to uncover a dangerous and murky world of corruption and co-operation between bent coppers and villains. *Out*, a serial rather than a series, showed that a working-class villain could take centre stage and that the audience need not necessarily ally itself with crime fighters in order for the conventions of the genre to be utilised.

SOME GENDER ISSUES

While the world of *The Sweeney* and its like was relentlessly macho, the uniformed police ensemble drama began to feature women in leading roles. *Juliet Bravo* (1980–5) and *The Gentle Touch* (1980–4) had more in common with the realism of *Dixon* than the naturalism of *The Sweeney*, showing that the conventions of the genre are sufficiently flexible to include a wide range of stylistic techniques. These series also demonstrated that shifting gender politics could (if rather belatedly) be accommodated by the crime fiction genre. The casting of Jill Gascoine (*The Gentle Touch*) and Stephanie Carter (*Juliet Bravo*) proved that while patriarchal values and gender stereotypes may have characterised previous crime fictions, they were not a *defining* characteristic of the genre.

Subsequently, many series have given prominent roles to women and some have explicitly addressed issues of prejudice and inequality based on gender. Principal among these was Lynda La Plante's *Prime Suspect* (1990–). In the first series of *Prime Suspect*, following considerable media coverage of the case of real-life policewoman Alison Halford and her claims of sexual discrimination against the force, Jane Tennyson

Figure 10.1
Prime
Suspect.
Source:
Granada
Television.

(Helen Mirren) became the fictional character through which the problem was mediated for audiences of the day.

These preoccupations can be seen in the first episode which deals explicitly with gender issues. Its structure is interesting in that the first twenty minutes set up expected narrative patterns with the discovery of a body (a young and beautiful woman found in a prostitute's bedsit). The man who arrives at the scene to take charge is DCI Shefford, an old-school copper who commands the total loyalty of his team. We discover that Tennyson was the senior officer on duty when the murder was discovered but Shefford was 'fished out of a club' to attend. The misogyny of the officers, young and old, is continually reinforced until Shefford dies unexpectedly of a heart attack. It may be that this narrative set-up was used so as not to alienate the traditional male viewer who could have been threatened by the representation of female authority in this environment. As the story develops Tennyson gradually wins the respect of the male team but only by being better at the job than any male officer and by adopting very masculine characteristics. Parallel to this is the storyline of Tennyson's home life that disintegrates as she gains professional acceptance. In subsequent series of *Prime Suspect* Tennyson makes it to the higher ranks but she is still excluded from the world of male camaraderie and is still without a fulfilling relationship. The implicit suggestion of *Prime Suspect* is that the police service expects and rewards masculine attributes and values and that only by adopting these can women (or men, for that matter) succeed in their careers. The inference is that sexism is a cultural problem for the police force and cannot be dealt with solely at the level of legislation.

Blue Murder (ITV, 2004) provided a few variants on the themes explored by *Prime Suspect*. Detective Chief Inspector Janine Lewis (played by Caroline Quentin) is undisputedly 'the boss' and her domestic life is certainly demanding (single mother with both a tiny infant and a fractious teenager). Lewis, though, deals with the pressures of home and work with an unfailingly cheery optimism. In some ways, the police force as represented

Figure 10.2 Blue Murder.
Source: ITV plc.

Figure 10.3
Publicity still,
55 Degrees
North.
Source: BBC.

in *Blue Murder* has moved beyond sexism: at least to the extent that male and female officers are equally likely to resort to gender stereotypes. Lewis's problems are not those of canteen culture sexism or the glass ceiling; they are the problems facing a career woman in any profession. She juggles the competing demands of work, children and (in her case) an ex-husband and several would-be boyfriends. Like DS Cole in *55 Degrees North*, DCI Lewis is a 'new cop' in the sense that a chaotic personal life does not prevent her from having a very clear and uncomplicated moral framework which applies to all areas of her experience.

ENTER THE EXPERT

A sub-genre of the crime fiction series may be identified as the 'expert' drama. Here, an outsider with a particular area of expertise assists the police in cracking complex crimes. Although such series closely conform to the narrative structure and value system typical of the genre, the relationship between the expert and members of the police force opens up a range of dramatic possibilities. In series such as *Cracker* (1993–5) and *Silent Witness* (1996–) we see many examples of the tensions which drive forward the narrative of crime stories. There may be friction between the intuitive, impulsive individual and the hard-working team relying on the patient and painstaking application of procedures. An understanding of criminals and their motivations can be contrasted with sympathy for the victim. Alternatively, the narrative may explore the use of science and technology as a foil for the virtues of traditional methods of criminal investigation.

Figure 10.4 Cracker.
Source: Granada Television.

The first really successful example of this sub-genre was *Cracker* written by Jimmy McGovern, produced by Gub Neale (who also produced *Prime Suspect*), and set in Manchester. The lead character Fitz (Robbie Coltrane) uses his specialist criminal psychology skills to help track down the villain. After intensive speculation into the motive behind the crime, the suspect invariably confesses to Fitz rather than the police. This in itself signalled a new shift in attitudes towards crime. In earlier decades the consensus seemed to be that villains were 'just bad'. In contrast, *Cracker* firmly re-inforced the view that criminal behaviour, however extreme, has its roots in the individual's background, childhood and social influences. *Cracker* storylines revolved around individuals propelled towards crime by the extreme circumstances of their personal experiences. In the three-part episode *Men Should Weep* (1994), Floyd, a young black man who rapes white women, is shown to be mentally and physically scarred by racist bullying as a child. Fitz discovers that Floyd would sit in a bath of bleach at the age of six in an attempt to make his skin white like his mother's.

In *To Be Somebody* (1994) we are drawn into a sympathetic understanding of Albie Kinsella (played by Robert Carlyle). Albie's killing spree begins when the death of his father triggers off memories of his involvement in the terrible Hillsborough football stadium tragedy of 1989. Jimmy McGovern's interest in the causes and devastating consequences of this tragedy was further explored in his highly acclaimed dramatised version of events, *Hillsborough* (1996).

The expert has remained a popular format, with many series of BBC's *Silent Witness* starring Amanda Burton as pathologist Sam Ryan. Other examples have included *Wire in the Blood* (2002–4) with Robson Green as clinical psychologist and *Sea of Souls* (2004–5) with academic Monaghan (Bill Patterson) heading up a paranormal investigation unit.

ECONOMIES OF SCALE AND LOCATIONS OF CHOICE

The expert series also conforms to institutional requirements which have seen individual episodes get longer and the series get shorter. Crime fiction plays an impor-tant role in the schedules and is often relied on to pull in big peak-time audiences. However, it is also an expensive form of programming, so producers are under pressure to achieve economies of scale. Longer episodes – sometimes two- or three-parters which nudge towards feature film length – help to achieve this. Of these longer dramas, *Inspector Morse* (1987–2000) played a particularly important role in acclimatising audiences to dramas of two hours or more.

The locations of *Inspector Morse*: in and around Oxford; the social milieu: upper middle class; his character: urbane and refined; his approach to investigation: intellectual and intuitive; not to mention his car: a classic Jaguar; all combined to tap into a very familiar reference point for British viewers: the country house murder mystery. The most famous exponent of this genre was the writer Agatha Christie, whose characters Hercule Poirot and Miss Marple have features which recur in numerous television and film dramas. In many senses, then, *Inspector Morse* rewarded the audience's nostalgic leanings. This was also incorporated into narratives which took a traditional 'whodunit' form with multiple suspects, red herrings and complex sub-plots all playing a part. The audience was

Figure 10.5 Inspector Morse. *Source: Carlton Television.*

flattered by references to high culture both in the dialogue and imagery and by clues in the theme music or in incidental shots of apparently irrelevant detail.

INTERTEXTUALITY: THE KNOWING AUDIENCE

Inspector Morse was an exercise in style with no real points of contact with either the social realism of *Z-Cars* or the action realism of *The Sweeney*. Nonetheless, *Inspector Morse* made extensive use of the genre series' richest resource: the audience's knowledge of the history and form of genre conventions. *Inspector Morse* has itself now become a part of this inventory of genre knowledge, so that it has helped to condition the form of successors such as *A Touch of Frost* (1992–) and *Midsomer Murders* (1997–). While *Midsomer Murders* retains the upper-class cast of characters and even the rural Oxfordshire locations, the intellectual pretensions of *Morse* have been replaced by something approaching parody. The scenarios and twists and turns of plot are barely plausible, but *Midsomer Murders* assembles familiar faces, familiar locations and familiar characters. As Jack Kibble-White (2003) puts it: 'Invoking the ghosts of some of television's most successful programmes seems to be a winning formula for *Midsomer Murders* with up to 8.5 million viewers tuning in to watch the most recent series.'

It seems then that a crime fiction series can succeed purely by invoking an audience's shared memory of former programmes, actors and stories.

THE BILL AND *THE COPS*

The uniformed police drama has been substantially redefined by *The Bill* (1984–). The viewer of *The Bill* is always aligned with the police. We never see any action or events which are unknown to the police. We are with the officers of Sunhill as they collect and sift information, interview suspects and apprehend villains.

The Bill began life as a weekly one-hour series with twelve-week runs, but in 1988 it became a twice-weekly half-hour series, ever present in the schedule. In its new incarnation, *The Bill* could be seen as the first television drama to erase the boundary between soap opera and crime fiction. Such hybrid forms can give producers and writers the scope for creative licence but against this could be counted the rather different relationship which each genre has with its audience. The soap opera tends to focus on the emotional relationships between characters and to derive the plot from them. The crime fiction genre, on the other hand, is more narrative driven, usually with an emphasis on investigating crimes. The narrative-based genre provides opportunities to tackle more controversial areas such as police corruption and institutional racism or sexism. This means that crime fiction has the potential to challenge the ideological consensus with powerful issue-based stories.

Soaps, too, can confront orthodoxy but are much more likely to do so at the level of representation rather than narrative. These two contrasting tendencies have certainly been evident in *The Bill*. In striving for a sympathetic and authentic representation of the Metropolitan Police there have been strong and positive roles for ethnic minority characters and for women. Gay and lesbian storylines have been featured and the Metropolitan Police's intention to build a 'customer friendly' ethic is evident in Sunhill.

In 2002 producer Paul Marquess was brought in to halt a steady decline in *The Bill*'s ratings. Here he makes clear his diagnosis of the problem and the solution:

> I had stopped watching *The Bill*, it was loved by people aged 50 and upwards.
> I didn't feel as a storytelling machine it was connecting . . . I also thought if
> you were black or Asian where were you?

> When I got here the Met was in a post-Lawrence universe policing London for its
> entire population, not just for the white property owning classes. *The Bill* had not
> got to grips with that. My cast is now a metropolitan dream full of women and
> minorities. It needed to change fast, it needed emergency surgery.
> (*Evening Standard* Media Section, 12 February 2003)

Clearly *The Bill* has become less of a crime fiction series and more of a soap opera with an increasing focus on personal relationships at an emotional and often sensational level. Marquess's surgery involved a widespread cull of established characters, many of whom met a sticky end when Sunhill police station was blown up. Ratings were certainly revived but, it could be argued, the ideological work of *The Bill* has firmly reverted to imparting a comforting and reassuring image of the police.

Kibble-White (2002) has suggested that recent cop shows have defined themselves 'in terms of their adherence or non-adherence to the soap opera genre'. If *The Bill* lies at one end of this spectrum then *The Cops* (1998–2001) was determinedly at the other end. Once again, economic factors exercised an important influence on the conceptualisation and realisation of this series. With pressures to keep the budget down, producer Tony Garnett shot the series on digital video rather than more expensive film. As well as yielding substantial savings, Garnett made a virtue of the video aesthetic, using hand-held camera techniques to lend a fly-on-the-wall style authenticity to the series. The inclusion of apparently random events and the improvisational style of the actors' performances also added to the realistic feel.

The Cops tested the boundaries of crime fiction by marginalising the actual investigating and solving of crimes. Instead, the narrative thrust was provided by the characters' quest for survival in a blank, alienating urban landscape. There was no sense of comradeship among the officers or evidence of ties binding the local community together. As each episode followed a working shift at a police station in a northern urban sprawl, we saw police officers as individuals coping with the demands of a difficult and demanding job in the context of their own complicated private lives. Their coping strategies included acts of petty malice or vindictiveness as well as occasional examples of compassion or kindness. Sometimes all of these were exhibited by the same character. Just like Regan and Carter, these were cops prepared to break the rules, but this time the objective was not to serve a code of 'natural justice' but to make their own lives a little bit easier or a little bit more bearable.

FURTHER READING

Akhtar, M. and Humphries, S. (2001) *The Fifties and Sixties; A Lifestyle Revolution*, Boxtree.

Clarke, A. (1992) '"You're Nicked!": Television Police Series and the Fictional Representation of Law and Order', in Strinati, Dominic and Wagg, Stephen (eds) *Come On Down; Popular Media Culture in Postwar Britain*, Routledge.

Cooke, L. (2003) *British Television Drama; A History*, BFI.

Leishmann, F. and Mason, P. (2003) *Policing and the Media; Facts, Fictions and Factions*, Willan.

Sparks, R. (1992) *Television and the Drama of Crime; Moral Tales and the Place of Crime in Public Life*, Open University Press.

Helpful critical accounts of many seminal cop shows can be found at: http://www.museum.tv/.

▼ RESOURCES

USEFUL DATA SOURCES

Advertising Association
Abford House
15 Wilton Road
London SWIV INJ
☎ 020 7828 2771
<http://www.adassoc.org.ub>

Advertising Standards Authority (ASA)
2 Torrington Place
London WC IE 7HW
☎ 020 7580 5555
<http://www.asa.org.uk>

BBC
Television Centre
Wood Lane
London W12 7RJ
☎ 020 7743 8000
<http://www.bbc.co.uk>

**British Board of Film Classification
(BBFC)**
3 Soho Square
London WIV 5DE
☎ 020 7440 1570
<http://www.bbfc.co. uk>

British Film Institute (BFI)
21 Stephen Street
London WIP IPL
☎ 020 7255 1444
<http://www.bfi.org.uk>

Channel Four Television
124 Horseferry Road
London SWIP 2TX
☎ 020 7396 4444
<http://www.channel4.com>

Film Education
Alhambra House
27–31 Charing Cross Road
London WC2H OAU
☎ 020 7976 2291
<http://www.filmeducation.org>

**National Museum of Photography,
Film and Television (NMPFT)**
Bradford
West Yorkshire
BDI INQ
☎ 01274 202030
<http://www.nmpftorg.uk>

Ofcom
Office of Communications
Riverside House
2A Southwark Bridge Road
London SEI 9HA
☎ 020 7981 3000
<http://www.ofcom.org.uk>

Press Complaints Commission (PCC)
1 Salisbury Square
London EC4Y 8AE
☎ 020 7353 1248
<http://www.pcc.org.uk>

▼ GLOSSARY

absent presence Barthes uses this term to refer to a state of affairs when the very invisibility of some groups becomes a significant issue.

active audience theory The idea that members of media audiences actively construct interpretations of media texts.

actuality Recordings of images and sounds of events made on location as they actually happen for inclusion in news reports or documentaries.

aesthetic To do with beauty, artistic merit or good taste.

analogue A continuous, unsegmented representation. In terms of broadcasting, analogue signals require greater bandwidth and, unlike digital, do not offer the sophisticated possibilities of interactivity.

anchorage The fixing or limiting of a particular set of meanings to an image. One of the most common forms of anchorage is the caption underneath a photograph.

archetype An original model on which subsequent models are based; particuarly used in relation to characters in fictional works such as film or broadcast fiction.

auteur Literally, author. Auteur theory, most likely to be applied to films, is the idea that the text is the work of an individual creator, usually the director.

binary opposition A device used in textual analysis to show how oppositions such as good/evil, male/female are explored within narratives.

bourgeoisie A Marxist term for the capital-owning class. In order to make profit, they purchase labour from the proletariat.

breaking news A news story, the details of which are unfolding while it is being reported.

bricolage The way signs or artefacts are borrowed from different styles or genres to create something new.

broadsheet Traditionally, a large rectangular newspaper, such as the *Daily Telegraph*. Broadsheets have always been associated with serious journalism, reporting important events at home and abroad. They are targeted at an upmarket, professional readership. However, former broadsheets, including *The Times*, are now often published in a tabloid format.

canon A list of cultural products which are traditionally held to be the best (if not the most popular).

CGI Computer-generated images.

connotation The meaning of a sign that is arrived at through the cultural experiences a reader brings to it.

construction Expresses the idea that people can be 'made' by what they see, hear and read. Can also refer to the components of a text which are 'built up' by the media institution.

contemporary Up to date as opposed to historical. Contemporary can also mean produced within the lifetime of a course of study for AQA coursework purposes (see p. 30).

convergence The coming together of different communication technologies such as the telephone, the computer and the television.

critique A critical review or commentary, especially one dealing with works of art or literature.

cultural capital The idea that knowledge of particular topics can confer advantages in the same way as monetary wealth.

cultural imperialism The idea that powerful and wealthy countries can exercise economic, cultural and social control over others through control of media industries.

Democratisation The act of making more democratic. Used in Media Studies particularly to describe the process by which new interactive technologies put more control in the hands of consumers/audience members.

demographics Population variables based on observable and measurable differences such as age, sex and region.

denotation What an image actually shows and what is immediately apparent, as opposed to the assumptions an individual reader may make about it.

deregulation The relaxing of state controls over an industry. In media terms this has meant the 'freeing up' of the airwaves and much looser rules about takeovers, mergers, cross-media ownership and the content of media output.

diegetic Of or about the events within a narrative. In *EastEnders*, jukebox songs in the Vic are diegetic, but the theme music at the beginning and end of the programme is non-diegetic.

digital Representations or signals which are reducible to a series of numbers (digits). Once information is in a digital form it can be processed by computers. This gives a great deal more opportunity and flexibility to store, retrieve, manipulate or interact with texts.

discourse Forms of language and communication which embody ideology. Can also mean 'the language associated with', so we use terms such as 'internet discourse' or 'news discourse'.

discourse of realism The 'conversation' texts have with audiences about the ways that reality will be represented within the text.

dissolve Film term for the transition between two images whereby one 'dissolves' into the next.

docu-soap A combination of documentary and soap opera, usually in the context of television. 'Real lives' are presented in ways which are usually associated with fictional narratives.

drama-documentary A hybrid television form which combines the conventions of drama with those of documentary.

encoding A process by which the media construct messages.

enigma A narrative device that teases the audience by presenting a puzzle or riddle to be solved.

feature In newspapers this is generally an article that concerns itself with a topical issue while not having any hard news content.

feminism A perspective based on the power relations in society which takes as a starting point the need to combat prejudice and discrimination against women. Feminists agree that society is patriarchal, with disproportionate power and influence concentrated in the hands of men.

freeview Digital television channels available without additional subscription payments.

genre The term used for the classification of media texts into groups with similar characteristics.

globalisation The process by which cultural products and media institutions show a decreasing respect for national boundaries. Some commentators link this process to the increasing domination of the Western media. Others see the growth of a collective, interdependent and inclusive global culture spurred on by technological developments.

hard news News that is important and is happening at the time it is reported. A rescue attempt on a cross-Channel ferry, the death of an important national figure or a rise in mortgage interest rates could all be classified as hard news.

hegemony The concept used by the Marxist critic Antonio Gramsci to describe how people are influenced into accepting the dominance of a power elite which imposes its will and world view on the rest of the population. Gramsci argues that this elite is able to rule because the rest of the population allow it to do so. It can be argued, therefore, that the ideological role of the media is to persuade us that it is in our best interests to accept the dominance of this elite.

high culture The cultural products and activities which enjoy enhanced status because of their perceived value and aesthetic merit. Some critics argue that high culture simply reflects the tastes and opinions of the most powerful groups in society.

hybridity The fusion of two or more genres to create a new sub-genre, for example docu-soap which fuses elements of documentary and soap opera.

hyperreality An aspect of the postmodern condition in which, according to Jean Baudrillard, simulation has displaced other forms of reality. Mediated images are not an alternative to reality or even a version of reality; they *are* reality.

hypodermic needle theory A theory that suggests that the media 'inject' ideas into a passive audience, like giving a patient a drug.

hypothesis An assumption or idea about something that research will investigate and, it is hoped, either prove or disprove.

icon A sign that works by resemblance.

iconography Those particular signs that we associate with particular genres, such as the physical attributes and dress of actors, the settings and 'tools of the trade' (for example cars, guns).

ideology A system of beliefs that determines how power relations are organised within a society.

index A sign that works by a relationship to the object or concept it refers to; for example, smoke is an index of fire.

institution Media institutions are the companies, bodies or corporations which produce and distribute media texts.

interpellation A term coined by French Marxist philosopher Louis Althusser, it describes the process by which ideology addresses the individual. According to Althusser ideology addresses us through texts and when we respond, in any way, we are subject to it.

intertextuality The way in which texts refer to other media texts that producers assume audiences will recognise.

Marxism A perspective which sees economic factors as the basis for all social explanations. In Marxists' view, capitalism is the root cause of the division between two classes, the bourgeoisie and the proletariat. Marxist theories of the mass media tend to focus on the ideological role of the media in maintaining the rule of one class and the subservience of the other.

media saturation A term used to describe the extent to which our experience of the world is dominated by the media, not only at an individual level but also nationally and globally.

media-savvy (slang) Knowledgeable about the way in which the media work.

mediation The process by which a media text represents an idea, issue or event to us. This is a useful word as it suggests the way in which things undergo change in the process of being acted upon by the media.

metanarrative These are the theories or explanations which make universal truth claims. Religions, Marxism, structuralism, feminism and Freudian psychoanalysis have all been described as metanarratives.

metaphor A sign which works by implicitly transferring meaning from one area to another. For example, in a film, a setting sun could indicate the end of a relationship.

methodology The system or manner used to carry out research; the different ways in which 'data' can be captured.

metonym A sign which works by allowing part of something to stand for the whole thing. An image of a tractor when used to signify agriculture is a metonym.

mise-en-scène All of the components which contribute meaning to a scene or a sequence of moving images. Includes the props, the setting, the participants, the lighting, the position and movement of the camera and the shot selection.

mode of address The way in which a media text 'speaks' to its audience. The text incorporates assumptions about its audience. If you can answer the question 'Who does this text think I am?' you are on the way to identifying its mode of address.

monochrome Black and white.

moral panic A mass response to a group, a person or an attitude that becomes defined as a threat to society.

multi-tracking The process whereby different instruments and voices are recorded separately and then mixed together in a recording studio.

myth A story or explanation which unites a culture. Although the 'everyday' meaning of myth is a falsehood, we use myth in a rather different way in textual analysis to describe a widely held belief.

narrative The way in which a story is told in both fictional and non-fictional media texts.

naturalism A style of television or film presentation which sticks to fictional conventions but which may use techniques such as improvised dialogue or jerky camera movements in order to 'seem more real'.

niche market A small target audience with specific interests, for example DIY, classic cars or royalty.

objectivity This is a balanced, rational and scientific approach to research or understanding. It is based on the search for uncontroversial facts and underlying truths. Critics of this approach argue that many 'facts' and 'truths' are really ideological constructs.

paradigm Used in textual analysis this is a list of signs from which a selection has been made to form part of a syntagm. Looking at the signs in the list which were rejected can help us to see the contribution made by the selected sign to the meaning of the text.

pastiche These are texts which are made up from various sources and which have rejected authenticity in favour of copying or simulation. Often used negatively to describe a text which simply borrows ideas without displaying originality.

pluralism A political perspective which advocates the tolerance of competing views, parties and politicians. This approach defends Western representative democracies against critics who attack the inequalities of wealth and power.

polysemic The way in which a text has a variety of meanings and the audience is an important component in determining those meanings.

popular culture The cultural preferences of the majority of people. Almost the entire output of the mass media could be described as popular culture. Some critics point out that while popular culture is made *for* the majority of the population, it is not made *by* them.

positioning (audience) This is the idea that media consumers are manoeuvred into a certain subjectivity by the text's mode of address. For example, a sitcom may position its audience by including canned laughter. A news programme may position its audience by the news reader's sober clothing and serious tone of voice.

postcolonialism A perspective which recognises divisions between people (particularly 'West' and 'non-West') based on the legacy of colonialism and imperialism. In Media Studies postcolonialist commentators have raised awareness of representations and perceptions of ethnic and national differences which are derived from the experiences of colonisers and the colonised.

postmodernism The social, political and cultural attitudes and images of the late twentieth and early twenty-first centuries.

poststructuralism A development from structuralism which shares some of its assumptions but rejects others. Poststructuralism sees meanings and identities as unfixed, unstable and in a constant process of change. The technique of textual deconstruction is strongly associated with poststructuralism. This technique tends to see significance in elements of the text which are right at the margins or even excluded altogether.

process model This model considers the audience's interaction with the media as part of a linear process (sender–channel–message–receiver) in which the meaning of the message is thought to be 'fixed' by the producer.

proletariat In Marxist terms, this is the working class; those who have to sell their mental or manual labour.

psychographics The techniques of categorising consumers in terms of their psychological attributes, particularly their aspirations. Psychographic profiling enables media producers or advertisers to target their audience in terms of lifestyle choices or personality types.

qualitative research A type of research that attempts to explain or understand something and may necessitate much discussion and analysis of people's attitudes and behaviour. It usually involves working with small numbers of people or 'focus groups'.

quantitative research A type of research, usually based on numbers, statistics or tables, that attempts to 'measure' some kind of phenomenon and produce 'hard' data. It often involves working with large groups of people.

reader An individual member of a media audience. The term is no longer confined to print-based media but is also used of film and broadcast media to imply a receiver who is engaging actively rather than passively with a text.

realism Representation by the media of situations or ideas in such a way that they seem real.

reality TV The television genre which deals with the behaviour of people in real or contrived situations where there is no script. Programmes may deal with 'ordinary people' at work or with celebrities in bizarre circumstances. Reality TV often encourages audience interactivity, for example voting.

representation The process by which the media present to us the 'real world'.

rhetoric Language which is intended to persuade or convince.

semantic Related to the meaning of words.

semiotics The study of signs and sign systems.

sign The sign consists of two components: the signifier and the signified. The signifier is a physical object, for example a sound, printed word or advertisement. The signified is a mental concept or meaning conveyed by the signifier.

simulacra Simulations or copies that are replacing the 'real' artefacts.

social class Any category based on power, wealth or income. Some approaches to social class claim to be objective and based on measurable data such as occupation. Others are more subjective and simply rely on individuals expressing their membership of one class or another.

soundbite A snappy and memorable quotation that can easily be assimilated into a broadcast news story (for example Tony Blair's 'Education, education, education').

spin doctor A person who tries to create a favourable slant to an item of news such as a potentially unpopular policy.

structuralism This approach argues that identifying underlying structures is all-important in undertaking analysis. In linguistics, for example, it can be argued that all languages have a similar underlying grammatical structure, which we are born with the capacity to learn. Similarly, certain social structures, such as the family unit, may be common to many cultures.

subjectivity The individual's sense of self or identity. Our positioning by media texts may change or reinforce our subjectivity.

symbol A sign that represents an object or concept solely by the agreement of the people who use it.

syntagm Used in textual analysis to describe a series of signs (each chosen from a *paradigm*) which are meaningfully linked together in accordance with the rules of a code.

tabloid A compact newspaper, half the size of a broadsheet, designed to appeal to a mass audience. Tabloids, particularly at the lower end of the market, are associated with sensationalising trivial events rather than with comprehensive coverage of national and international news.

text Any media product such as a magazine or TV news programme or a coherent part of that product such as an editorial feature or a news item.

uses and gratifications theory The idea that media audiences make active use of what the media offer. The audience has a set of needs, which the media in one form or another meet.

vox pop The voice of the people. A device used by broadcast journalists in which recordings of 'ordinary' people are included in a news item to show their opinions.

voyeurism The sexual (or pseudo-sexual) pleasure gained from observing people without their knowledge.

▼ BIBLIOGRAPHY

Abercrombie, N. (1996) *Television and Society*, Polity Press.

Althusser, L. (2003) *The Humanist Controversy and Other Writings*, ed. F. Matheron, trans. G.M. Goshgarian, Verso.

Barthes, R. (1967) *Elements of Semiology*, Cape.

Barthes, R. (1977) 'Rhetoric of the Image', in R. Barthes, *Image, Music, Text*, ed. and trans. Stephen Heath, Hill and Wang.

Bell, M. (1995) *In Harm's Way*, Penguin.

Benn's Media Directory, CMP Date and Information Services (annual), Miller Freeman.

Berger, J. (1972) *Ways of Seeing*, Penguin.

Bernstein, B. (1971) *Class, Codes and Social Control*, Routledge.

Brown, M. (2004) 'Calling the Slots', *Guardian*, 20 September.

Butler, J. (1990) *Gender Trouble: Feminism and the Subversion of Identity*, Routledge.

Casey, B., Casey, N., Calvert, B., French, L. and Lewis, J. (2002) *Television Studies: The Key Concepts*, Routledge.

Chippendale, P. and Horrie, C. (1993) *Stick It up Your Punter!*, Pocket Books.

Chomsky, N. (1988) *Manufacturing Consent: The Political Economy of the Media*, Pantheon Books.

Cohen, S. [1972] (2002) *Folk Devils and Moral Panics: Creation of Mods and Rockers*, Routledge.

Cohen, S. and Young, J. (1973) *The Manufacture of News*, Sage.

Coleman, S. (nd) 'Review of Government Communication: From the Megaphone to the Radar Screen', http://www.gcreview.gov.uk/evidence/coleman.pdf, accessed 1 November 2004.

Culler, J. (1975) *Structuralist Poetics: Structuralism, Linguistics and the Study of Literature*, Routledge.

De Fleur, M.L. and Ball-Rokeach, S.J. (1989) *Theories of Mass Communication*, 5th edn, Longman.

Dyer, G. (1982) *Advertising as Communication*, Routledge.

Evans, H. (1972) *Newsman's English*, Heinemann.

Fiske, J. (1987) *Television Culture*, Methuen.

Fiske, J. (1989) *Reading the Popular*, Routledge.

Fiske, J. and Hartley, J. (1990) *Reading Television*, Routledge.

Fowles, J. (1969) *The French Lieutenant's Woman*, Cape.

Galbraith, J.K. (1969) *The Affluent Society*, Hamish Hamilton.

Gauntlett, D. (2002) *Media, Gender and Identity: An Introduction*, Routledge.

Gitlin, T. (2002) *Media Unlimited*, Owl Books.

Guardian Media Directory (2005) ed. Chris Alden, Guardian Books.

Hall, S. (1981) 'Encoding and Decoding in the TV Discourse', in Centre for Contemporary Cultural Studies (ed.) *Culture, Media, Language*, Hutchinson.

Hartley, J. (1982) *Understanding News*, Routledge.

Herman, H.S. and Chomsky, N. (1994) *Manufacturing Consent: The Political Economy Model of the Media*, Vintage.

Hesmondhalgh, D. (2002) *The Cultural Industries*, Sage.

Jenkins, H. (2003) 'Interactive Audiences', in V. Nightingale and K. Ross (eds) *Media and Audiences: New Perspectives*, Open University Press.

Keeble, R. (1994) *The Newspapers Handbook*, Routledge.

Kibble-White, J. (2002) 'And the Beat Goes On: *The Bill* and Police Ensemble Dramas', http://www.offthetelly.co.uk/drama/cops.htm, accessed 14 June 2004.

Kibble-White, J. (2003) 'Crimewave: *Inspector Morse* and Long-Form Crime Dramas', http://www.offthetelly.co.uk/drama/cops2.htm, accessed 14 June 2004.

Lewis, J. (1991) *The Ideological Octopus: An Exploration of Television and Its Audience*, Routledge.

Livingstone, S. (1990) *Making Sense of Television*, Routledge.

Lyotard, J.F. [1979] (1984) *The Postmodern Condition*, Manchester University Press.

McLuhan, M. [1964] (2001) *Understanding Media*, Routledge.

McLuhan, M. and Fiore, Q. (1967) *The Medium Is the Message*, Bantam.

McNair, B. (1994) *News and Journalism in the UK*, Routledge.

McNair, B. (1998) *The Sociology of Journalism*, Arnold.

McQuail, D. and Windahl, S. (1981) *Communication Models for the Study of Mass Communications*, Longman.

McRobbie, A. (1991) *Feminism and Youth Culture: From Jackie to Just Seventeen*, Macmillan.

Marx, K. [1848] *A Contribution to the Critique of Hegel's Philosophy of Right*, available at http://www.marxists..org/archive/marx/works/1844/df-jahrbucher/law-abs.htm

Marx, K. and Engels, F. [1848] (2004) *The Communist Manifesto*, Penguin.

Marx, K. and Engels, F. [1886] *Treatise of Feuerbach*, available at http://www.marxists.org/archive/marx/works/1845/theses/theses.htm

Medhurst, A. (1998) 'Tracing Desires: Sexuality and Media Texts', in A. Briggs and P. Cobley (eds) *The Media: An Introduction*, Longman.

Miller, D. and Philo, G. (1999) 'The Effective Media', in G. Philo (ed.) *Message Received*, Longman.

Moore, A. and Gibbons, D. (1987) *Watchmen*, DC Comics.

Morley, D. (1980) *The* Nationwide *Audience*, British Film Institute.

Morley, D. (1986) *Family Television*, Comedia.

Morley, D. (1992) *Television, Audiences and Cultural Studies*, Routledge.

Mulvey, L. [1975] (2003) 'Visual Pleasure and Narrative Cinema', in W. Brooker and D. Jermyn (eds) *The Audience Studies Reader*, Routledge, Chapter 13.

Orwell, G. [1949] (1990) *Nineteen Eighty-Four*, Penguin Books.

Orwell, G. (2000) 'Politics and the English Language', in G. Orwell, *Essays*, Penguin.

Peace, M. (1998) 'The Construction of Reality in Television News', http://www.aber.ac.uk.

Perkins, T. (1997) 'Rethinking Stereotypes', in T. O'Sullivan and Y. Jewkes (eds) *The Media Studies Reader*, Arnold.

Philo, G. (2004) 'Media Effects and the Active Audience', http://www.gla.ac.uk/departments/sociology/units/media/effects.htm, accessed 20 November 2004.

Pope, R. (1998) *The English Studies Book*, Routledge.

Postman, N. (1985) *Amusing Ourselves to Death*, Methuen.

Rayner, P., Wall, P. and Kruger, S. (2004) *Media Studies: The Essential Resource*, Routledge.

Ross, K. (2000) 'Whose Image? TV Criticism and Black Minority Viewers', in S. Cottle (ed.) *Ethnic Minorities and the Media*, Open University Press.

Ross, K. and Nightingale, V. (2003) *Media and Audiences: New Perspectives*, Open University Press.

Said, E. (1978) *Orientalism*, Pantheon Books.

Selby, K. and Cowdery, R. (1995) *How to Study Television*, Macmillan.

Voloshinov, V.N. (1973) *Marxism and the Philosophy of Language*, Harvard University Press.

Williams, N. (2004) *How to Get a 2:1 in Media, Communication and Cultural Studies*, Sage.

Williams, R. (1962) *Communications*, Penguin.

Williams, R. (1963) *Culture and Society 1780–1950*, Penguin.

Williams, R. [1974] (1989) 'Drama in a Dramatised Society', in R. Williams, *On Television*, Routledge.

Wolf, N. (1991) *The Beauty Myth: How Images of Beauty Are Used Against Women*, Vintage.

Woodward, K. (1997) 'Concepts of Identity and Difference', in K. Woodward (ed.) *Identity and Difference*, Sage.

 **INDEX**

Note: page numbers in *italics* denote references to illustrations or tables

ABC (Audit Bureau of Circulation) 125
Abercrombie, N. 77, 80
Abramovitch, Roman 11
absent presence 81
Abu Ghraib prison photographs 147
action genre 41
Adorno, Theodor 132–3, 197–8
advertising: audience research 118, 120,
    125, 126, 127; cultural stereotypes 238;
    Galbraith on 14, 61; lack of consumer
    choice 141; news media 167, 237;
    television 7; visual icons 225; women
    in car advertising 23–4, 26, 27, 229
aesthetic pleasure 66
Affleck, Ben 61, *62*
age 118, 146
Airport 109
Althusser, Louis: ideology 48, 61, 87, 197,
    235; representations 93; structuralism
    222, 234
American Beauty 82
anchorage 12, 56, 60, 188
Anderson, Gerry 202, 204
Anderson, Pamela 98
Andre, Peter *59*
annotation 243–4, 247–8
Arafat, Yasser 159
archetypes 98
Arsenal FC 11
aspirational types 119
assessment criteria 20–1, 246–7
Atwood, Margaret 209
audience 1, 16, 27, 113–54; active 134–42,
    151, 224; context of consumption 207–8;
    demographic variables 118–19, 120, 129;
    'effects' theories 133, 134, 138, 140;

encoding/decoding model 143–8; focus
    groups 126–7; genre 38, 41, 47–8;
    hegemony theory 142–3; interactive 9,
    152, 153; Internet 152–3; live 115–16,
    117; magazine readers 47, 120–5;
    Marxist analysis 233–4; mass 113, 116,
    117, 130; media messages 129, 133,
    134, 135–7, 143–7; mediation 76;
    news 159, 160; poststructuralism 224;
    psychographic variables 119, 120, 129;
    reception theory 148–9; research on
    117–28, 129, 131, 151–2; resistant
    151–2; segmentation 47, 118–19,
    129–30, 131; semiotics 222; television
    schedules 150; two-step flow model
    134–7, 138; uses and gratifications
    model 138–9, 140, 141; voyeurism 66
audience–producer–text triangle *41*
Audit Bureau of Circulation (ABC) 125
Auf Wiedersehen, Pet 52, 82
Austin, Mark 179–80, 182
Austin Powers films 101
Australia 94
auteur theory 233
authenticity 170, 172, 178, 182, 260–1
award ceremonies 148, *148*

Baby's Breakfast 84
BAFTA award ceremony 148, *148*
Baker, Tom 48
BARB (Broadcasters' Audience Research
    Board) 125
Barbie Magazine 53
Barclay Brothers 165
Barlow at Large 253
Barthes, Roland 56, 79, 81, 86, 94, 187–9

Baudrillard, Jean 75, 86, 201, 225–6
BBC (British Broadcasting Corporation):
    audiences 129, 130; Charter of the 173;
    crime fiction 65, 66, 252; *El Dorado* 42;
    entertainment vs education 112; licence
    fee 129; news 157, 159, 163, 165, 171,
    175; prison service ban 254; production
    values 206, 207; state investment 237;
    website 16, 64
BBC News 24 171
BBC Radio Four 172
BBC3 171, 176
The Beatles 5, 6, 11
beauty industry 107
Beck, A. 35
Beckham, David 10, 56, 166, *177*, 178, 179
Beckham, Victoria 177–8, *177*, 179
Bell, Martin 166–7
Bell, Tom 254
Bennett, P. 35
Benn's Media Directory 18
Berger, John 106
Bergg, David 150
Bernstein, Basil *51*, 201
Bertolucci, Bernardo 5
Best, George 11
BFI Film Library 16
bibliographies 31, 34, 35
Big Brother 7, 8, 38, 109, 111–12
Big Country 93, 94
Bigley, Kenneth 180
The Bill 52, 64, 80, 259–60
Billy Liar 7
binary oppositions 71, 221, 230
'black' definition 87–8
Black and White Minstrel Show 143, *145*
Blackadder 45, 46, 47, *51*
Bladerunner 111
Blair, Tony 174, 180, 188, 195
Blair Witch Project 137
Blake's Seven 47–8
blaxploitation 101
blogs 159
The Blue Lamp 115, 252
Blue Murder 64, 255–7, *256*
Blue Peter 141
Bolter, J. 34
Bon Jovi 82
Bosnian war 166–7
Bowling for Columbine 143, 197

Boyle, Danny 97
Braveheart 99
Briatore, Flavio 61, *63*
bricolage 101, 225
British Sign Language 88–9
Broadcasters' Audience Research Board
    (BARB) 125
broadsheets 24, 156, 200–1
Brown, John 95
Bruce Almighty 92
BSkyB 7
Buffy the Vampire Slayer 80
Burton, Amanda 258
Bush, George W. 137, *138*, 147, 188
The Business 160
Butler, Judith 101, 230

C4 (Channel Four) 8, 109
cable television 7
capitalism: dominant ideology 88; Frankfurt
    School critique of 132–3; hegemony 143;
    liberal pluralism 236; Marxism 198, 231,
    232, 233–4, 236; political positions 17;
    postfeminism 229; resistant audience
    concept 151; strengthening of global
    capitalism 236
Captain Scarlett 202
Carlyle, Robert 258
Carrey, Jim 92
Carry On. . . films 84, 218
Carter, Angela 89
Carter, George 69
Carter, Nina 64
Carter, Stephanie 254
cartoons 77
Casey, B. 176
Cathy Come Home 131
CAVIAR (Cinema and Video Industry
    Audience Research) 125
celebrity 8, 9; lifestyle magazines 47, 55,
    56–64; news 163, 178; public relations
    162
Celebrity Fat Club 109
Channel Five 171, 176
Channel Four (C4) 8, 109
Chapkis, Wendy 107
Chelsea FC 11
Choi, Chris 182
Chomsky, Noam 167–8, 221, 237
Christie, Agatha 258

Cinema and Video Industry Audience
    Research (CAVIAR) 125
cinemas 115–16, 207
Citizen Kane 27, 30
Clarke, Roy 52
class *see* social class
Cleese, John 46
Clifford, Max 162
Clough, Brian 180–1, 183
Club Reps Uncovered 109
CNN 197
Cohen, S. 165
colonialism 224, 238
Coltrane, Robbie 258
comedy: live audiences 115; mavericks 52;
    progressive 50, 52; regressive 50; women
    107; *see also* sitcoms
comic books *44*, 45
'common sense': changes over time 143;
    ideology 71, 90, 233, 235; male gaze
    105; mediated world 77; stereotypes 81
communication: audiences 113; mediation
    76, 77; persuasive 95, 96; representation
    75, 92; signs 187; *see also* language
Communism 85, 231
competition 129
computer games 86
'conative' communication 46
conclusion of essay 31, 245, 250
connotation 46, 145, 235
consensualism 165–6
Conservative Party 17, 253
consumer sovereignty 139
consumerism 229, 230
consumption 2, 12, 207–8
context: of consumption 207–8; independent
    studies 21–2, 26, 28; media reception
    149; Media Studies exams 245; sitcoms
    51; television crime series 65; wider 4–18,
    208–9
convention 94
convergence technology 9
Cook, Robin 152
Coolio *188*
The Cops 64, 260–1
Coronation Street 28, 39, 42, 79–80, 179;
    'absent presence' 81; audience for 47,
    116–17; idealised reality 77; uses and
    gratifications model 138–9, 140
cosmetic surgery 107

Cosmopolitan 53, 86
Countdown 8
Country Living 121–2, *124*, 130
Cracker 64, 257, *257*, 258
Craven, Wes 39
crime 35, 69–70, 162, 165, 181, 251–2, 253
crime fiction 35, 64–71, 251–61
critical autonomy 21, 245, 246, 247
critical order 72
Cruise, Tom 60
Cruz, Penelope 60
CSI 67
Culler, Jonathan 45
cult TV shows 47–8
cultivation theory 133
cultural distance 164
cultural imperialism 237–8
cultural relativism 221
cultural value 217–18, 225
culture: definitions of 219; high 38, 217,
    218, 259; low 38, 217, 218; popular
    11, 38, 151, 202, 217–19, 225; systems
    of representation 75; transmission of
    5, 18
'culture industry' 133, 198

Da Vinci, Leonardo 217
Dad's Army 45, *51*
Daily Express 160, 174
Daily Mail 17, *160*, 174
Daily Mirror 136, *160*, 201, 251
Daily Record 160
Daily Star 160
Daily Star Sunday 160
Daily Telegraph 160, 165, 174
data collection methods 117, 125, 141
dating shows 111
De Fleur, M.L. 48, 77
deaf sign language 88–9, *90*
decoding *see* encoding/decoding model
deconstruction 191, 223–4
democracy 152, 239
denotation 145
Derrida, Jacques 224
developing countries 79, 237–8
Di Caprio, Leonardo 84
Diaz, Cameron 205
diegesis 189
digital technology 7, 110–11, 155–6, 159,
    176

digital television 7, 9, 39, 115, 130, 155
Dirty Harry 253
disabilities 80–1
Disney World 34
disruptive pleasure 67
Dixon of Dock Green 64, 252
documentaries 84
La Dolce Vita 211
The Doors 6
Dr Who 48
drama: crime fiction 64–71, 251–61; 'expert' 257–8; reality TV 110; structuralist analysis of 221–2; Williams on 78
The Dreamers 5
drug metaphor 133–4
drug taking 97–8, 134, 145, *146*, 165, 166–7
Duffy, Carol Ann 196
DVDs 114, 115, 128, 208
Dyer, Gillian 26, 95
Dylan, Bob 52

Eastenders 28, 80, 81
Eastwood, Clint 2
Eccleston, Christopher 48
economic issues 231, 232, 235, 237, 238
Edward, Prince 61
'effects' theories 133, 134, 138, 140
El Dorado 42
election campaigns 134–5, 137
elitism 218
Emmerdale 179
encoding/decoding model 143–8
Endemol 38
Eriksson, Sven Goran 10
essay structure 30, 31–4, 248, 250
etc. magazine *212*
ethnicity: audience segmentation 118; encoding/decoding approach 146; postcolonialism 191; representation of minorities 79, 81; sports journalism 13; *see also* racism
ethnocentricity 164
ethnographic research 141
Evans, Harold 169
Evening Gazette 126
exams 240–50; assessment criteria 246–7; checklist for 243–5; essay structure 248, 250; examples of questions 242; planning grid for textual comparisons 248, *249*;

preparation for 241, 242–3, 244; unseen texts 247–8
exhibitionism 8
'expert' drama 257–8

Fahrenheit 9/11 143, *144*, 197
'false consciousness' 232, 233–4, 235
fandom 47
Farrelly Brothers 84
Fascism 17
The Fast Show 52
Fathers4Justice 162
Fawlty Towers 45, 46, *51*, 217–18, 244
femininity 101, 227, 229; *see also* women
feminism 89, 101, 191, 193, 226–30; *see also* gender; women
FHM 53, 54
55 Degrees North 64, 65–6, 68, 69, 70–1, *256*, 257
figure of accumulation 95
Film Studies 39
films: audience research 125, 127–8; auteur theory 233; BFI Film Library 16; British films of the 1960s 6, 7; cinema audiences 115–16; codes 221; contexts of consumption 207–8; cultural imperialism 238; cultural stereotypes 238; deep structures 221; genre 41, 42; individualism 233; internet marketing campaigns 137; Internet Movies Database 15, 30; media reviews 135–7, *136*; naturalism 85; oppositional views 143; pleasure from 222; referencing 35; Tarantino 45; women's representation in 103
Finding Nemo 77
Fireball XL5 202
Fiske, John 88, 89–90, 151, 201
focus groups 126–7, 128
football 10–12, 14, 114–15
football fans 99
Footballers' Wives 84
foregrounding 223–4
Foster, Barry 70
Fowler, Robbie 12
Fowles, John 247
Fox News 197, 198
Frankfurt School 132–3
free market economics 17, 236
Freeman, Morgan 92

freeview 7
The French Connection 253
Freud, Sigmund 93
FT 160
functionalism 139–40

Galbraith, J.K. 13–14, 61
Galtung, J. 13, 163
game shows 8, 81
gangster films 42, 43
Garnett, Tony 260
Gascoine, Jill 254
Gauntlett, David 133, 228
gay men 81, 89–90, 91–2, 143, 230,
    260
Gaye, Marvin 217
gaze 103, 105, 228
gender: audience segmentation 118; crime
    fiction 254–7; domestic power relations
    149; encoding/decoding approach 146;
    feminism 191, 193, 226–30; news 156;
    queer theory 230; representation of
    101–8, 191, 193, 228; sports journalism
    13; television preferences 149–50;
    see also feminism; men; women
genre 2, 4, 34, 37–73; audiences 38, 41,
    47–8; celebrity lifestyle magazines 55,
    56–64; definition of 40; functions of 41;
    historical context 43–5; hybrids 50, 52–5;
    sitcoms 45–6, 49–51; social values 48;
    structuralism 222; television crime fiction
    64–71, 251–61
The Gentle Touch 64, 254
Gervais, Ricky 52
Gibbons, Dave 45
Gibson, Mel *99*
Gitlin, Todd 78
Gladiator 207–8
Glasgow Gallery of Modern Art *100*
Glasgow University Media Group 151–2,
    173
'global village' 156
globalisation 237
God 92–3
The Godfather 104
Goebbels, Josef 132
Goethe, Johann Wolfgang von 206
Goffman, Erving 58
The Good Life 45, 50, *51*
Goodbye Lenin! 231

Gramsci, Antonio: hegemony 13, 90, 142,
    234–5; naturalisation 197; structuralism
    234; unconscious ideology 92
graphic novels *44*, 45
Green, Robson 258
Groening, Matt 83
Grusin, R. 34
Guardian 17, 24, 158, *160*, 201
Guardian Media Directory 18
Guardian On Line 64
Guardian Unlimited 14, 157, *158*

Halford, Alison 254
Hall, Stuart 143, 146, 147, 190
Hamlet 205
Harcup, Tony 163
Harry, Prince 180, 181, 184, *194*
Hartley, J. 201
Harvard referencing system 34
Have I Got News for You 53
Hawkes, Terence 47
Heartbeat 5, 225
Heat 55, 56, 60, 61, *62*
Heath, Ted 253
hegemony 13, 90, 142–3, 234–5
Hello 55, 56–8, *57*, 60, 61–4, *63*, 84–5
Herman, Edward 167–8
heroin users 97–8, 145, *146*
Hesmondhalgh, Desmond 130
heterosexuality 101, 230–1
high culture 38, 217, 218, 259
Hillsborough 258
Hitler, Adolf 17, 132, *132*
Hollyoaks 47
Hollywood 42, 127, 203, 204–5, 222,
    238
homophobia 143, 167, 225
homosexuality 81, 89, 90, 91–2, 230–1;
    see also gay men; lesbians
Horkheimer, Max 132–3
horror 41
human interest 161, 170
Humperdinck, Engelbert 202
Humphrys, John 7, 172
hybridity 50, 52–5
hyperreality 13, 75, 86, 225, 226
hypothesis framing 23–4

Ibiza Uncovered 80
iconic signs 74, 79, 94

iconography 60, 68

identity 79, 219; queer theory 230; Scottish 101; uncertainty about 201, 224

ideology 16, 27, 80, 193, 209; Althusser 48, 61, 197, 235; celebrity lifestyle magazines 61; crime fiction 66, 69, 71; dominant 49, 71, 88, 90, 143, 197; gender representations 107–8; hegemony theory 13, 142, 234–5; heterosexual 230; Marxism 232, 233–4, 235–6; news media 165, 166, 173, 184; patriarchal 227; representation 48, 61, 87–92; stereotypes 81, 83; *see also* values

illustrations 36

I'm a Celebrity Get Me Out of Here 7, 8, 47, 109, 111, 131, *131*

imperialism: cultural 237–8; deconstruction of imperialist discourses 224; military 238, 239

implosion 225, 226

Independent 160

independent study 19–36

individualism 233

inequality 101

infotainment 161

Inspector Morse 64, 70, 79–80, 258–9, *259*

institutions 1, 16, 27; audience research 117, 118, 120, 125, 127; functionalism 139–40; Marxist analysis of 232; uses and gratifications model 139

interactivity 8, 9, 152, 153

Internet: audiences 152–3; critical perspectives 153; marketing campaigns 137; news 157, 159; plagiarism 29; research 14, 15–16, 64; television 8, 9; weblogs 159; *see also* websites

Internet Movies Database 15, 30

intertextuality 17, 259

introduction to essay 31, 245, 250

Iraq: abuse of Iraqi prisoners 147; invasion of 205, 235, 238–9; kidnap of Kenneth Bigley 180

irony 201, 202, 204, 205, 225

Irwin, Steve 60

Islam 173, 238

The Italian Job 101

ITN news 176, 179–84

ITV 7, 103, 130

ITV News 176, 179–84

J17 105, *106*

Jackie 228

Jagger, Mick 5

Jakobson, Roman 46

James Bond films 190

Jameson, Fredric 73

Jamie's Kitchen 109–10

Jason, David 46

Jenkins, H. 153

JICNARS (Joint Industry Committee for National Readership Surveys) 118

JICREG (Joint Industry Committee for Regional Press Research) 126

Johns, Stratford 253

Johnson, Samuel 58

Joint Industry Committee for National Readership Surveys (JICNARS) 118

Joint Industry Committee for Regional Press Research (JICREG) 126

Jonsson, Ulrika 111

Jordan *59*, 61

journalists 74, 161–3, 164, 166–8, 169, 170

Juliet Bravo 254

Katz, E. 134–5, 137, 201

Kaye, Peter 52

Keaton, Buster 84

Keeble, Richard 162

Keegan, Kevin 12

Kennedy, Charles 183

Kerry, John 137, *138*

Kibble-White, Jack 259, 260

Kirwin, Dervla 71

Klein, Paul 41

Kojak 253

Kubrick, Stanley 207

La Dolce Vita 211

La Plante, Lynda 254

labour 232

Labour Party 17, 253

lads' magazines 16, 54, 101, 225

language 16, 27; codes 220–1; ideological basis of 87–8; register 12–13, 32; representation 75; sports headlines 12–13; structuralism 221

Last of the Summer Wine 52, 55

Law and Order 254

Lazarsfeld, P. 134–5, 137

The League of Gentlemen 52

'least objectionable programme theory' 41
Leigh, Mike 85
lesbians 143, 230, 260; *see also*
    homosexuality
Lévi-Strauss, Claude 221
Lewis, Justin 146
Liberal Democrats 183
liberal pluralism 139, 236–7
libraries 18
Lie Detector 206, 207
lifestyle 56, 119, 120, 121
Literary Studies 4
live performances 115
LIVE TV 206, 207
Livingstone, Sonia 21
Loach, Ken 85
Loaded 54
'lobby system' 162, 167–8
Loch Ness *100*
Lopez, Jennifer 61, *62*
The Lord of the Rings 86
Love Thy Neighbour 50
low culture 38, 217, 218
Lucy, Gary *106*
Lull, James 141, 149
Lyotard, J.F. 86, 204

MacArthur, Colin 95
McGovern, Jimmy 258
McLuhan, Marshall 75, 77–8, 150, 156, 187
McNair, Brian 34, 166
McQuail, Denis 110
McRobbie, Angela 228
Madonna 92–3, 151
magazines: audiences 47, 120–5, 126, 127,
    129–30; celebrity lifestyle 47, 55, 56–64;
    codes 221; genre 42, 53; girls' magazines
    228; hybridity 53, 54; lads' magazines
    16, 54, 101, 225; mediated reality 78–9;
    mediation of media messages 135–7; news
    156; popular culture 217; status levels
    147; structure of 223; textual analysis
    209–13; TV listings 54–5, 130; women's
    magazines 38, 53, 120
Mail on Sunday 160
Major, John 174
male gaze 103, 105, 228
Manchester City FC 12
Manchester United FC 11
Manson, Marilyn 47

marketing campaigns 137
Marple, Miss 258
Marquess, Paul 260
Marsh, Jodie 61
Marx, Karl 14, 17, 92, 198, 231–3, 236
Marxism 227, 231–5, 237; Frankfurt School
    132, 133; hegemony theory 142, 234–5;
    ideological manipulation 13; news media
    197, 201; politics 17; popular culture
    217; structuralism 222; tabloid celebrity
    stories 178; textual analysis 191, 196,
    197–8
masculinity 6, 101, 227; *see also* men
Match of the Day 11
mavericks 52
MCS website *25*
meaning 92, 93, 147, 216; anchorage
    188; encoding/decoding model 145, 147;
    paradigmatic analysis 190; polysemy 145,
    206; poststructuralism 223, 224; relay
    189; semiotics 145, 219, 220, 221, 222;
    structuralism 223; struggles over 143;
    Voloshinov 234
Medhurst, Andy 81
media: alternative representations 83;
    audiences 113–17; choice 140–1;
    construction of reality by the 74, 75,
    80; cultural imperialism 237–8; cultural
    transmission 5, 219; drug metaphor
    133–4; encoding/decoding model 143–8;
    feminism 227; functions of 200–1;
    hegemony theory 142–3, 234–5; liberal
    pluralism 236; Marxist perspectives
    198, 232–5; postcolonialism 238–9;
    postmodernist perspective 201, 225;
    power of the 131–2, 133, 146;
    proliferation of mass media 77–8;
    realism 77; representation of 'place'
    93; self-referentiality 17–18, 135, 137;
    sport 10–14; textual analysis 1, 4, 15;
    two-step flow model 134–7; uses and
    gratifications model 138–9, 140, 141;
    see also magazines; newspapers; radio;
    television
media institutions 1, 16, 27; audience
    research 117, 118, 120, 125, 127;
    functionalism 139–40; Marxist analysis
    of 232; uses and gratifications model 139
Media Studies: assessment criteria 20–1,
    246–7; audience 113; critical skills

29–30, 186, 203, 245; exams 240–50;
independent research studies 19, 20;
referencing 34; relativism 218–19;
synopticity 27; textual analysis 4, 200;
theory 1–2, 215–17; websites 15
Media Studies: The Essential Resource 26
mediation 76–8, 79, 135, 137
men: lads' magazines 16, 54, 101, 225;
male gaze 103, 105, 228; news 156;
representation of 103, 104, 105–6,
107–8; television watching 149; *see also*
gender; masculinity
Men Only 53
mental illness 152
Merchant, Steven 52
metanarrative 201, 204, 225
Midsomer Murders 259
Miller, D. 151
Milton, John 217
Mind Your Language 50
Minogue, Kylie 60, 64
minority groups 79–82, 88–91, 92
Mirren, Helen 255
mise-en-scène 67, 189, 206
The Missing 128
Mission Impossible 187
mobile phones 157, 158
modality judgements 85
mode of address 33, 40, 60–1
modernism 202
Mona Lisa 79, 217
Monroe, Marilyn 98
Moore, Alan *44*, 45
Moore, Bobby 10, 12
Moore, Michael 143, *144*, 197
Moores, Shaun 26
moral panic 165, 253
Morley, David 148–9, 150
motivation 94, 98
*The Movies: An Illustrated History of the
Silver Screen* 210
Mr Bean 52
Mr Right 111
MTV 103
Mulvey, Laura 105, 228
Murdoch, Rupert 195, 198
music: audiences 47; bricolage 225; dance
52–3; folk 52; genre studies 72; live
audiences 115; mass audiences 130; news
bulletins 174; of the 1960s 5, 6, 202;

pop videos 225; popular culture 217;
rap 191, 225; recording technology 86;
resistance and subversion 151; rock
bands 104; rock and roll challenge to
conservative values 133; simplicity of
three-minute pop song 218; song lyrics
6, 82–3, 93; status levels 147
music halls 115
musicals 42
My Weekly 53

narrative: news stories 168–70, 178; realism
86; sitcoms *51*; structuralist analysis of
221–2; Todorov 43
Nation, Terry 48
National Readership Surveys (NRS) 126
nationalism 17, 231
Nationwide 148–9
naturalism 85, 254
The Navigator 84
Nazism 17, 132
Neale, Gub 258
Neeson, Liam *99*
negotiated reading 146, 190
New Labour 17, 174, 195
news 92, 155–85; alerts 158–9;
celebrity 176–9; headlines 169, 177;
informalisation 175, 176; *ITV News*
case study 179–84; Marxist critique 197,
198; narrative structure 168–70, 178;
news room roles 162–3; newsworthiness
163–4; presentation trends 13, 172,
176; presenters 143, 172, 175, 176;
profitability motive 237; realism 86;
sports 10; textual analysis 171
news conferences 162
News Corporation 195, 198
news groups 159
News International 158
News of the World 130, *160*, 176–8, *177*,
195
newspapers 156, 159; audience research
126; circulation figures *160*; codes
221; functions of 200–1; infotainment
161; Internet databases 14, 15; local
198, *199*, 200; mass audiences 130;
mediation of media messages 135–7;
narrative structure 168, 169, 223;
newsworthiness 163–4; on-line editions
157–8; oppositional views 143; political

viewpoints 174, 235; popular culture
217; profitability motive 237; referencing
35; representation 74; sports headlines
10; textual analysis 193–201; *see also*
journalists; tabloid newspapers
NHS careers advertisement *108*
niche marketing 53
Nightingale, Mary 179–80
Nightingale, V. 153
Nineteen Eighty-Four 10
Nixon, Richard 236
Norton, Graham 91–2, *91*
Now 56, 61
NRS (National Readership Surveys) 126
Nu-metal music 47
NWA 91

objectivity 173, 174, 197
Observer 101, *102*, 107, *160*
Ofcom 129
The Office 52
OK 56, *59*, 61, 64
Oliver, Jamie 109–10
One Foot in the Grave 45, *51*
Only Fools and Horses 45, 46, 47, *51*
Open All Hours 45, *51*
opinion leaders 135, 137
oppositional reading 146, 190
Orwell, George 10, 13
Out 254

paradigms 39, 72, 87, 171, 189–90
Paradise Lost 217
paragraphs 32, 33, 169, 244–5
parental control 141
Parker, Alan 7
parody 73, 86, 201, 202, 204
pastiche 52, 201, 204
patriarchy 224, 226, 227, 229
Patterson, Bill 258
Paycheck 43
PC Format 53
PC Gamer 53
Peace, Mark 173
People 160
People Leaving a Factory 84
The People's Friend 213
Perkins, Tessa 81
phatic communication 56
Philo, G. 151, 152

Phoenix Nights 52
Pink Floyd 6
place, representation of 70, 93–101
plagiarism 28–9, 34
Play for Today 131
Playboy 53
playfulness 204, 225, 226
pleasure 38, 66–7, 222, 224
Poirot, Hercule 258
polemic 196
police 65, 70, 181, 253–4, 255–7, 259–61
Police Camera Action 9
political correctness 16
political economy approach 167, 237
politics: Communism 231; crime policies
253; election campaigns 134–5, 137;
ideological struggles within the media
235; Iraqi prisoner abuse 147;
left-wing 17; liberal pluralism 236;
news coverage 161–2, 164, 167–8,
183; newspaper partisanship 174, 195,
197; right-wing 17; spin 165, 183
polysemy 145, 206
Pope, Rob 223
Pope, Val 85
popular culture 11, 38, 151, 202, 217–19,
225
pornography 8, 54, 130
Porridge 45, *51*
postcolonialism 191, 193, 227, 229, 238–9
postfeminism 229, 230
Postman, Neil 77, 201
'postmodern condition' 86, 204, 218
postmodernism 13, 191, 201–5, 224–6;
bricolage 101; feminism 229; high/low
culture 218; progressive comedy 52;
reality 77, 86
poststructuralism 191, 222, 223–4
power: cultural value 218; domestic power
relations 149; feminism 226–7, 229;
of the media 131–2, 133, 146; and
representation 88; ruling class 142;
see also hegemony
Practical Photography 53
preferred reading 146, 147, 151, 190
preparation for exams 241, 242–3, 244
Presley, Elvis 133
press briefings 161–2
press releases 161
Prima 120, 121, *123*, 130

primary research 21
Prime Suspect 64, 254–5, *255*
production: conditions of 206–7; genre 2, 37–8, 43; news 155; wider contexts 5
The Professionals 253
profitability 237
progressives 50, 52
proletariat 232, 233, 234
propaganda 10, 132, 168
Propp, Vladimir 222
psychological realism 86
public relations 162
public service broadcasting 129, 173
publicity stunts 162
The Puzzler 53

Q Magazine 105
qualitative research 141
Queer Eye for the Straight Guy 108
Queer as Folk 91
queer theory 229, 230–1; *see also* homosexuality
Quentin, Caroline 255
Question Time 109
quiz shows 8

racism: changes in television entertainment 16, 143, 234; right-wing parties 17; television crime fiction 252, 258, 260; *see also* ethnicity
radio: audience research 126; codes 221; football commentaries 114, 115; mediation of media messages 135; news 157, 159–60; *Today* programme 172
Radio 5 Live 157
Radio Joint Audience Research Limited (RAJAR) 126
Radio Times 54, 55, *130*
RAJAR (Radio Joint Audience Research Limited) 126
Ramsay, Gordon 109
Ray, John 183
Read, Mike 111
realism 77, 79, 80, 84–7, 205; films of the 1960s 6, 253; reality TV 109; socialist 85; television crime fiction 252, 253, 254, 259; types of 85–6
reality 79, 84–5, 86, 92; consensualist model 166; construction of 74, 75, 80; mediation of 77, 78; postmodernist

perspective 201, 225–6; *see also* hyperreality
reality TV 7–9, 10, 22, 38, 127; audience voting 47; playfulness 226; pleasure from 222; representation 78, 109–112
Rebel Without a Cause 133
reception theory 148–9
referencing 26, 28, 29, 34–5
regionalism 12
regressives 50
regulation of news media 163
Reith, Lord 112
relativism 218–19, 221, 222
relay 188–9
religious fundamentalism 173, 231
representation 3, 16, 27, 74–112; alternative 83–4; definition of 74–5; gender 101–8, 191, 228; ideology 48, 61, 87–92; mediation 76–8; minority groups 79–82, 88–91, 92; reality TV 109–12; Scotland 93–101; television crime fiction 64; women 22–3, 92, 101–3, 105, 106–8
research: AQA Unit 5 specification 36; assessment criteria 20–1; audience 117–28, 129, 131, 151–2; ethnographic 141; independent study 19–36; Internet 14, 15–16, 64; libraries 18; presentation 35–6; primary 21; reception theory 148–9; referencing 26, 28, 29, 34–5; secondary 21, 22, 29; structure 30, 31–4; title 24–5; wider contexts 14, 15–18, 21–2, 28
resistant audience 151–2
retro 5, 101
revision 241, 242
rhetoric 95, 96
Richard, Cliff *192*
Right to Reply 109
Rob Roy 99
Roberts, Yvonne 107
rock music 104
role models 79, 83, 229
The Rolling Stones 5–6
Ross, Jonathan 88
Ross, Karen 79, 153
Ruge, M.H. 13, 163
ruling class 6, 142, 232–3, 234–5, 237
Russian Revolution 231
Ryall, Tom 39

Said, Edward 238
satellite television 7, 9, 130, 156
Saussure, Ferdinand de 188, 220, 221
Schwarzenegger, Arnold 98
Scorsese, Martin 42
Scotland 93–101
Scott, Ridley 207
Scottish shortbread *96*
Scream 39
Sea of Souls 258
Seagal, Steven 98
secondary research 21, 22, 29
segmentation 47, 118–19, 129–30, 131
self-referentiality 2, 17–18, 135, 137
self-reflection 82
'semiotic democracy' 151, 153
semiotic guerrilla warfare 229
semiotics 56, 87, 145, 187–90, 219–21,
    222–3; *see also* signs
sex 8, 130
sexism: changes in television entertainment
    16, 143, 234; lads' magazines 16; police
    dramas 255, 257, 260; *Thunderbirds*
    205
sexuality 91, 92, 101, 133, 228, 230–1;
    see also heterosexuality; homosexuality
Shakespeare, William 205, 225
Shankly, Bill 10, 14
Shrek 2 205
sign language 88–9, *90*
signified 56, 79, 94, 145, 187, 225
signifiers: anchorage 56; dominant 189,
    209; motivation 94; postmodernism
    225; relationship with signified 79,
    145; semiotic guerrilla warfare 229;
    textual analysis 187, 189, 190, 209
signs 87, 97, 216, 222; encoding/decoding
    model 143, 145, 147; genre 39;
    hegemony theory 235; iconic 74, 79,
    94, 188; indexical 79, 94; meaning 219,
    221; poststructuralism 223; primitive
    communication 75; simulation 225;
    structuralism 223; symbolic 79, 94, 188;
    textual analysis 187–90; Voloshinov 234;
    see also semiotics; syntagms
Silent Witness 67, 257, 258
Silvestedt, Victoria 107
The Simpsons 77, 80, 83–4
simulacra 52, 201
simulation 225–6

sitcoms 38, 45–6, 47, 49–51; absence
    of minority groups 81; mavericks 52;
    progressives 50, 52; racism and sexism
    16; regressives 50; top ten British sitcoms
    45, 51
Sky 11, 13, 195, 198
Sky News 171
Smith, Cath 89
soap opera: audiences 21, 47, 116–17; *The
    Bill* 260; gay and lesbian characters 143;
    genre 38–9, 42; magazine synopses 137;
    realism 79; representation of 'place' 93;
    uses and gratifications model 139, 140;
    women 149; young people in 3
social change 5, 16, 65
social class: audience segmentation 118–19,
    120; class struggle 198; crime fiction
    70; encoding/decoding approach 146;
    hegemony theory 142; Marxism 191,
    198, 232, 233–4; sitcom characters *51*;
    sports journalism 13; youth culture of
    the 1960s 5
social control 234
socialisation 140, 201, 227
socialism 17
socialist realism 85
Softly, Softly 253
software 32
song lyrics 6, 82–3, 93
The Sopranos 141
Spartacus 207
Spender 70
Spice Girls 83
Spielberg, Steven 233
spin 165, 183
Spooks 187
sport 10–14, 115, 116
Stanislavsky, Constantin 85
Star Trek 47
Star Trek: The Next Generation 84
Stars in Their Eyes 110
Starsky and Hutch (film) 204
Starsky and Hutch (TV show) 204, 253
stereotypes 79, 81–2, 83, 84; audience
    profiles 119; feminists 230; gender 101,
    227–8, 254, 257; ideology 90; Islam 238;
    non-Western cultures 238–9; Scotland
    98; sign language 89; television light
    entertainment 234
Stingray 202

Stourbridge News 199, 200
structuralism 221–2, 223, 234
style over substance 225
Sugar 53
Sun: circulation figures *160*; mass audience
    for 130; on-line edition 157; political
    alignment 174, 195, 197; sports headlines
    12; textual analysis *194*, 195–8, *196*, 200
Sunday Express 160
Sunday Mail 160
Sunday Mirror 160
Sunday Sport 84
Sunday Telegraph 160
Sunday Times 160, 169
surveillance 9, 110, 153, 155
The Sweeney 64, 253, 254, 259
symbols 79, 94, 188
synoptic ability 21, 27
syntagms 87, 96, 171, 188, 189–90, 209
syntax *33*

tabloid newspapers 38, 156, 176–8;
    controversial issues 24; sports coverage
    10, 11, 12; *see also* newspapers; *Sun*
Tarantino, Quentin 45, 233
Tarrant, Chris *57*
tartanry 95
taste 53
A Taste of Honey 7, 253
Taylor, Damilola 50
technology: communication 113, 140, 150;
    convergence 9; digital 7, 110–11, 155–6,
    159, 176; Internet 8, 9; media audiences
    114; news 155–6, 157, 158; realism 86
teenagers 11
telenovelas 221
teletext 156, *157*
television: audience research 125, 127, 129;
    audience segmentation 130; codes of
    220–1, 223; conditions of production
    206; construction of reality 75; crime
    fiction 35, 64–71, 251–61; cult shows
    47–8; cultural imperialism 238; digital 7,
    9, 39, 115, 130, 155; drug metaphor
    134; films on 208; functions of 201;
    gender differences in TV preferences
    149–50; genre 39, 42; iconic signs 74;
    'least objectionable programme theory'
    41; listings magazines 54–5, 130; live
    sports events 116; mediation of media

messages 135–7; naturalism 85; news
    155, 156, 159–60, 168–9, 171–6,
    179–84; oppositional views 143; popular
    culture 217; public service broadcasting
    129, 173; realism 77; referencing 35;
    relational/structural uses of 141–2;
    representation 77, 78; schedules 150;
    social values 48, 77; sports coverage
    11–12; standards of acceptability 143,
    234; status levels 147; TV Ark website
    16; *see also* reality TV
10 O'Clock News 159
terrorism 92, 172, 180
test screenings 127–8
text messages 158
texts: audience interpretations of 116;
    audience-producer-text triangle *41*;
    conditions of production 206–7;
    contemporary 2–3, 20, 21, 27, 30;
    contexts of consumption 207–8; genre 2,
    37, 38, 40, 47, 48–9, 72; independent
    studies 20, 25–6, 28; mode of address 40;
    poststructuralism 223–4; semiotic analysis
    187–90, 222; two-step flow model 135;
    value of 217–18; wider contexts 4–5, 6,
    14–15, 17, 21, 208–9
textual analysis 1, 4, 15, 26, 186–214;
    audiences 207–8; conditions of production
    206–7; feminist 191, 193; magazines
    209–13; news bulletins 171; paradigms
    189–90; signs 187–90; *Thunderbirds*
    202–5
TFI Friday 101
Thaw, John 254
Thelma and Louise 193
theory 1, 2, 26, 33, 215–17, 219
This Sporting Life 253
Thoreau, Henry David 52
Thunderbirds (film) 203–5, *203*, 206
Thunderbirds (TV show) 202–5, *202*, 206
time management 243, 245
The Times 160, 195
Titanic 84
Today programme 172
Todorov, Tzvetan 43, 46, 48, 222
tone 33
Tonight with Trevor McDonald 84
top ten British sitcoms *45*, *51*
A Touch of Frost 259
Trainspotting 97–8, *97*

'Trekkies' 47
Triumph of the Will 132
TV Ark 16
TV Quick 55
TV Times 54, 55
two-step flow model 134–7, 138
typefaces 32

U2 105
uncertainty 201, 202, 224
Unforgiven 2
uses and gratifications model 138–9, 140, 141

values 16, 77, 87, 90, 92, 187; *Country Living* magazine 121, 122; crime fiction 66; genres 48; news media 165, 166, 167; prejudicial 89; rock and roll challenge to conservative values 133; transmission of 5, 219; *see also* ideology
Van der Valk 70
The Vicar of Dibley 45, 46, 47, *51*
vicarious pleasure 67
Victoria, Queen of England 95
violence 130
'viral' campaigns 137, 153
virtual communities 152, 159
visceral pleasure 66
Vision, Shelly 251
Voloshinov, V.N. 198, 234, 235
voting 9, 47
vox pops 109, 170
voyeurism 8, 9, 66

war 147
Warner, Jack 252
Washington Post 236
Watchmen 44, 45
Watergate scandal 236
Waterman, Dennis 254
We Love Telly 136
webcams 8
weblogs 159
websites: football 115; interactive audiences

152; referencing 28, 29, 35; research 14, 15–16, 24, 28; *see also* Internet
Welles, Orson 27
Western cultures 237–8
westerns 2–3, 39, 42, 253
What's New Pussycat? 7
What's On TV 130
'white' definition 88
The Who 5, 6
Who Wants to Be a Millionaire 8
The Wild One 133
Williams, Andy 101
Williams, Noel 29–30
Williams, Raymond 78, 92, 110, 117
Williams, Robbie 110
Wimbledon FC 11
Winslet, Kate 84
Wire in the Blood 258
Wisdom, Norman 110
Wolf, Naomi 228
Woman's Own 53
women: car advertising 23–4, 26, 27, 229; crime fiction 254–7; female body 228; high heels 89–90; magazines 38, 53, 54, 120; representation of 22–3, 92, 101–3, 105, 106–8; role in sitcoms 49, *51*; soap operas 149; *see also* femininity; feminism; gender
Woodward, K. 79
word processing 32, 35, 36
working class (proletariat) 5, 6, 232, 233, 234
World Cup (1966) 10, 11, 12

Yahoo 157
Yes, Minister 45, 51
Young, Jock 165–6
Young, Kirsty 176
The Young Ones 52
youth culture 5–6, 133

Z-Cars 64, 252–3, 259
ZOO 107

Related titles from Routledge

Media Studies: The Essential Resource
Philip Rayner, Peter Wall, Stephen Kruger (eds)

A unique collection of resources for all those studying the media at university and pre-university level, this book brings together a wide array of material including advertisements, political cartoons and academic articles, with supporting commentary and explanation to clarify their importance to Media Studies. In addition, activities and further reading and research are suggested to help kick start students' autonomy. The book is organized around three main sections: Reading the Media, Audiences, and Institutions and is edited by the same teachers and examiners who brought us the hugely successful AS *Media Studies: The Essential Introduction*. This is an ideal companion or stand alone sourcebook to help students engage critically with media texts. Its key features include:

- further reading suggestions
- a comprehensive bibliography
- a list of web resources

Hb: 0–415–29172–0 **£65.00**
Pb: 0–415–29173–9 **£16.99**

Available at all good bookshops
For ordering and further information please visit:
www.routledge.com